To

Larry,

with thanks,
again,

Paddy

LITERATURE AND PERSONAL VALUES

Literature and
Personal Values

PATRICK GRANT
Professor of English
University of Victoria, Canada

St. Martin's Press

First published in Great Britain 1992 by
THE MACMILLAN PRESS LTD
Houndmills, Basingstoke, Hampshire RG21 2XS
and London
Companies and representatives
throughout the world

A catalogue record for this book is available
from the British Library

ISBN 0–333–54159–6

Printed in Hong Kong

First published in the United States of America 1992 by
Scholarly and Reference Division,
ST. MARTIN'S PRESS, INC.,
175 Fifth Avenue,
New York, N.Y. 10010

ISBN 0–312–07548–0

Library of Congress Cataloging-in-Publication Data
Grant,Patrick.
Literature and personal values / Patrick Grant.
    p.   cm.
Includes bibliographical references (p.   ) and index.
ISBN 0–312–07548–0
1. Literature—Philosophy.   2. Literature—Aesthetics.   3. Values
in literature.   4. Social values in literature.   5. Philosophy,
Modern.
PN49.G639   1992
801—dc20   91–32343
                                                         CIP

To the helpers

Gloria, Tom, Dennis, Marilyn, Terence, Jim, Elaine,
Larry, Nat, Marvin, Sarah, Rodger, Sandy, Robin, Ken
and the community at Mission

Contents

Preface

This book attempts to set out the theory of a particular critical practice: it attempts, that is, to give an account of some of the values that have remained more or less implicit in several earlier critical books of mine. This perspective is worth establishing at the start, because one assumption in the following pages is that we frequently need to do things by practice before coming to understand the principles and values underpinning what it is we do. Literature, I want to say, especially shows how this is so by foregrounding the gaps and contradictions, as well as the unlikely bridges, between practice and explanation in human behaviour. In so doing, literature also makes us pressingly aware how language itself operates through an elusive dialectic of presence and absence, participation and objective distancing – knowing *how* and knowing *what*. I want to suggest that one way to approach the idea of the person – an idea that literature and criticism have done much to produce and confirm – is by interpreting it within just such a dialectic.

In broad terms, my position might be described as something like a 'hermeneutic realism,' if this label is used to define the root paradox which language forces on us, simultaneously giving us a world and separating us from it. 'Hermeneutic' then implies that our descriptions are value-laden, and we participate in a human world by learning how to grasp and shape certain meanings. By contrast, 'realism' implies that things exist over and against us, and our descriptions of them can be assessed as more or less adequate. Neither of these poles should usurp the other, and the idea of the person is sustained by a tension between the contending valances: a person is neither entirely subjective nor entirely objective, neither entirely private nor just one thing among others.

The main sections of the book bring to bear on these issues the vocabularies of hermeneutics and phenomenology (Chapter 2), scientific verification (Chapter 3), philosophy of imagination (Chapter 4), Judæo-Christian religion (Chapter 5) and Marxism (Chapter 6). Also, and with a view to maintaining my own recommended dialectic between practice and theory, each chapter offers exegesis of one or more literary texts.

The footnotes indicate my particular indebtedness to various sources, but the pervasive influence of a small number of books and authors calls for special acknowledgement, if only because, being pervasive, such influence is frequently impossible to footnote adequately. This I have come especially to realise by having attempted, throughout, to be as adequate as I can. Briefly, as a means of approaching the diversities of modern literary-critical debate, I have found (at least) the following lines of enquiry indispensable: Martin Heidegger's account in *Being and Time* of our pre-possession by the world and by language, especially as this account is developed by Maurice Merleau-Ponty; Michael Polanyi's re-direction of phenomenology to the history and procedures of science, and his notion of a 'tacit dimension' in human thinking; Paul Ricœur's analysis of the relation and distinction between metaphor and reflection; Richard Miller's account in *Fact and Method* of hermeneutic and positivist approaches to the natural and social sciences; Rudolf Bultmann's development of Heidegger, especially as it passes over to Jürgen Moltmann's *Theology of Hope* on which, in turn, Edward Schillebeeckx draws to develop the implications of his theory of 'negative contrast'; Ernst Bloch's Marxism, with its analysis of hope, the 'humanum,' and the not-yet conscious, complementing Antonio Gramsci's account of contradictory consciousness and transformational value. Charles Taylor's *The Sources of the Self* was published when a first draft of this book was all but complete, and I have attempted to integrate some of his important arguments into the final version. Taylor's ideas about the historical development of the self and about tacit evaluation complement Polanyi suggestively, and what I refer to as a 'personal signature' combines Taylor's 'personal resonance' with Polanyi's 'personal coefficient,' as I make clear in the text.

I am aware that in the broad context of 'postmodernism' and the ultra-nominalist trends of much recent literary theory, some aspects of the argument I am proposing will appear unfashionable. Partly for that reason I feel urged all the more to press my case, not so much against a specific set of antagonists as against the exaggerations that thrive within a certain, widely-dispersed climate of opinion. Those who dwell in such a climate move with easily-imitable alacrity to undermine or 'deconstruct' explicit affirmations of value, claims to personal identity, responsibility, judgement, intention, and so on, yet often without pausing much to question the latent evaluations and personal commitments enabling their own procedures. My intent is to put the case for personal values as also hard-won, requiring confirmation and calling for clear description upheld by shrewd assessments of well-foundedness. My aim is not to discount a salutary energy in the thoroughgoing scepticism of many recent theorists, but merely to avoid the stultification of thinking that follows upon an insufficiently reflective application of the 'hermeneutics of suspicion.'

I would like to thank Rodger Beehler especially for his comments on the chapter on Marx: some of his felicitous re-phrasings remain as he wrote them. Once again, Mike Doyle, Laurence Lerner and A. D. Nuttall have read the entire typescript. I appreciate increasingly how generous they have been over the years, attending with care and acumen to the improving of a variety of sows' ears. Also, without the patience, goodwill, and judicious surveillance of Sue Mitchell, I would scarcely have come to see even half so clearly what I meant to say.

Permission to reproduce excerpts from articles of mine already in print has been received from the University of Ottawa Press, for 'Redeeming the Time: *The Confessions* of St. Augustine,' ed. D. L. Jeffrey, *By Things Seen: Reference and Recognition in Medieval Thought* (Univ. of Ottawa Press, 1979); from Edinburgh University Press, for 'Imagination in the Renaissance,' ed. James P. Mackey, *Religious Imagination* (Edinburgh Univ. Press, 1986); and from Macmillan Ltd., for 'Knowing Reality: A Reading of *Four Quartets*,' ed. Shyamal Bagchee, *T. S. Eliot. A Centenary Volume* (Macmillan, 1990). I am grateful to the Association of Canadian University Teachers of English for the invitation to present before a discriminating audience a verison of my thoughts on *The Merchant of Venice* (now part of Chapter 5), at a plenary session of the Learned Societies Conference, May, 1990. I would like also to acknowledge with gratitude the Social Sciences and Humanities Research Council of Canada for awarding a Research Time Stipend which enabled me to complete the typescript.

PATRICK GRANT

1
Introduction

Debate about the meaning and identity of persons is intricate and vexed. Recently, it has been much invigorated by Derek Parfit,[1] who offers a powerful new challenge to the notion that personal identity is continuous over time. Parfit suggests that there is no more to a person than psychological and physical connectedness, and, like nations, people are subject to changing boundaries. Consequently, it is reasonable to propose that we can be different persons at different times in our lives.

The implications of such arguments are considerable, affecting our assessment of responsibility, practices of distributive justice, and the respect we accord to others as autonomous moral agents. Yet for literary theorists, all this has a familiar ring. Derridean deconstruction aims precisely at undermining a spurious 'metaphysics of presence' that assumes the existence of a unified self. Foucault and Barthes attack the idea that an author is the single, originating source of a text, and Lacan ponders the illusions and misrecognitions entailed by the idea of a self-identical subject. Lacan's arguments are repeated in another mode by Althusser, and then by a wide variety of critics with psychoanalytic and Marxist interests. In short, Parfit's general claims are grist to the mill of many 'post-modernist' literary scholars.

Assessments of Parfit have come mainly from other philosophers who tangle with his close-grained, abundant arguments, and among these Shirley Robin Letwin ventures a larger view. She suggests that 'most of what we value in our civilization becomes inexplicable without the concept of personal identity', and then condemns Parfit's account of this identity as nothing less than 'a profound attack on Western civilization'.[2] However, as Charles Taylor[3] points out, Parfit's discussion falls within a particular philosophical tradition deriving from Locke and stressing continuity of self-awareness

1

as a principal criterion of the personal. Such a tradition is not simply identifiable with everything that is meant by the person in Western thought, and needs to be assessed accordingly.

Indeed, as Locke says, some capacity for reflection and self-awareness is an attribute of persons and should be examined closely; yet, as Taylor urges, we need also to notice that the idea of a person has evolved historically, and is basically evaluative, indicating the human qualities we hold most distinctive and worthwhile.[4] The meaning of persons thus does not stay still, and self-consciousness itself emerges through particular judgements of what is significant and valuable. Such judgements in turn assume the human use of language, through which people become aware of their individual separateness, but by means of which they seek shared understanding and mutual recognition. Through language, people make plans and set standards – the 'self-set standards' Polanyi describes[5] – which call for commitment. Yet this does not imply that we can believe just what we want: we enter into consciousness through a language and history where standards and obligations already exist as shaping forces of that same consciousness. Thus, although individual receptivities remain intricately unique, persons are not just private individuals. Rather, personal identity is established through others, and however highly one values human autonomy, it is less than personal if it fails to recognise itself as formed in relation to a human culture and as part of a material world, both of which make claims on us.

As Ricœur[6] points out, symbolism enables our recognition of some of these fundamental claims and ties between our bodies, the world, and other people, and just as human self-interpretation changes in time, so symbols are formed into myths through narrative. Jonathan Glover,[7] a philosopher in the Parfit tradition, likewise stresses the significance of narrative for personal identity, as does the theologian Don Cupitt,[8] and in the same spirit George Steiner describes critical commentary on literature as producing its own 'fables of understanding'.[9] The present book is basically an attempt to construct a kind of fable in Steiner's sense, and my main point is that literature and criticism make available and confirm a view of the person as constituted within the play of presence and absence fundamental to language. This entails an assessment of persons as historically situated and in process of becoming through time; as autonomous and self-creating to a degree, yet shaped by prior commitments; and as called to recognition, evaluation, and obligation to standards. It follows that, as persons, we begin only from where we already are, and however far back we look, we find that earlier beginnings are themselves marks of a narrative already under way, directed into the world by agents able to plan, to interact, to work towards a goal.

At first, *Homo faber* laboured reflectively as man-maker-of-tools, leaving relics or fragmentary signs of himself: Oldowan choppers from half a million years ago, hand axes and cleavers of the Acheulian, struck from prepared cores by techniques enduring through the long sojourn of *homo erectus* and Neanderthal; then the leaf-points and burins of the Cro-Magnon peoples before the making of metals. Cro-Magnon learned also to propitiate the hunt by painting the underground limestone at Les Combarells and Lascaux, Font de Gaume and Cap Blanc and at almost a hundred sites in the Dordogne alone, beginning perhaps thirty thousand years ago. Nor were these painted animals just to kill. They are depicted fecund, pregnant, lactating, as well as speared and trapped: painted over and over, layer upon layer in a ritual mimesis of the fragile interdependency between the human and its sustaining environment.

Whatever changes in language accompanied such developments across the millennia remain unrecorded until literate cultures provide a window, especially onto the primordial myths and tales already developed in oral tradition. Beginning in approximately the third millennium BC with protoliterate pictograms and hieroglyphics, written language slowly found its way to the flexibility of alphabetic script, so that something of the ancient sagas and myths of Mesopotamia, Egypt, and Canaan survives in forms recorded in the second millennium BC. In such a context, the Hebrew Bible provides a unique narrative of a people and culture discovering itself before God in history through repeated transgression and exodus, beginning with the nomadic *khabiru* of some four thousand years ago. Yet the account we have today is itself a result of intricate workings and reworkings of old stories and cult wisdom by a variety of hands from the ninth to the second century BC. Not surprisingly, laminations and echoes blend with more ancient and foreign texts from surrounding cultures, themselves echoes of even more shrouded beginnings.

Again with momentous import, alphabetic writing came to Greece in the eighth century BC when the songs of blind (perhaps, that is, illiterate) Homer were set down. Like those of the Bible, Homer's tales also recede through the further reaches of memory to old campaigns against the Mycenaeans, to Troy sacked in the thirteenth century BC (Troy VII.b, that is), to volcanic eruptions on Thera triggering a series of disasters, especially by tidal flood, that wrecked established coastal civilizations and caused mass migrations and conquering expeditions through the Mediterranean basin. Perhaps the exodus from Egypt and the story of unusual tidal behaviour at the Sea of Reeds are part of this general pattern, as are the wanderings of Odysseus through Homer's strangely a-chronological, half-enchanted mythical time, still haunted by echoes of pre-historical matriarchal cults and dreams of lost ways of life.

To some scholars, Odysseus has seemed to make his way with remarkably little self-consciousness, and it has been observed that Homer has no notion of a person in the modern sense. For instance, as Bruno Snell claims, Homer has no word for 'mind', but rather a variety of words (*psyche, thumos, nous*) indicating the functions of bodily organs and their affects.[10] Although Snell's thesis is questionable and needs to be carefully hedged, it is clear that Greek speculation discovered the concept of mind in a philosophical sense, and with it the distinction between body and soul. In so doing, the philosophers in one way left Homer behind, but in the manner of the Biblical redactors of the ancient sagas, they also appropriated in their search for certainty the great themes already implicit in him: the relationships between change and permanence, words and truth, reality and illusion, appearances and judgement. In short, the ancient myths and symbols penetrate to enveloping recesses where our bodies take hold of a world. If such myths and symbols do not touch us where we all belong, they cannot bring us where we need to go, and speculation based on them is futile.

Here then the argument turns upon itself, for the old stories help us to see that the human ego before the discovery of mind is not simply equatable with the ego we take for granted as naturally our own. 'I' is not given once and for all as a kind of searchlight to look out on things, but is discovered through labour among things. Descartes' attempt in the seventeenth century to found himself indubitably in the *cogito* after having called everything in doubt is therefore itself part of a story rather than the beginning of the true story, as he supposed. A retrieval of the antique past and of the shrouded realms of prehistory can therefore add a great deal to our understanding of how 'I' is historically produced, shaped by the uncertain processes of becoming through which knowledge is made. In this process, language gives us a world, though things in themselves reserve their secret, as words like probes search out the hidden interiors, and culture then is a means to an end, a community *en route*, finding itself out.

As Ernst Bloch says, the human is constituted within a dynamic of 'is and not-yet',[11] for 'is' entails the presence of the past and the fact that knowledge is traditional; 'not yet' that the present is drawn, as by gravitational pull, to a condition that would repair its deficiencies, relieving it of scandal and contradiction. Literature and criticism, I want to suggest, are produced also within such a dialectic, extending our bodies and making us present to one another, while confirming also our strange opaqueness and mutual separations, the conditions of our habitation within history's narrative.

WORDS AND DEEDS: ON READING SWIFT AND SYNGE

Literary criticism has come late into the arena of rigorous epistemology, but the widespread impact during the past fifteen years of structuralist and deconstructionist arguments upon the study of literature has introduced a far-reaching interest in the broadly post-Kantian problem of what words do and do not give us. This is a complex debate, and for the moment I want to hold to the elementary observations I have made in the previous section: language is another kind of tool, a means not only of shaping a world, but of possessing and finding ourselves within it, and within history. Language moreover gives us our most distinctly human purposes, but we follow these gropingly, feeling our way and modelling a sense of personal identity through the signs, symbols and reflections which, gathered together as a way of life, we call culture.

In this context, I take literature to be, among other things, one complex expression of the making of culture and of the idea of the person. In this process, literature affords also a singular means for coming to know and investigate a certain, twofold danger of misunderstanding the interplay within language of presence and absence, transparency and opacity. On the one hand, we need to avoid thinking that words are simply transparent to things and therefore make things present; on the other, we need to avoid thinking that words are produced by consciousness alone and do not refer to things, which therefore remain entirely opaque. This joint error is broached in both Jonathan Swift's satire in Voyage III of *Gulliver's Travels*, and in J. M. Synge's *The Playboy of the Western World*.

Voyage III is generally considered the least satisfactory part of *Gulliver's Travels*[12] because it is episodic and slapstick, but it thematises satirically the dangers of treating words as if they refer exactly to things. Everywhere, Swift's dearest preoccupation is how such an attitude to language blinds us to human inconsistencies and breeds cruelty and oppression.

In the opening episode of Voyage III, Gulliver's ship is seized by pirates, one of whose leaders is Dutch and another Japanese. Gulliver initially appeals to the Dutchman, on the grounds of 'our being Christians and Protestants, of neighbouring Countries, in strict Alliance' (154), but this only increases the pirate's homicidal rage. Gulliver's life is saved by the Japanese, so that Gulliver is set adrift rather than tied back to back with another man and thrown into the sea, as the Dutch pirate wishes.

In principle, the English and Dutch are allies, but principle here is inadequate to the complexity of actual human dealings. This at once reflects Swift's opinion that the Dutch had been false allies (acting counter to principle, that is) in the War of the Spanish Succession, and also that progressive Dutch ideas on science, religion and trade would breed a materialism that Swift feared as distortive of common sense and humane practice.[13] Almost everything in Voyage III follows from this opening in which theory and practice, word and deed, language and body, are at odds.

The stranded Gulliver is soon picked up by the astonishing flying island of Laputa. But the Laputans have their feet off the ground in more senses than one, for their lives are given over to speculation based on the assumption that reality conforms to concepts. In one sense, however, the Laputans are right, because the island does indeed fly, and is a technological *tour de force*. Yet their very success and power make their lack of common sense about language and things all the more disturbing, and not just silly. Still, they certainly are silly: they make Gulliver a suit of clothes by taking elaborate measurements with complex instruments, but the clothes do not fit. Likewise, they praise women's beauty 'by Rhombs, Circles, Parallelograms, Ellipses, and other Geometrical Terms' (163), but the women have affairs with strangers whose presence is more immediate than that of their absent-minded, speculating husbands.

Swift's account of Laputa is perhaps a satire specifically on Cartesianism, but it is part also of his general parody of the *Philosophical*

Transactions of the Royal Society.[14] Thus Gulliver's Laputan tutor explains with an abundance of technical, 'scientific' detail how the island flies (167), and it is no surprise for the reader to learn that the Laputans do not have a word for imagination (163). (One recalls Sprat's famous advice on 'so many *things*, almost in an equal number of *words*', and on 'clear senses . . . bringing all things as near the Mathematical plainness, as they can').[15] In short, Laputan faith in naming is so complete that common nouns come to have the reality of things, which are taken as the only reality. But such beliefs are disastrous, for one result of denying the body's complex unreasonableness and need for relationship is that the body takes revenge. Thus the Laputans suffer from chronic anxiety caused by their astronomical calculations, and they inhabit hopelessly ill-built houses and dress in foolish, ill-fitting clothes while their wives betray them. Meanwhile, at the distinguished Academy at Lagado on the island of Balnibarbi (to which the flying island is attached),[16] scientists struggle with a variety of absurd projects marked by uselessness, filth and absurdity.

This state of affairs, as Swift brilliantly sees, leads inevitably to a catastrophic diminishment of language itself. Because things in fact resist appropriation by words, it follows that attempts to explain all experience exactly along Cartesian or Newtonian lines end up in confusion and absurdity. Thus, the mechanical language-frame set up at Lagdano to improve knowledge through the objective process of automatic combination produces only chaos. The target here is Bacon's attempt to make a system from aphorisms, pieces of 'knowledge broken' (as Bacon says) and restructured on a mechanistic model.[17] So the 'School of Languages' sets out to clarify language but ends up abolishing it: 'since Words are only the Names for *Things*, it would be more convenient for all Men to carry about them, such *Things* as were necessary to express the particular Business they are to discourse on' (185). This absurd project is stopped only by the threat of rebellion from 'Women in Conjunction with the Vulgar and Illiterate' (185), those 'common People' who, Swift suggests, bring plain sense to bear on the matter. In short, attempts to mechanise language end up making another Babel: as everyone knows, Laputa means 'whore', and the satire on a new idolatry of the Whore of Babylon in the form of a false science imposing its reified abstractions reaches for inspiration all the way to Genesis.[18]

A further negative consequence of taking words as 'only the

Names for *Things'* is intimated by the common people's rebellion, for there is an inevitable link in Voyage III between reified language and political oppression. To the extent that one holds that names simply correspond to things, one is likely to impose one's ideas in the name of reality itself. Thus the flying island is used to suppress the rebellious Lindalinians (the Irish, in Swift's political allegory), and it is usual practice for Laputa to block out the sun and cause disease and famine in dissident townships (171). In short, it is easy to be cruel on principle, and it is easy to be confident about principles when common nouns are taken naively as referential. Swift's concern here, and elsewhere from the Drapier's Letters to *A Tale of a Tub* and *The Mechanical Operation of the Spirit*, is that oppression, cruelty and the evils of colonisation depend on distortions of our singular cultural advantage, namely language.

Taking words for things in a Laputan manner has, however, as its mirror image the error of seeking in imaginative word play an escape from things. J. M. Synge's *The Playboy of the Western World*[19] makes a useful comparison to Swift because it mainly explores this second kind of distortion and how it also contributes to political oppression – again in Ireland.

Synge's playboy is Christy Mahon, a timid young man who travels in the company of his bullying father. Christy is at last driven to strike old Mahon with a spade, and runs off leaving him for dead. He then stops off at Michael James Flaherty's public house, where he quickly finds his story puts him in the limelight. So he embellishes it and is treated as a hero, especially by Pegeen Mike, the publican's daughter. Christy grows more confident and assertive as his story takes hold, and even starts living up to the expectations others have of him. But things change when old Mahon turns up, nursing a wounded head. Christy's admirers quickly turn against him ('I'll set the young lads to destroy him here [163]', says his true-love, Pegeen). In his extremity, Christy attacks old Mahon again, and leaves him again for dead. This time the locals apprehend their playboy, intending to hand him over to the law, and in a frenzy of resentment Pegeen burns his leg with a piece of turf from the fire. But once more old Mahon survives. Christy is freed and is now, at last, in charge. He leaves with his father, while Pegeen laments.

As Christy comes to realise late in the action, 'you're after making a mighty man of me this day by the power of a lie' (165). The lie is mainly his own imaginative extension of an event nobody else has seen, but he depends also on the indulgence and co-operation of his audience.[20] Christy's 'poet's talking' (149) or 'eloquence' (147) takes on a life separate from the event he supposedly describes, and induces in others a fantasised sense of freedom from the constraints of law and institutional control. In short, 'poet's talking' can be escapist, as becomes evident when the real, conspicuously anti-poetic old Mahon appears and Christy's assault on him dispels the heroic illusion.[21] Fear of the authorities then rushes in to fill the void.

The play invokes absent but menacing authority in various ways. For instance, Shawn Keogh awaits the dispensation from Father Reilly and the bishops to permit him to marry Pegeen. There are several kinds of licences (for dogs, marriages, the public house), while 'Peelers', militia, 'loosèd khaki cut-throats' (75) and dispensers of English justice shadow the conversation, as do stories of hangings. The splendour of fine words and tall tales is thus an antidote and to some degree a protest against juridical authority, but it is also, ironically, a disengagement from real issues, confirming the hold of the oppressors. Christy discovers something of this when he realises 'there's a great gap between a gallous story and a dirty deed' (169), and the knowledge helps to liberate him from servility to his father. Meanwhile, Synge renders the whole complex. The entrancing coloratura of Christy and Pegeen's language is romantic but also treacherous because escapist from actual, common concerns. Their indulgence covers up fears and resentments which then in turn engender hatred and confusion, as when Christy is set upon by his erstwhile admirers. As Synge well knew, the peasants of Mayo and the Congested Districts lived on the edge of starvation and in distressing conditions about which he wrote despairingly in his essays and notebooks.[22] The reality was not romantic at all, and yet Synge also admired the poetry of Western Irish speech. As is often remarked, the perplexing, dynamic interplay between reality and fantasy is central to *The Playboy*, which celebrates the joyous language while dramatising an un-poetic social reality.[23]

Synge's achievement in all this was scarcely understood by the rioters who felt insulted during the first performances at the Abbey Theatre and later in the United States, so that the play (ironically) could proceed only with police protection.[24] But such lack of understanding is not surprising, for Synge's effects are brilliantly mixed, and, as he himself pointed out in a canny letter to the Times,[25] the pattern of praise and blame in *The Playboy* is not straightforward.

For instance, the 'loy' or spade with which Christy strikes his father ('I just riz the loy and let fall the edge of it on the ridge of his skull' [73]) is a complex motif. As Christy says, 'the blow of a loy' taught him about the difference between the 'gallous story' and the 'dirty deed' (169). But in dialect speech 'lie' is pronounced almost exactly like 'loy'. Thus the loy with which Christy strikes is also the lie by which he contrives to escape the consequence of his action. In this context, the depiction of Christy as a parody of Christ ('Christy Son of Mahon', says Hugh Kenner)[26] takes on an added dimension, for the law here also is transcended by the power of the word, Christy's tall story.

In short, Synge partly shows us how people can co-operate with their oppressors as do Pegeen and the others who first indulge Christy's romantic energy as an escapist distraction, and then shut out its transforming potential in order to return to the Western World ruled by Father Reilly and the peelers. Paradoxically, Christy re-shapes himself through imagination, though he is forced also to curtail its scope, adjusting his 'lie' to a disenchanting reality before he leaves, in charge of himself and (relatively) independent.

Altogether, Christy's career shows how imaginative language needs engagement with events, an objective state of affairs, a common condition. In this, Synge is at one with Swift, for cruelty and oppression find their way through the 'gap', or absence between words and things of which Christy speaks and of which the Laputans are unaware. Language, it seems, can be neither the thing itself nor just consciousness, but is a productive synthesis, a continuing dialectical upheaval, making and unmaking, present and absent simultaneously.

CRITICAL PRACTICE: RECENT CONTEXTS

The present then already is the past, a tradition of knowing, and yet the present is also fugitive and slips away on a trajectory plotted by the energies of desire towards the 'not yet' of a longed-for possibility. Literature, I am suggesting, teaches us how to grasp such a fugitive but real sense of presence, and it does so today in a critical climate especially taken up by epistemological problems of a broadly post-Kantian sort, relating to how words make things present, and what they occlude. The story of the recent rise of critical theory engaging these issues is generally acknowledged to owe much to the joint impact upon literary criticism of Saussurian linguistics and Lévi-Strauss's structuralist anthropology.

As is well known, Saussure makes a fundamental distinction between 'langue' and 'parole'[27] to indicate the general system of a language as distinct from the individual use of that system by a speaker. For Saussure, linguistics is concerned with 'langue', and the key to studying linguistics is the sign. A sign combines a signifier and a signified: the former is a sound-image; the latter the concept to which the signifier refers. Signs are made up of signifier and signified but have no direct reference to reality and are chosen arbitrarily: for instance, there is no inherent reason why the letters p, i, and n should signify the idea of a metal object used as a fastener. The word 'pin' gets its meaning rather because of its difference from other signifiers within the system: 'in language there are only differences without positive terms', as Saussure says in a much-cited phrase. Thus the signifiers 'pin', 'bin' and 'sin' gain meaning not because they describe discrete, actual things, but because of how they are distinguished from one another. A pin, after all, can refer to a metal fastener, a hold in wrestling, or a wooden peg. We come to know these meanings through a complex series of differences among signifiers, and from the fact that the signified does not have a stable relationship with either the signifier or the referent. For Saussure's linguistics, referents are not important: he prefers to study the structure of signs.

Claude Lévi-Strauss set out to explore how the 'langue' of culture at large contains various kinds of further coded relationships enabling societies to cohere. Kinship systems, cooking, religious practices, face-painting, and so on, are ways of classifying and ordering society and of mediating its contradictions. The same is true of myths, which embody a basic algebra, or set of relations which show us some fundamental ways in which humans organise themselves socially. Again, this structural algebra is more important for Lévi-Stauss than what a myth, or story, might seem to mean in a more obvious sense.[28]

One advantage of all this when applied to literary criticism has been to promote a certain liberation from the dogmatisms of literal-mindedness. Real significance we now know might be otherwise than the plain meanings of a text indicate, and we all might act and judge in accord with deep-seated structures, despite the variety of our circumstances and apparent freedoms. Freud, Marx, and Darwin have in common the principle that deep structures operate as codes challenging the received pieties of common sense. To this degree they are forerunners of a structuralism that has since returned to them for sustenance by a variety of roads. Another way of putting this is to say that submerged laws of the text are essential: laws beneath the surface do not change but operate in a perpetual present, which is hypostasised.

Just so, Newton's followers likewise thought he had discovered the immutable structure of the universe once and for all: 'God said, *Let Newton be*! and all was *Light*,' as Pope burstingly put it. But then came Einstein. In some such fashion, post-structuralist criticism has taken structuralism to task in the name of indeterminacy, and especially by attacking the idea of presence. In the words of Robert Young, post-structuralism in general aims to fracture 'the serene unity of the stable sign and the unifed subject':[29] that is, it calls in question claims made in the name of truth, or metaphysics, or the stable subject, or essential structural principles. Indeed, structuralism's own idea about the perennial shifting of meaning within networks of differences is turned back upon structuralism itself and, as need be, on the history of metaphysics – which is to say, on most of Western philosophy. Consequently, post-structuralism is less adequately described as a movement than as a kind of vigilant and solvent attitude. It is bent on demonstrating how self-authenticating knowledge, like the stable knowing subject, is based on nostalgia for unity which is never attainable through language because meaning is never stable but dispersed through differences along a perennially shifting chain of signifiers. Thus, Derrida isolates Rousseau's key assumption that speech is a natural source of language and writing its secondary distortion, just as civilization is a secondary distortion of nature. Derrida argues instead that language is always already in a sense 'writing' (écriture) because always already alienated from nature and other than present to itself in the transparency of a definitive meaning. Consequently, common-sense assumptions about authors and critics, or authors and readers, or the primacy of the 'text' to discourse about the 'text', are all found to depend on distinctions that, under scrutiny, betray an unacknowledged desire for stability, closure, and presence. If Lévi-Strauss hypostasiscs the presence of structural laws, Derrida celebrates the freedoms attendant on the absence of any enduring law whatever.

As is frequently pointed out, extreme scepticism at last cannot state its own principles, for to do so is to make an absolute statement and thus to capitulate to the enemy. But this often is not the main issue to raise with sceptics. Rather, there is a baleful scepticism (as with the philosopher in Keats' *Lamia* whose gaze freezes the lifeblood of thinking), and an energising kind (like Montaigne's) that opens what has already been frozen over. There are thus refrigerating and thawing scepticisms; the first is destructive of thinking, but the second is its regenerator. The pressing question with recent developments in literary theory is whether they are freeing the waters or freezing them.

Further aspects of this debate will be taken up as this book progresses. For the moment, and with intent to free rather than freeze, I have tried in this introduction to sketch an approach to literature that occupies a place between those who tend to reify language (and so lean towards the excesses of Laputa) and those who see truth as something made by consciousness in an endless play of metaphor (who lean towards the excesses of 'poet's talking'). In so doing, I have suggested that a sense of self or of personal identity is historically produced by continuing engagement with others in a world where we are at once prepossessed and alienated. The foundation myths and symbols by which cultures enter history reflect the multivalency of this prepossession and separation: the fragility of life, the dark radiances of birth, death, loss, cleansing, feeding, journeying, and so on. Such myths and symbols then call for clarification, if only because, irreducibly, they compel our recognition and concern. Yet the languages of clarification and the institutions these languages engender discover themselves in turn less than adequate to experience. Therefore they keep returning to the symbols for revivification, while in turn developing their own rhetoric to persuade, both about their truth claims and inadequacies, thereby engendering fresh metaphors, new narratives.[30] Culture is thus the history of a perpetual dialectic between symbol and understanding, image and idea, carried on within a complex play of mimesis and occlusion, presence and absence, 'is and not-yet'.

To summarise briefly: the sense of one's self is historically produced in a dynamic of prepossession and development towards a possible future. The great poetry by which a culture enters history leaves its mark on this process, and on the kinds of literature through which it develops. This being the case, symbol and clarification require one another, as do literature and criticism, exegesis and theory. Only by preserving the tension between metaphoric and reflective languages are fresh metaphors developed to express the inadequacies as well as the potential of what is made clear. Finally, literature and criticism make accessible a complex knowledge of the development of culture and language, and I want to invoke this idea as a way of assessing what it means to be a person capable of a degree of self-presence and presence to others, able to make plans entailing commitment and calling for clarification. But first, I would like to turn to some fundamental issues touched on by this introduction and which need examining in more detail, precisely because they are the underpinnings of what I take a person to be. These are the experiences of belonging (the sense of presence and participation), of alienation (the sense of absence), and the consequent desire for wholeness and plenitude, recovering for the future what we have lost from the past.

2

Fundamentals

BELONGING: ON HERMENEUTICS AND PHENOMENOLOGY

One belongs, albeit unwittingly, and reflection brings this fact to light. But every attempt at recapturing the beginning even of reflection leads to perplexity, and 'I' thus seeking itself is thrown back inevitably among the scattering lights of its own facets. The means by which reflection might imperfectly recover some such intuition of belonging are explored by a broad movement in philosophy during this century associated with hermeneutics and phenomenology.

The term 'hermeneutics' was first widely used in biblical criticism to set out rules for approaching a text and for distinguishing between its various senses.[1] Biblical manuals typically divide hermeneutics into noematics (the senses of scripture), heuristics (how to discover what sense is appropriate) and prophoristics (how to convey the sense to others). These manuals aim to establish guidelines for fixing a right understanding of sacred scripture in line with shared traditions of exegesis.

A crisis for this kind of hermeneutics occurred during the Enlightenment, when a widespread critical interest in the Bible as a set of historical documents forced interpreters to regard the sacred scriptures not just as revealed, but as one element in a whole complex of cultural experience. It lay then especially with Friedrich Schleiermacher (1768–1834) to establish the watershed distinction between special and general hermeneutics, the latter dealing with knowledge in the widest sense, and in relation to the totality from which it is inseparable.[2] Schleiermacher was particularly interested in relationships between individual speakers and their language: 'Accordingly, each person represents one locus where a given language takes shape in a particular way, and his speech can be understood only in the context of the totality of language.' Psychologically, that is, the person is 'a constantly developing spirit'

15

(99), but the inner totality can be grasped only in terms of an inherited language-system, with which the speaker interacts by a kind of organic fusion or synthesis.

Schleiermacher's most influential student, Wilhelm Dilthey (1833–1911), developed his mentor's theory in a more technical direction by attempting to provide a foundation for knowledge across the spectrum of human sciences. Dilthey proposed that understanding is a 'category of life' (*Lebenskategorie*) originating in what we take life to be in the largest sense. Human beings 'understand' life situations by immersion, and react appropriately without being fully conscious of how they do so. Acts of understanding are lived experiences not entirely reducible to language, but rather reflecting the complex ways we take up a place in society, culture and history. These understandings are 'expressed' (a key term for Dilthey) in different kinds of behaviour.[3] Yet Dilthey's work did not come to maturity before he had read Edmund Husserl's *Logical Investigations*, and since Husserl (1859–1938) is usually hailed as the father of modern phenomenology, we might see already in Dilthey's hermeneutics the beginnings of a convergence leading to the so-called 'phenomenological hermeneutics' of Husserl's student, Martin Heidegger.

The etymological root of 'phenomenon' is 'a thing appearing', and philosophical preoccupation with relationships between sensible appearances and real essences has marked the course of Western thinking since Plato's thematising of the problem in his teachings on 'forms' and 'copies'. Throughout ancient and medieval thought, metaphysics remained the regulating science for studying sense perception, and hence also for studying physical nature. From such a perspective, language was trusted to disclose some aspect of the divinely established order of things.[4]

As with hermeneutics, a major crisis occurred for the medieval, metaphysically-grounded way of thinking in the Renaissance and Enlightenment, when mathematics replaced metaphysics as the governing science for studying nature, thus bringing about what we now call the scientific revolution. In its wake, all talk of metaphysical 'substances' or 'essences' and the like was widely relegated to the dungeon of medieval obscurantism. Notions about language participating in a divinely-scripted book of the world were increasingly replaced among those influenced by the new scientific method by a view of language as a tool for controlling a recalcitrant and inert physical nature.

Among the new philosophers, Descartes (1590–1650) pre-eminent-ly was concerned to place the mathematico-physical approach to nature on a secure footing. Although he clung still to medieval talk about substances, he used this terminology mainly to confirm a split between human 'thinking substance' and the 'extended substance' of material nature. Categorically separate from an inert, mechanical world, the Cartesian ego now becomes free to contrive means to subject and control nature by experiments governed by mathematical calculation. The results would change the face of the earth more radically, rapidly, and extensively than anything else in history.

I mention Descartes because modern phenomenology has been especially concerned to reject as naive his distinctions between thought and extension, subject and object. Thus, for Husserl, the Cartesian *cogito* is highly problematic, even though Descartes' method of systematic doubt, holding apperances and common sense in suspension is also, precisely, Husserl's own. However, in contrast to Descartes, Husserl wants to describe various modes of human presence in the world. Science is to take its place within the varieties of human consciousness, and Husserl aims to present consciousness as a kind of transcendental foundation for different kinds of knowledge.[5]

One key means for achieving his purposes derives from Husserl's teacher Franz Brentano (1838–1917), who in turn drew upon scholastic philosophy for the notion that mental acts are distinct because they are 'intentional'. Husserl also stressed the importance of intention, arguing that every thought is about something, and so 'intends' its object. Consciousness therefore can be said partly to constitute its object, and strict distinctions between subject and object are untenable. Phenomenology for Husserl is then basically an attempt to reduce phenomena to the stream of consciousness, the basic forms of conscious presence. He proceeds by way of the so-called *epoche* or suspension of judgement, until the essential forms or *eideia* are disclosed to reflection in their absolute being.

To explore the mystery of Being, Husserl therefore re-deploys the key scholastic concept of intentionality to address his own specifi-cally post-Cartesian circumstances. But also, in describing Being from a point of view that attacks the separation between subject and object, Husserl is forced upon a language that itself evokes the kind of presentness with which he deals. One result is a diminishment of the difference between the languages of philosophy and poetry, a point that returns us to hermeneutics, and especially to Martin Heidegger.

As we have seen, for Husserl the main point of enquiry is consciousness and its contents. Heidegger (1889–1976) carefully redirects this enquiry towards existence, the world of things, 'being-in-the-world', as he says. He does so partly by insisting on a strong identity between hermeneutics and phenomenology: 'The phenomenology of Dasein is a *hermeneutic* in the primordial signification of this word, where it designates this business of interpreting.'[6] That is, our understanding of being-in-the-world comes through the process of interpretation, which for Heidegger (as for Schleiermacher) is intimately connected with language. Through language, human beings are uniquely able to question their own existence, and with this power of questioning comes an experience of dread (*angst*), but also of hope, the projection of one's self towards what Heidegger calls authentic existence. By this he means choosing resolutely a fullness of being in face of one's possibilities and temporal limits, which is to say, death. Thus, for Heidegger the process through which hermeneutics discloses being-in-the-world is temporal, or historical. Human existence (*Dasein*, 'being there') is thrown into a situation where meaning is discovered through the merging of past, present and future horizons. In this context, Being is not an object set over against a subject, and Heidegger looks especially to the pre-Socratics for an example of authentic speech without the modern subject-object cleavage. He tells us that Western metaphysics has forgotten this original presence of Being to language, and the post-Cartesian technologists and controllers of nature are the worst offenders.

In *Being and Time*, Heidegger sets out to restore our sense of Being, partly by argument but partly also by breaking through the familiar concepts and mental constructs by which our culture has brought about its own amnesia, its forgetfulness of belonging. Typically, Heidegger conducts us by way of powerful indirections whereby language digs back through the sediment of its own conventional sense to a revelatory moment where words give us a world – a sense of Being. The shock and wonder produced by poetry recover this sense also, and Heidegger the philosopher often contrives to produce a poetic effect of felt strangeness as a means of recovering the primordial 'unconcealedness'. By refusing in this way to treat Being as an object, Heidegger also develops the idea (deriving from Dilthey) that our 'thrownness' (*Geworfenheit*) into the world entails pre-understanding. That is, we belong beyond our conscious knowing, and in the anxious process of interpreting, questioning and choosing, we must learn again to listen to the rich presentness of Being that constitutes us, and not alienate ourselves from it by the designs of control and power.

Heidegger's 'phenomenological hermeneutics' has had far-reaching effects on a wide range of twentieth-century thinkers, and I will return to *Being and Time* in the third section of this chapter. Meanwhile, I want simply to notice how hermeneutics and phenomenology help to establish anew, and in terms appropriate for a post-scientific, secular culture, a pre-linguistic intuition of belonging. By reading these philosophers we might better come to recognise how we have complex pre-understandings through our bodies, to which we must strive to make language responsive. The claim that such recognition is evoked or made present in a singular way through the symbols and metaphors of art and culture remains fundamental to this study. Yet certain liabilities attendant upon phenomenological hermeneutics in general call also for a word of caution. Especially, it is important not to treat in too cavalier a fashion the processes of scientific verification and empiricism with which phenomenology and hermeneutics often take issue. Nor should we ignore how history is fraught with struggle, contradiction and ideologically-manipulated injustice. But these matters are the topics of later chapters; meanwhile, let us return to the idea of belonging, and how it is fundamental to the description of a person.

For Heidegger, the discovery of Being is never complete, but is effected in momentary irradiations, or 'clearings' in the labyrinths of experience. One compelling explanation of how we might integrate the perpetual, unknown surplus of Being into a theory of cognition and personal knowledge is offered by Michael Polanyi (1891–1976),[7] who draws broadly on the phenomenological tradition to distinguish between what we attend *to*, and what we attend *from*. Polanyi draws on Gestalt psychology, basically to argue the Heideggerian point that we always 'know more than we can tell'. He then goes on to analyse the 'tacit dimension' upon which we rely in order to attend *to* anything at all. For instance, we can recognise a person's face among a million others, and yet we usually cannot tell how we do so. This is because we 'attend from a large number of clues, most of which we cannot identify, to the physiognomy which they indicate'.[8] The focus of attention (the physiognomy) is the meaning of the clues that make up the shape we recognise. But we are only subsidiarily aware of the clues as we attend to the face, and if we focus on one of the clues, we lose sight of the whole.

Polanyi analyses numerous such examples, emphasising how they pertain to acquiring skills, using tools, and making complex discriminations. Basically, he wants to show how the body is a ground *from* which we focus when we use language, and which therefore can never be fully attended to. Even in turning language back on a part of the process (as we are now doing) we find ourselves still attending from a further tacit ground: the immense, unconscious complexity of our being in the world, through which language mysteriously blossoms and which is always more than we can say. For Polanyi, as for Heidegger, we cannot finally make articulate what we know, and we are always committed 'passionately and far beyond our comprehension'.[9] Consequently, even in the sciences knowing is an art involving apprenticeship, a set of skills learned by participation and immersion. Knowledge then is also connoisseurship, the roots of which are not available to clear explanation, but acquired only by belonging in a working community. Knowing by doing is the key to all learning even though we cannot fully know what we do.

Polanyi extends these principles to art, and here his theory comes even closer to Heidegger's, for Polanyi's main point is that art shows afresh how subsidiary elements in perception are engaged and assumed in our knowing and recognising a familiar world.[10] Art forces us to discover anew the ground from which we attend and which informs and energises what we think of as ordinary. Through art, that is, we are enabled to re-experience something of the bodily-rooted, emotionally-charged, intuitively-felt, inexact sense of belonging: the ontological mystery from which language arises to focus on its object, naming and thereby fashioning the thing named as part of a world. The making-force of words thus is perpetually remade through literature, as metaphor and symbol disclose new dimensions of our familiar world, and in so doing forge new meanings. As Heidegger says, poetry 'takes place in language because language preserves the original nature of poetry'. In short, poetry gives us again the sense of wonder and surprise that is the 'Being of beings in the sense of presence'.[11] And it does so from the very heart of ordinariness – the things and people around us we always thought we knew.

Polanyi and Heidegger are carefully responsive to the intimacy between body and language, and the paradoxical separateness from the body that language effects. They also draw attention to an unspeakable surplus, a nebula of pre-understanding, informative yet unformulated. Consequently, the search for an absolute place to start and to ground our certainties is as vain as the quest for a complete final system. It seems that although we can posit a totality in which we belong, we know it imperfectly, being always in the midst, and riven, attending from an unspecifiable complexity to a particular focus. This also is our situation as persons in history, for the past likewise is a tacit ground informing the present with a set of assumed, often ignored, pre-understandings.

For instance, it is commonplace in literary history that a 'medieval world view' was displaced during the Renaissance and Enlightenment. Certainly, the shift from a Ptolemaic to a Copernican heaven and from an Aristotelian to a Galilean physics is, in the broadest terms, sufficiently decisive that today the old scheme has largely to be re-learned from the outside: approached, in C. S. Lewis's terms, as a discarded image. Modern students are likely to see it as a quaint set of metaphors and fanciful beliefs rather more unlike our sense of the world than like it. And yet, we have departed from this past less decisively than we might think, and it remains a constitutive part of our selves. Let me now make this more clear.

As I have noticed, pre-Renaissance natural science was governed by metaphysics rather than mathematics, and everywhere assumed a supreme Being in whose hands we and the world belong together. This does not deny that medieval people experienced anguish and despair: starvation, tyranny, plague, high infant mortality, superstition, and so on, meant that terror and misery were sufficiently immediate. Yet all this was accounted for by a set of universally promulgated assumptions. Our history, it was said, begins in original sin, and our inheritance is mortality, broken will, and delayed intellect. Suffering therefore has a cause and is to be taken up in the larger design of the second Adam, Christ, who gathers the faithful at the end of our earthly pilgrimage, which is also history's pilgrimage. In short, we are to have faith in a personal belonging, even through our most negative and alienating experiences. No doubt, the victim on the rack or the patient enduring the operation without anaesthetic would have found minimal relief in such doctrine, but the doctrine stood to guarantee publicly an all-embracing meaning and order.

These teachings were further characterised by the familiar broadcast theories about participation, teleology and hierarchy. By participation I mean a felt identity with the interior energies informing our everyday world, and which language apprehends (the very sense, indeed, that phenomenologists would have us recover in terms appropriate for our modern circumstances). The general notion can be grasped through the intuition everywhere evident in medieval literature and philosophy, that thinking is not confined to the human mind in a Cartesian manner, with the ego set over and against an inert material world. Rather, as in Plato's *Timaeus* and Aristotle's *De Anima*, medieval metaphysicians assumed that movement itself manifests spirit. Thus the rotating heavenly bodies as well as ordinary growing, living things show forth spiritual activity indicating God's presence and purposes. Moreover, everything in heaven and earth, including ourselves and our history of suffering, is directed teleologically to appointed ends, to fulfilments appropriate to their created natures. All of which in turn confirmed a further confidence that these ends can be known and hierarchically ordered along a chain of being whereby vegetable, animal, human and angelic natures are arranged on a scale of increasing purity. Just so, in each human individual, the soul's reasonable element should rule its appetitive and animal parts, so that here also a hierarchy is maintained whereby the human corresponds to and participates in the creation as a whole.

In various ways, these principles were adapted and translated into theories of monarchy, feudalism, the family, monasteries, guilds, the arts and a host of other – indeed virtually all other – areas. Again, I do not suggest that people's behaviour conformed simply to the theory, but rather, through the multiple, symbolic manifestations and endless exegesis of such principles, a human world declares itself in the form of a distinctive culture. Thus from Augustine to Aquinas, among the encyclopaedists, allegorisers of the classics, commentators on scripture, homilists, spiritual masters, and Galenic interpreters of the body's temperaments, the intricate classifications of hierarchies, ends, and patterns of participation were worked out according to an infinitely pursuable *analogia entis*, the analogy of Being in which all things declare their belonging and consequently their hope in the face of suffering.

Such is the old, forlorn picture, and we have departed far enough from it, and yet it in turn constitutes a dimension – albeit tacit , as Polanyi would have it – of the culture that has developed from it.

My sketch of the historical development of pheonomenology and hermeneutics itself indicates something of how this is so. But to develop this idea of cultural continuity and difference in relation to the notion of belonging, let us look at a literary example from the Middle Ages, and compare it to one from our own century.

The *Secunda Pastorum* (c. 1400)[12] by the so-called Wakefield master is perhaps the most distinguished single work of medieval English cycle drama. It celebrates Christ's nativity, and offers an engaging amalgam of coarseness and sophistication, farce and theology. The play opens with some shepherds gathered on the wintry moors, watching their sheep and complaining about their lot in life. Mak, a well-known thief, joins them, and while they are asleep he steals a sheep which he brings to his wife and hides in a cradle: if he is pursued he will pretend his wife has just given birth. The shepherds suspect Mak and search his hut, but they cannot find the lost sheep, and so they leave. But one of them has a qualm of conscience and returns to offer a gift to the newborn child, at which point the theft is discovered. Rather than turn Mak over to the authorities, the shepherds toss him in a blanket. Later, as they sleep, they are awakened and summoned by an angel to visit another hut (presumably at the side of the stage opposite to Mak's) and this time they witness the birth of Christ, to whom they offer gifts.

One striking thing about *Secunda Pastorum* for a modern audience or reader is the way in which it deals with history. The shepherds inhabit fourteenth-century England, complaining about English weather, contemporary social conditions, and commenting on Mak's fake southern accent (215); yet they are supposed to visit the newborn Christ. This anachronism is scarcely concealed; rather, it is paraded and indulged. Elsewhere, the shepherds invoke 'oure Lady' (19), they swear by Christ's cross, by St. Nicholas (118) and St. Thomas of Kent (458), and refer to bells ringing lauds (180). As Eric Auerbach says, Medieval drama characteristically creates the sense of a timeless present in just this way, by placing key scriptural events in the context of the audience's own historical consciousness and social concerns. One effect of this technique is to suggest how Christian truth is always contemporary. Thus in the present example we are to see how Incarnation is perpetually re-enacted. Moreover, the play strongly suggests that the moments of charity wherein the shepherds offer a gift to Mak's 'child' and then spare Mak from a legal trial that would surely condemn him to death, are themselves incarnational: in these moments Christ also is born. Far from wanting to conceal anachronism, the author forces it upon us, for it is the vehicle of his message about what Christ's birth means. We are to 'come awake' to this significance and the play is, accordingly, punctuated with scenes where sleeping people awaken. The crucial moment of recognition, the significance of a redeeming Christ, is always imminent, always now.[13]

This strong sense of God's presence invites (indeed enables) the exploration and discovery of analogies, for individuals participate in general principles that sustain us all and guarantee meaning to which language and symbol give public access. Thus Mak, a particular rogue, is not the devil even though he behaves in a diabolical manner and is described accordingly: 'What dewill shall he hatt, Mak? / Lo, God, Makys ayre!' (604), says Coll of the 'hornyd lad' (601) discovered in the cradle. Likewise, the scene in Mak's hut is typical because it parodies the holy family at Bethlehem, farcically reversing the orthodox significance. So also, the general plot development from the shepherds' complaints on the storm-lashed moor to their singing with angels describes the typical course of a Christian life: one must suffer the consequences of the Fall, but then find reconciliation and harmony through patient endurance and the practice of charity. As one commentator points out, history here is salvation history, and its course from a Biblical past to English present and eschatological future[14] is reduplicated in each of us as a perpetual, present drama. These meanings are, as it were, publicly dependable, and we need only learn to read them.

Nonetheless, it is hard to avoid feeling that the strong farce and coarse exuberance in *Secunda Pastorum* also effect a counterpoise to such grave and soaring significances. The baby with the 'long snowte' (585), Gill's mock birthpangs, and the blanket-tossing are robustly unperturbed by theological aerobics. Indeed, resorting to Bakhtin, one critic sees the play's carnivalesque elements as disrupting the totalising tendencies of official dogma, and therefore as a force of renewal.[15] Also, it is worth noticing how such disruption is strengthened by the opening scene, where the shepherds are cold, ill-clad, and complaining about 'gentlery-men' (18) who 'hold . . . vs hunder' (24). Those in authority, we learn, are as proud as peacocks and take what they want: 'Thus lyf we in payne, anger and wo' (40). Transgressions are viciously punished, and much is made of the hanging which is Mak's fate if he is caught.

We might read these passages in two ways. First, the protest of the weak and afflicted shepherds is vindicated by God's showing them favour, and so the play calls for social renewal. Second, the shepherds' sufferings (like the weather) are a consequence of the Fall and therefore must , like Christ's cross, be endured.[16] In this case, the disruptive effect of protest is re-appropriated by the prevailing orthodoxy.[17] Still, like the farce, the protest does register, and throughout *Secunda Pastorum* we can recognise a certain vigour and exuberance confronting complacency in a manner that the analogies and icons do not fully absorb. In short, the theology stays sufficiently accessible for us to feel how complex is its alienation from what it would explain. In one sense indeed we do not 'belong' in the cultural world that produced *Secunda Pastorum*, but, in another, we continue to detect there something of ourselves, our history, and our continuing concerns.

If a typically Medieval sense of participation or belonging is assumed in *Secunda Pastorum*, then Samuel Beckett shows himself a connoisseur of the kind of alienation Heidegger describes as endemic in the twentieth century. Beckett's Nobel Prize [18] attests his acceptance by (that is, belonging in) a culture whose profound incapacity for belonging is his main subject. Thus *Endgame*,[19] perhaps Beckett's masterpiece, is a play about disrelationship rather than relationship, alienation rather than belonging, the death of meaning rather than its birth. In short, we might consider it a thoroughgoing inverse of *Secunda Pastorum*.

As Hugh Kenner[20] points out, the stage set for *Endgame* seems to represent the inside of a skull, with the two high windows as eyes. The ashbins containing Nagg and Nell are then perhaps memory. Clov (who looks out and provides information) is intellect, and Hamm (blind and confined to a wheelchair) is the will. As the play opens, Nagg and Nell are sealed in the ashcans, and Hamm is covered with a sheet which Clov removes after the curtain rises, but before any words are spoken. The effect is of a kind of waking up, but also of a set being uncovered for yet another performance. Throughout, Beckett goes on drawing attention to the play in this manner, not as an 'action' in the conventional Aristotelian sense, but as merely playacting: another in a round of daily performances that mean nothing and will cease by and by. 'Finished' (1) is the first word spoken; 'remain' (84) is the last, and together they catch the two poles of hopelessness and entrapment within which *Endgame* takes its course. Insofar as we are inclined to search for some kind of mimetic dimension, it is simply that all our routines are playacting, or mere behaviour. Several jokes are directed at the audience to remind them that they really belong in the world of the play, which is to say, in an arbitrary, empty, and peculiar world bereft of meaning, and where belonging is illusory. As the allusion to chess in the title suggests, people are fixed in combative interaction, each confined to a separate space. Moreover, in the endgame phase the main action is, as it were, played out; indeed, it approaches stalemate, with the same final moves as endlessly repeatable as the play's performances, returning the characters to the same positions, the same predictable routines, the same final impasse. As Kenner says, Beckett might be responding to such notions as T. E. Huxley's, that man is an irrelevance whom 'an indifferent universe engages in chess'.[21]

Already, however, the suggestion that the characters represent the mind's faculties (memory, intellect and will) gives the play meaning – and in this instance a rather medieval one. Yet I have been tentative: 'perhaps' this is a sense to be derived; perhaps not. For *Endgame* is full of fugitive allegories barely distinct enough to enliven curiosity and never consistent enough to satisfy it. Intimated significance (solipsism, chessgame, the playactng theme) combines with frustrating randomness to create the unique perplexities that are Beckett's hallmark. As we grasp at meaning it peters out, comically, inconsequentially, inevitably. Perhaps the black toy dog with a leg missing is God; perhaps the small boy outside, detected (or so Clov says) through the telescope, is hope, but perhaps not, for not all wandering children are figures of hope, and not all black toy dogs with a leg missing are theological symbols. Indeed, our reaching to make something of these has a comic desperation about it, confirming the arbitrariness of the enterprise. 'Mean something! You and I, mean something!' (33) says Clov, in incredulous protest, again, as it were, catching the audience in the act. Rather, a remorseless, nihilistic litany comments on how futile are such efforts: 'Zero . . . zero . . . and zero' (29), says Clov. There is 'no more' nature, nor bicycle wheels, coffins, sugar plums, navigators, rugs, or pain killer: an improbable list, its very disconnectedness confirming the randomness of entropy and the inevitable common denominator, 'nothing'. 'There is nothing to say' (79) Clov pronounces at last.

It is tempting to link all this to a general twentieth-century pre-occupation with alienation and absurdity, especially as formulated by existentialist developments of Heidegger's analysis of death, nothingness, 'thrownness', and the acts of choice by which we make a world. Indeed, scholars have suggested that Beckett and Heidegger share a number of basic concerns and dwell in the same ontological atmosphere.[22] For instance, both have a similar sense of contingency, of our simply 'being there' in a world, thrown into the midst without explanation. Thus Malone finds himself in his mother's room, which, absurdly, is his world, and *Act Without Words* begins with 'The man flung backwards on stage', the very index of our condition. Likewise, Heidegger's account of action and choice in a world where we are confronted by the twin abysses of alienation and unrealised possibility evokes many a Beckett scenario. So in *Endgame*, Hamm's name suggests that he is an inept actor, called to play a part like Heidegger's *Dasein* and also to be as he is not, like his near namesake, Hamlet. Clov's name is a version of cloven, suggesting our inevitable separateness from one another, and the incompleteness of our identities and projects despite our interdependency (as Hamm[er] to *clou*, or nail).[23] All this is recognisably the world of Heidegger, Sartre and their followers.

Still, despite these affinities, Beckett cannot simply be labelled Heideggerean or existentialist. As T. W. Adorno says, Heideggerean ontology has a place in *Endgame* but only to be parodied.[24] Heidegger uses the idea of 'thrownness' as Sartre does 'absurdity', to transform 'senselessness itself into sense' (19). But Beckett does not admit this redemptive move, and the meaning of *Endgame* is, precisely, that it does not have any such sense: 'Understanding it can mean nothing other than understanding its incomprehensibility, or concretely reconstructing its meaning structure – that it has none' (10–11). For Beckett, the identity of subjects remains illusory (a preoccupation that haunted him from his early essay on Proust), and 'the ontological tendency of every existentialism, even that of *Being and Time*', as Adorno says, is abandoned in *Endgame* 'like an obsolete bunker' (17).

Adorno's point about parody reminds us that *Endgame* is also wonderfully humorous. Indeed, Harold Bloom uses this fact to criticise Adorno's despairing assessment, and insists that an 'extra-ordinary gusto informs *Endgame*', however much 'indistinguishable from an acute anxiety attack'.[25] It is but a short step from Bloom again to Bakhtin's 'carnivalesque', invoked this time by Sylvie Debevec Henning to suggest that Beckett challenges both the modern sense of despair (which *Endgame* indeed shows us) and also our lingering, 'familiar teleological hermeneutics'.[26] Rather, Beckett's comedy offers a certain resistance to philosophical interpreters. This, we might suggest, is a product of the play's marvellously perplexing and anguished tone as a whole, but it is caught also in flashes, as when Hamm remarks about God, 'The bastard! He doesn't exist!' (55); or when he asks if the black toy dog is white, and Clov replies 'Nearly' (40); or when Clov turns the telescope on the audience (I see . . . a multitude . . . in transports . . . of joy' [29]). 'Nothing is funnier than unhappiness, I grant you that' (18), says Nell, voicing the paradox with a wry and dispassionate mournfulness, to which Beckett amazingly gives life.

Secunda Pastorum and *Endgame* present different assumptions about the world and about belonging, and these assumptions are characteristic of different phases of cultural development. *Secunda Pastorum* shares certain metaphysical premises with the other cycle plays, cathedral sculpture, woodcuts, homilies, encyclopaedias and poems which, taken together suggest the lineaments of a culture, a communal way of being in the world. Likewise, from Beckett we might move through Sartre to the existentialists and Joyce, the theatre of the absurd and a characteristic sense of fragmentation in twentieth-century culture constituting that *anomie* and alienation which Heidegger especially diagnoses. In short, for the author of *Secunda Pastorum* the sense of a personal presentness is incarnational; for Beckett, it is an empty repetitiveness frustrating our will to significance.

And yet, these two works are not just mutually exclusive. We have noticed how, in *Secunda Pastorum*, the protest and comedy remain as a residue unabsorbed by the theologising vision. The gap between symbol and world opens up, that is, in the resistance within the play to how the incarnational, 'participatory' symbolism represents the world. In this tension is a poignancy that we can only recognise as pertinent to ourselves and to how we belong in the world, and that we can affirm as a hallmark of poetry, a complex meaning made present by the singular means of art. Likewise, the whimsical and farcical elements of *Endgame* create a sense of solidarity, a certain fraught nobility that in turn protests against the play's insistent nihilism. It seems that the human, whatever it might or might not be, cannot be just reduced to nothing, and poetry cannot present it as such. Beckett knows all too well about the failure of symbols to overcome our alienations, but alienation itself is not all there is, and a strange poetry survives even from the ashes. Moreover, Beckett's focus on alienation is itself the product of a particular cultural history, and as we have seen from the brief outline of phenomenological hermeneutics, this history assumes the metaphysical presuppositions of the author of *Secunda Pastorum*. Beckett's critique of metaphysical certainty depends on the fact that such certainty was once culturally sustaining. Just so, Heidegger's attack on Western metaphysics aims to restore a sense of the world that gave rise to metaphysics. Heidegger especially would have us understand the Cartesian contribution to modern thinking, but, as we see, we cannot do that without understanding Descartes' relationship to scholasticism, and so the story of the presence of our historical past leads us, as it leads Heidegger, to the very origins of speculation.

For, as Heidegger says, we enter into a conversation already in progress and the present is known only through the past. We are in dialogue with our cultural inheritance, and not only with its theories and ideas, but with its symbols and metaphors, its energies of will and desire, its literature and art. Yet this past, which flickers and changes under our attentive gaze, is not a stable or uniform guarantor of certainty and exists also as an open wound in the flesh of the present, an inheritance of suffering and contradiction. Literature especially lets us into both the conversation and the wound, as we have seen, because through literature we can recover a sense of the prevailing orthodoxies of past times, and also of the joys and sorrows, freedoms and constraints attendant on those orthodoxies. And so history and literature alike confirm at once how necessary is a sense of belonging to the sense we have of ourselves as persons, and how inseparable is such a sense of belonging from the experience of woundedness and flaw, to which I will now turn in more detail.

FLAW: ST. AUGUSTINE AND ORIGINAL SIN

A flaw is a defect and also a gap or crack. In an obsolete sense it is an outburst, as of anger. In awakening to evil out of a sense of shame or guilt, terror or compassion, we find the Flaw already there, outside and in. A central task of culture is to guide our response – whatever indignation is awakened by our awakening.

By the time Plato gave his attention to them, Homer's epics had been accorded the respect due to sacred texts and Plato remains everywhere concerned with the problem of detecting truth beneath the shifting appearances, a key theme also of the *Odyssey*. Thus, in *The Republic*, where Plato reflects carefully on the problem of suffering, he centers again on the relationship of truth to appearance, reality to illusion. Briefly, he proposes that we are fallen from a perfect, transcendental world and have chosen to live in this place of shadows, illusions and forgetfulness to expiate the sins of past lives. The Real world, which is also Good, remains supremely desirable and we must try to recover our innermost connection to it amidst the painful wanderings of our sojourn in the obfuscating thickness of our material habitation. For Plato, we are fallen creatures.

By contrast, in the Book of Genesis, Adam is thrust out into the wasteland after an act of disobedience. By and by he is joined in the deserts of painful experience by others whose misdemeanors are also described in the opening chapters of Genesis, and whose offences against God stand in need of pardon and reconciliation. The subsequent history of Israel records a series of such evictions or settings forth caused originally by broken promises and guided by divine intervention. History itself becomes the story of travellers and exiles struggling for reconciliation and stability in a shifting, cruel world.

For the ancient Hebrews the Flaw is thus first explained as a consequence of infidelity, but by the time of Isaiah and Job, consciousness of the scandal of evil had become intensely problematic: the innocent everywhere suffer for no apparent reason, and the Hebrews resisted Plato's essentially a-historical theory of pre-existence as a way of solving the problem. Rather, they held to the conviction that God alone knows the reason for suffering, and must be trusted to show the way out, a last exodus at the end of time. Apocalyptic literature – the main biblical example being the Book of Daniel – speaks especially to these issues, suggesting that the powers of this world will be undone in the end by a greater power. Innocent suffering will be revealed then for what it truly is, namely a spiritual victory by which the monsters of affliction and tyranny are smitten even as they smite.

In Chapter 5 I will return to the relationship between Christianity and apocalyptic eschatology. Meanwhile, I would like to notice how, despite their differences, the philosophical monotheism of ancient Greece and the religious montheism of ancient Israel come together in Christianity, where the perfect world of Platonic Forms and the holy city of Jerusalem both suggest a single ideal of happiness beyond time. Our access to it is through redemptive suffering endured on the model of the Incarnate Christ in the conditions of our fall or exile, and, in brief, this combination of elements is the foundation of St. Augustine's influential contribution to Western theology. For Augustine draws on the Bible and the Greeks to conflate the story of Adam's loss of Eden with Plato's fall from an ideal world, which he equates in turn with the city of God, the apocalyptic New Jerusalem of the end times. By combining these elements, Augustine develops at once a body of metaphor and a theory of a primordial Flaw offering to explain our sense of absence from our true selves and others, a condition giving rise to the hope of recovery, a desire to belong without alienation.

The *Confessions*[27] is St. Augustine's spiritual autobiography, written from the point of view of a converted Christian who believes that God was present in his life from the start, even though this presence went unrecognised by the young man wandering, like Aeneas, in search of home, or truth. As commentators have noticed, the story proceeds through a kind of dual vision, at once recreating the young man's blindness, and also showing how God's hand was already present, but undetected.[28] Augustine's unusual inventiveness resides then in the way he contrives to open up his own particular failures to larger, typical patterns of divine Providence within which the reader might also discover a true course. Consequently, even the most singular autobiographical incidents turn out to conform to an encompassing, typical design, though the reader (like the author as a young man) only discovers this from a vantage point later in the story, when the design is disclosed. Reading the *Confessions* is therefore a mimesis of the course towards illumination that the book describes as autobiography. A brief redaction of the narrative can help to make this clear.

The autobiographical section begins with Augustine's recollections of childhood. He cannot remember anything about his infancy, but reconstructs it from observation of other infants, regretting that he must have been as selfish and greedy as they (I, 11). He describes his early schooling at Thagaste and Madauros, and the pleasure he took in 'vain shows' (I, 30), in stealing food from his parents' cellar, and in a 'vain desire for pre-eminence' (I, 30) among his companions. He talks of his sexual awakening and, in a celebrated passage, he recalls robbing an orchard of pears and then flinging the unripe fruit to hogs (II, 9).

Augustine then tells how he went to Carthage to study, and took up with a woman who bore him a son. He recalls his arrogance as a student, his love of the theatre, and the company of disruptive and subversive companions. But at this point he discovered the (now lost) *Hortensius* of Cicero, which awakened in him 'an incredibly burning desire for an immortality of wisdom' (III, 7). One consequence was his decision to become a Manichaean, an event that especially distressed his pious and solicitous mother, Monica.

For a while, Augustine taught rhetoric at Thagaste, but after the death of a close friend, he returned to Carthage. There he met the Manichaean bishop, Faustus of Milevis, whose arguments left Augustine dissatisfied. He tells us of further discouragements caused by his dealings with students, and so he set out for Rome. Though he took his mistress and child, he contrived to leave his mother behind.

From Rome, Augustine proceeded to Milan, where he met Ambrose, the bishop whose allegorical interpretations of the Old Testament provided answers to certain problematic Manichaean doctrines (IV, 23). Consequently, Augustine made a final break with the Manichaeans, and for a while joined the Academy. Monica meanwhile had caught up with him, and although she was pleased with his spiritual progress, she found him in an unhappy frame of mind. Under her influence, he was persuaded to dismiss his concubine and become betrothed to a girl as yet under age for marriage (VI, 25). He duly sought out another concubine.

Augustine tells us that about this time he was reading 'certain books' (VII, 13) of the Neo-Platonists, which scholars now think were some of Plotinus' *Enneads* and parts of Porphyry. From these he learned especially that evil is not, properly speaking, a thing, and so could not be said to exist. It is, rather, a privation of good. The story then records Augustine's struggle to submit his will to the Christian truth that he had now accepted intellectually. At last, one day in a garden he cast himself under a fig tree and heard from a neighbouring house a child singing 'tolle lege', take up and read' (VIII, 28). He opened a nearby book to St. Paul's letter to the Romans (13:13–14):

Not in rioting and drunkenness, not in chambering and wantonness, not in strife and envying: but put ye on the Lord Jesus Christ, and make not provision for the flesh, in concupiscence.

This was his answer: the gift unlocking his will was delivered through the voice of a child, and not found by the questing intellect alone. Augustine then became a Christian, and set out to return home with his mother and child, both of whom died *en route*.

At this point, at the close of Book IX, the autobiographical section ends, but the *Confessions* does not. Book X continues with a treatise on memory, which develops into an extended examination by the author of his own conscience under the threefold heading 'the lust of the flesh, the lust of the eyes, and the ambition of the world' (X, 41). Books XI and XII are an elaborate examination of the first chapter of Genesis, and contain an equally elaborate meditation on the nature of time. Book XIII, the last, contains a further commentary on Genesis, and develops into a prophetic statement on the church in the world.

Structurally, it is odd that the last four books (that is, the section following the autobiographical part) should take up almost half of the whole work. Several theories have been advanced to explain this, but whatever their point of view, scholars tend to agree that Augustine deals with the story of his life in a highly artificial manner, fitting it into a total theory of human experience in time, under God's providence.[29] The general principles of this theory become increasingly clear in the last four books, but the point is that the principles were already implicit in the autobiographical section. We must learn to discover this by re-reading, and for this reason I have offered the above redaction, reproducing something of the deceptive straightforwardness of the narrative.

Augustine's opening words assure us, plainly, that God is at the centre: 'Great art Thou, O Lord' (I, 1), but then immediately he describes God's presence in paradoxical terms: 'Most merciful, yet most just; most hidden, yet most present; most beautiful, yet most strong; stable, yet incomprehensible' (I, 4). We are assured, that is, of God's immediacy and our own, fundamental belonging, but are warned also that we will be baffled by our own alienations. And indeed it is difficult to see what God's presence has to do specifically with the greedy infant, the theatre-going youth anxious for pre-eminence in school, and the pear stealing. Yet the answer becomes clear from the vantage point of Book X, where Augustine's subject is the examination of conscience under the headings of 'lust of the flesh, the lust of the eyes, and the ambition of the world' (X, 41). These headings correspond to the key sins of concupiscence, curiosity, and pride, for, as Augustine tells us elsewhere, 'these three kinds of vice namely, the pleasure of the flesh, and pride, and curiosity, include all sins'.[30]

Now we can reconsider why he says what he does about his boyhood. The gluttonous baby, the boy raiding the cellar, and the incontinent youth are examples of concupiscence. The boy taken with stage plays and spectacle exemplifies the sin of curiosity. The envious baby and the arrogant schoolboy are proud. The theft of pears, which to some readers has seemed disproportionately emphasised, is now seen to warrant that emphasis because stealing fruit from a garden reminds us of Eden, and thus represents the mystery of iniquity in general, encompassing the other three types of transgression. And we can now also see why Augustine provides that peculiar meditation on memory as a preface to the examination of conscience in Book X: through memory, the meaning of the present itself is discovered.

As Robert J. O'Connell[31] has shown, the threefold sin, concupiscence-curiosity-pride, indicates the basic pattern of our flawed moral condition. It is the key to many incidents in the *Confessions*, and corresponds also to the three main divisions of the human mind. Drawing broadly on Platonism, Augustine holds that people have a higher reason (*sapientia*), a lower reason (*scientia*) and sense-knowledge (*sensualis animae motus*),[32] and these are hierarchically ordered. The sin against the higher reason is pride; against the lower reason, curiosity, and against the senses, concupiscence. Because human beings participate in the meaning of the whole creation, the structure of the human mind is reflected in various ways in the heavens and on earth. For instance, the sun stands for wisdom, the moon for knowledge, and the sea that brings forth teeming life for the senses (XII, 15–16). The animal creation itself is a book wherein we can read ourselves:

> Contain yourselves from the ungoverned wildness of pride, the sluggish voluptuousness of luxury, and the false name of knowledge: that so the wild beasts may be tamed, the cattle broken to the yoke, the serpents harmless. For these be the motions of our mind under an allegory; that is to say, the hautiness of pride, the delight of lust, and the poison of curiosity, are the motions of a dead soul. (XIII, 30)

Thus we see ourselves symbolically in the heavens above as in the earth beneath. The world, in short, is a book of signs hierarchically ordered to lead us to God, could we but read correctly. And it should now become clear why Augustine expends so much effort in those final books on the exposition of Genesis, for the young man's journey to God entails also the meaning of God's temporal creation, which is good, and not evil as the Manichaeans hold.

It is customary to point out that Augustine's use of the verb *confiteri* is also a clue to the structure of the *Confessions*, and can itself refer to the divisions of time: a confession of sins indicates time past, a confession of faith time present, and a confession of praise, time future.[33] Confession of sins would then correspond to the first nine books, which make up the autobiographical section; confession of faith to the present examination of conscience in Book X; confession of praise to a future of eternal rest. Thus the young man's journey in search of salvation is akin to the process of time itself, with its enfolded complexities of past, present and future. As Augustine says, there is not really a separate past and future, but rather the presence of things past and future gives us a sense of ourselves in the perilous undertaking of our lives, along the flawed courses of history. The very elusiveness of the past and the opacity of signs are themselves conditions of our fallenness, of the Flaw in nature and in ourselves which we come to know by experience but which does not yield to rational explanation. The soul, as Augustine says, 'whose pilgrimage is made long and far away' is fallen first into 'changeableness of times' (XII, 13).

The recovery of a sense of belonging and purpose (what St. Paul calls 'redeeming the time') depends, as Augustine's autobiography confirms, not on reason but on the will's 'conversion' or turning to the truth in recognition. Thus, at the beginning of Book II, Augustine tells us: 'I was torn piecemeal, while turned from thee, the One Good, I lost myself among a multiplicity of things' (II, 1). And at the beginning of Book V: 'Let them be turned, and seek Thee; and behold, Thou art there in their heart, in the heart of those who confess to Thee, and cast themselves upon Thee, and weep in Thy bosom, after all their rugged ways' (V, 2). These passages illustrate not only the two main Augustinian senses of turning (aversion and conversion), but they describe also two different *modes* of turning. The first derives from the Greeks, and its meaning is metaphysical, describing a Platonic fall from the single Good into shadowy multiplicity. The second is the return of a wandering and guilty son, and is distinctly Biblical, stressing pardon and reconciliation. One index of Augustine's achievement in the *Confessions* is that these two kinds of language are so effectively synthesised to represent and evoke the many-sided enigma of our flawed condition.

As I have indicated, the Neo-Platonist idea of a single Good, the supreme reality from which we are departed into multiplicity, illusion, and not-being, afforded Augustine an effective means of rebuking his Manichaean opponents: 'That evil then which I sought, whence it is, is not any substance: for were it a substance, it should be good' (VII, 8). And yet, although the Greek philosophers lifted the scales from Augustine's intellectual eyes, their ideas were insufficient to convert his will: 'Thus did my two wills, one new, the other old, one carnal, the other spiritual, struggle within me; and by their discord, undid my soul' (VIII, 11). The final answer lay not in philosophy, but in a personal relationship involving the whole man, and which Augustine found in Christ who is both the Good of Plotinus and the suffering servant of Isaiah and of the gospels, and whose life has the complex multivalency of a parable. Thus, by charity (*caritas*) Augustine means both the kind of clarification that frees us from illusion, and also a blessed experience of release from anguish. The opposite is *cupiditas*, the nightmare embroilment in worldly distractions scattering us amidst multiplicty without design, causing guilt, homelessness and anxiety. The meaning of *caritas* and *cupiditas* is thus not confined to their conceptual distinctness, but is conveyed also in the felt urgencies of confusion and anguish, release and clarification that we encounter throughout the book.

In this context, Monica, with whom Augustine experiences a moment of mystical reconciliation at Ostia (IX, 24), represents the spirit of charity and the protective (if imperfect) solicitations of mother church, *mater ecclesia*.[34] This, in turn, helps to explain her influence in the concubine episode, and in attempting to have Augustine betrothed in a regular manner. His affairs are examples of *cupiditas*, the identity-dissolving opposite of love. Thus Augustine tells us he loved his mistress 'in a wayward passion, void of understanding' (VI, 2), and consequently he wanders 'severed amid times', as he says, 'whose order I know not'.

A whole series of correspondences now begins to open up. Cupidinous love represents fallenness, anxiety and self-division. Charitable love represents a return to God, the discovery of time's design, belonging, and singleness of purpose. People either love God or the world, and their allegiance is symbolised by the two cities, Jerusalem and Babylon.

Although he does not say much about the fall of Adam and the loss of Eden in the *Confessions*, when he develops his best thinking

on the subject Augustine draws on all the main implications of
his spiritual autobiography. Thus, as we learn in *On the Trinity*,
the story of Genesis 3 itself depicts the threefold structure of the
human mind. Adam stands for *sapientia*, Eve for *scientia*, and the
serpent for the sensual movement of the soul. Consequently, every
sin duplicates and repeats the structure of the first sin in Eden,
and as a result of that sin, humankind was thrust forth from a
perfect world (Eden is now imagined as a kind of Platonic realm of
ideal perfections), into our 'lower' world of strife, death, sickness,
and confusion. Here the soul wanders until it finds reconciliation
through Christ, the second Adam who gives shape and meaning
to the human story which will be made complete in Jerusalem,
the Holy City of the Apocalypse. Meanwhile, the radical Flaw
consequent upon the loss of Eden remains with us through the
divisions of time, for the serpent, which represents concupiscence,
belongs with memory or past time; Eve, who represents curiosity,
belongs with the future; Adam, who represents pride, belongs with
the present.

Augustine's last major controversy was against the Pelagians,
who attacked his ideas about the Fall and Original Sin by arguing
that we can attain to saving knowledge and action by our own
efforts. From the time of his own acute experience of the bound
will, Augustine never flinched in his conviction that saving insight
is a gift of grace, and yet in controversy with Pelagius, the poetry of
the *Confessions* is largely gone, and Augustine's treatises on original
sin, famous for their descriptions of the *massa damnata* and the
traducianist notion of evil inherited through the flesh, are stark
and fierce reminders of how easily ideas might harden, forced out
of touch with the living springs of metaphor.[35]

The deleterious effects of Augustine's anti-Pelagian writings are
beyond calculation, but his impact on medieval culture comes
especially through the extraordinary power of suggestiveness that
we find in those works best combining reflection and imagination
to explore the dialectic between our experience of the Flaw and our
belonging in God's plan. Pre-eminently, these are *Confessions* and
The City of God, but also (among others) *On the Trinity*, *Enchiridion*,
and the *Commentaries on the Psalms*. Certainly, in the first two of
these Augustine's thinking about time and the problem of the
Flaw is a central concern, and the idea, derived from St. Paul,
that we are to 'redeem the time' through Christ, is developed to
suggest how a present sense of significance and belonging entails

a meaningful past projecting us towards future expectation. But, as we see, this explanation is carefully ambivalent, for we are also fallen amidst changeableness of times, imperfectly able to explain ourselves, inheritors of a primordial alienation. The resistance of our fallenness to rational explanation stays alive in the sense of personal anguish and God-given release that the poetry communicates, and in the multivalent appeal of images and metaphors that illuminate and obscure, confirm and qualify one another repeatedly.

The extraordinary impact of Augustine's contribution to Western culture during the Middle Ages devolves centrally from his concern for the problem of the Flaw and its relationship to how and where we belong in the world. Everywhere in his work, Odysseus still journeys homeward, and Israel still wanders in search of reconcilement. Greek philosophy combines everywhere with Biblical religion to provide a certain interpretation of the Incarnate Christ, developed then through the further images of bride and concubine, mother and child, Eden and the ideal city, through theories of typology and allegory, and of correspondences between the great myths and our individual psychology. Such elements are massively synthesised and yet perpetually in tension with the sense of imperfect understanding and fascination with the mystery that our awakening to the problem of unjust suffering sets in motion.

Without this poetry, Augustine would be a negligible figure. Indeed, in those works where his power of explanation hardens and poetic complexity diminishes, Augustine's theory increasingly takes on a formidable, unlovely caste. But at its best, his writing develops in Christian terms the explanatory power of the great myths of origins and ends, of belonging and fallenness, inherited from Greece and Israel. And already we can feel even in the struggle itself for explanation a new kind of literary self-consciousness, about what it means to be human.[36] Even St. Paul in his intensest conversion experience shows little evidence of the soul-searching we find in the *Confessions*, and the event on the Damascus road is not described as happening in the context of any introspection on the Augustinian model. In short, Augustine's kind of spiritual autobiography is more acutely aware than any work preceding it, of the internal contradictions and powerful alienations of a person seeking to recover a sense of belonging while simultaneously encountering the abyss of self-alienation, the joint elements that I am arguing are fundamental to what it means to be a human person.

In conclusion, I want to confirm again how reflection discovers the Flaw inextricably bound up with the experience of belonging, and how the idea of a person entails this fact, which no culture can ignore: consequently, no culture can live without contact with a poetry or symbolism keeping this fact alive. Such medieval ideas about teleology, hierarchy and participation as I discussed in the previous section with special reference to *Secunda Pastorum*, derive largely from the Augustinian synthesis which gives these fundamentals a powerful and influential form. But, as we have also seen, with the attack on scholastic metaphysics during the Renaissance, this Augustinian model was largely abandoned, and the fierce Augustinian poetry about our fraught belonging in a flawed world has not been well re-assessed until recent times. Notably, however, modern phenomenology has sought to recover some sense of the belonging and participation surrendered with the demise of medieval metaphysics, but in Medieval culture that sense of belonging is inseparable from the Augustinian doctrine of Original Sin. By contrast, the rise of Cartesian rationalism was accompanied by a marked neo-Pelagian confidence whereby the *cogito*, flawless in its certainty, might set no bounds to its shaping and controlling designs. As Michael Polanyi points out, traditional Christian moral aspirations for a perfect city on a renewed earth remained to drive a new scientific and secular culture, but this culture might now be dangerously unrestrained by traditional teachings about the Fall and Original Sin. And so in retrieving some equivalent to the relinquished metaphysical sense of belonging, the phenomenological and hermeneutic movement must find also a way to make present a new, balancing sense of Flaw, absence, and alienation. In attempting to do this, Heidegger's explorations of anxiety are worth considering in more detail.

RETRIEVAL: HEIDEGGER AND THE STRUCTURES OF CONCERN

It is difficult to say exactly when the Augustinian doctrine of Original Sin lost its grip, but in a broad way it did so under the impact of the Renaissance and Enlightenment. I do not mean that the ideas of the Fall and Original Sin were somehow disproven or banished in the same way as the ideas of Ptolemy; many people continued to believe in Original Sin, as many still do. Yet with the

Age of Enlightenment this doctrine ceased to provide assumptions about human nature upon which a culture could explicitly stand.

In teaching our inherited depravity and dependency on unmerited grace for salvation, Augustine had laid the foundations both for an institutional church whose central function was to mediate grace, and also for a set of social institutions assuming that one's lot in life, however cruel, might be explained as a consequence of the Fall. For church and state alike, we are all guilty before God, and our earthly responsibilities are prescribed by those whose authority is from God. These responsibilities are then delegated within a series of hierarchies extending to all walks of life and, as we have seen, by analogy these hierarchies extend to the non-human world, so that Augustine regards the world as a book wherein things signified in turn become signifiers of a higher order.[37] Thus we are led towards an eternal destination where signs themselves pass away before the vision of an originating and pre-existent meaning – our true home or place of belonging – that we are called upon to love and know. One consequence of such a view is that a proper understanding of the natural world turns the beholder's gaze heavenwards in contemplation, and not towards the object as something to be examined for itself. Not even the revival of Aristotle in the thirteenth century served to modify this hierarchical and metaphysical attitude to things as signs of a transcendent Reality. As Etienne Gilson says, for Thomas Aquinas in the thirteenth century as for Augustine in the fourth, 'if a physics of bodies exists, it is because there exists first a mystical theology of the divine life'.[38] According to this view, excessive curiosity about natural causes is idolatrous, and we have seen how Augustine argues that Eve's temptation centered on *curiositas*. In the English Renaissance, the moral tale of the ill-starred Faustus likewise confirms the traditional lesson that preferring knowledge and power to God will capsize us into self-destruction and despair.

At first, Faustus acts as though he might be free from guilt and sin, but these ironically energise his most compulsive aspirations, as his own blasphemies attest. And yet, although unable to stand free of his cultural past, Faustus also impresses us as a character asserting that he will not any longer just occupy a traditional place in society, but will offer to make society anew and in his own image by a magically-acquired power, the fruit of illicit *curiositas*:

I'll have them wall all Germany with brass

And make swift Rhine circle fair Wittenberg;

.   .   .

'Tis magic, magic that hath ravished me!
(I,i,85–104)[39]

Although the rebellious Faustus, like the complaining shepherds of *Secunda Pastorum*, is finally contained by an orthodox morality he offers to criticise, he leaves us nonetheless with a dangerous sense of some new charter in the making.

The sense of novelty and rebellion voiced by Faustus was gathered by Marlowe from a variety of antecedents. The development of printing, the recovery of manuscripts promoting a new interest in the Greek and Hebrew languages, the emergence of Italian city states, the development of banking, mercantile capital, and colonialism all contributed to a spirit of enquiry wherein a new *studia humanitatis* was pitted against traditional moral prescription with its deep reliances on metaphysics, hierarchy, and teleology. The like of Erasmus, Vives, Valla, and Reuchlin, among many others, unsettled the foundations by offering philological and textual criticisms of scripture, thereby revealing the several fallibilities of traditional moralising and anagogical interpretation. Moreover, the Humanists thought of themselves primarily as educators, and believed that learning is morally improving. Consequently, however much they professed the doctrine of Original Sin, one certain implication of their heavy emphasis on a morally improving education was that human beings are responsible and self-determining: in short, there was more of the Faustian impulse in Humanism from the beginning than most Humanists realised. Martin Luther (once Erasmus's disciple) saw this with complete clarity when he accused Erasmus of Pelagianism.[40] Meanwhile, Luther himself insisted on as strong and traditional a version of the Augustinian Original Sin as he could.

It is difficult to assess the encroachments of what might loosely be called a new Pelagianism during the Renaissance, but they are part of a pervasive criticism of medieval orthodoxy, and Ernst Cassirer sums up the prevailing mood when he talks of Nicholas of Cusa:

Although Cusanus never doubted the doctrine of original sin, it seems to have lost for him the power that it had exerted on the whole of medieval thought and on its sense of life. The Pelagian spirit is reawakening now, that spirit so bitterly fought by Augustine, whose polemics became the basis of medieval religious doctrine.[41]

Among other things, the Humanist spirit of self-sufficiency pervades the new science, which attempted to vex nature, as Francis Bacon says, to discover its hidden secrets – unlocking nature's power, in a Faustian manner, for the empowerment of humankind. Yet, as with Cusanus and Erasmus, and also again like Faustus, the new scientists often conducted their innovative business within the pale of the very orthodoxy that they threatened. Thus, Descartes piously draws attention to God's transcendence in order to confirm God's incomprehensibility. Then, with the swift neatness of a stage magician he draws the famous conclusion: 'this is enough by itself to show that what are called final causes are of no use at all in Natural Philosophy.'[42] Precisely the same argument is used by Francis Bacon,[43] and so the chief spokesmen of scientific rationalism and scientific empiricism alike managed to break with an older view of nature wherein things are signs to be referred in praise to God, even while contriving to maintain an allegiance to the teachings of orthodox Christianity.

Humanism and the scientific revolution are therefore bound together at least by the critical spirit with which they question the idea of our fallenness, our capacity for self-improvement, and our attitude to nature. Not surprisingly, during the Renaissance and Enlightenment a fresh interest developed among poets and philosophers in the state of childhood. Thomas Traherne breathlessly describes his infancy as a time when he was as innocent as Adam, until corrupted by the 'Dirty Devices of this World'. Henry Vaughan writes provocatively of the soul's pre-existence in a world of purity and light still accessible to children, as does John Earle.[44] With Rousseau, the idea that we are born good but are corrupted by civilization becomes the mainspring of a full-blown reformative zeal bent on undoing society's repressive mechanisms, and Rousseau returns everywhere to the idea that we are originally sinless and basically free, honest, and capable of acting reasonably. Yet Rousseau (like Voltaire) was no facile optimist: in the *Discours sur l'inégalité* he does not present the primitive state as the kind of unfallen, higher perfection we might associate with the Garden of Eden in the Augustinian tradition. Rather, Rousseau's primitives are dull and simple: yet they have the potential to develop a happy condition marked by morality, justice and community. The tragedy of history lies in the perversion and degeneration of this potential, and civilization must be reformed to enable us to recover ourselves as responsible, free citizens. The point is that we do not simply return to the original state, but develop its promise self-consciously, under the guidance of education. Moreover, it is our duty to do so.

Rousseau's arguments are highly secular, and in this he inherits the full force of the Englightenment's critical spirit. Yet he, like Voltaire and Montesquieu, Lessing and Thomas Paine, retained a belief in God. At least part of the reason was polemical: the conviction of absolute goodness could serve all the more powerfully to show the moral depravity of humankind and the hypocrisies of the churches. Thus, Voltaire's favourite means of attacking the Bible was to show that it is morally objectionable and inconsistent with the idea of a good God. Following Tindal and Bolingbroke, Voltaire thought the story of the Fall not only absurd and degrading, but also an insult to the supreme being. In the *Philosophical Dictionary* he offers a strong moral objection in the voice of the Socinians and Unitarians: 'It is an insult to God, they say; it is accusing Him of the most absurd barbarity to have the hardihood to assert, that He formed all the successive generations of mankind to deliver them over to eternal tortures, under the pretext of their original ancestor having eaten of a particular fruit in a garden.'[45] The institutional church with its childish mythology seemed to Voltaire first and last a means of entrapping and enslaving the credulous, and our conviction of radical guilt especially plays into the hands of rapacious and exploitative ecclesiastical institutions. Rather, the new Enlightenment emphasis is on independent judgement ('My own mind is my own church', as Paine says)[46] and moral responsibility. 'We lie under no necessary Fate of sinning,' says John Toland: 'There is no Defect in our Understandings but those of our own Creation, that is to say, *vicious Habits easily contracted, but difficultly reformed*. 'Tis just with us as with the Drunkard.'[47] The general Deist principle that revealed theology should be conformable to reason contributed to the same 'neo-Pelagianism' as the *philosophes* also promoted. Not surprisingly, Methodism reacted as vigorously against the Deists as Luther did against Erasmus, and Augustine against Pelagius.

Although the developments outlined here are complex, it remains the case, as Peter Gay says, that during the eighteenth century 'Both Christians and philosophes recognised that the Enlightenment's anthropology was revolutionary', and that the new, general 'insistence on man's original innocence was a decisive break'.[48]

As Ernst Cassirer insists, there could be no reconciliation on this point: the doctrine of Original Sin was the foundation of Christian orthodoxy, and was part of the generally received explanation of what it means to be a person. With Rousseau (and others) all that changed. In short, a medieval culture rooted in the conviction of radical guilt yielded to an Enlightenment culture stressing critical reason and moral responsibility. Yet the stress on human progress and perfectability soon enough assumed its own menacing aspect as untrammeled aspiration found increasing confidence to declare our human right to fashion meaning absolutely in a universe from which God is increasingly absent.

Traditional religion of course continued to offer resistance, or to provide a leaven in various forms, but the Augustinian theory of Original Sin with its metaphysical explanations and governing symbols had decisively surrendered its privileged position under the weight of the Englightenment critique. Yet the problem of the Flaw in relation to our sense of belonging persisted, as it still does, demanding an assessment appropriate for the cultural phase we both inherit and are called to fashion. What kind of reflection or metaphor or mythology will serve for the conditions in which we find ourselves today, sophisticates of alienation, guilty and respon-sible beyond conception, poised now with sufficient technological power to destroy everything? In the first part of this chapter, I sug-gested that phenomenology and hermeneutics provide one kind of approach to these issues, and I turn now again to Martin Heidegger.

As we have seen, Heidegger's main work, *Being and Time* (on which I continue mainly to draw in the following pages) is self-consciously difficult, written in a style often resorting to unusual language and terminology. Basically, Heidegger examines *Dasein* ('There-being'), his name for the human person. Dasein can wonder about the possibility of not being, and can question its own presence in the world. Heidegger attempts especially to catch a sense both of the mystery of Being disclosed and of Being withdrawn from full presence even as it reveals itself. Like Husserl, he seeks to retrieve the revelatory moment, the lighting-up or clarification at the point where things first become intelligible and which we have lost through habit and forgetfulness. Heidegger does this partly by stressing *Dasein*'s limitations, its being 'thrown' (*geworfen*) into a world to discover itself always already engaged and circumscribed. The world thus prepossesses *Dasein*, who can engage it through concern (*Sorge*).

These are the general positions outlined in my earlier summary, which I want now to develop in relation to Heidegger's special interest in the temporal stucture of our flawed and anxious condition. Characteristically, *Dasein* makes use of tools, extending the body into the world through skilled performance, and Heidegger distinguishes between tools that are 'at hand' (*Zuhandensein*, 'at handness'), and 'on hand' (*Vorhandensein*, 'on handness'). In the first case, the tool is part of an action, taken up in a task wherein knowledge and performance are inseparable. In the second case, it is an object that we can describe and discuss. But for Heidegger the subject-object dichotomy is a disastrous consequence of the history of metaphysics and our present technological culture is based on the control and manipulation of objects by subjects, cutting us off from the mystery of Being and reducing *Dasein* to a mere on-hand entity. Thus alienated, *Dasein* lives inauthentically, which is to say, in a state of separation from the world and from community, following along in conformity to habit and convention, deprived of the freedom out of which care arises. Nonetheless, to be able to question one's existence – to realise the possibility of not-being and the fragility of our present state – gives rise to a salutory anxiety out of which authentic care arises. Unlike fear, which has an object, the Heideggerean *angst* arises from contingency itself, the possibility of not-being, which is death, a non-specific negativity pervading all our concerns. Authentic *Dasein* is being-unto-death, choosing its projects and engagements resolutely.

Heidegger's analysis of *angst* lies close to the core of *Being and Time*, and is connected to the fact that *Dasein*'s concern is basically temporal . Time, however, is not the 'on-hand' experience of clock time, a quantifiable series with the present instant regarded as, somehow, most real. Authentic time is the very structure of concern itself, taken up with being-unto-death and with the sense of 'thrownness'. Because we inherit (or find ourselves in) a specific situation, our past remains present. Likewise, in taking up present concerns, we direct ourselves towards future possibilities which are therefore also present. Indeed, for Heidegger the future is the most present dimension of time and occupies a privileged position, for care and concern are primarily directed to it. Thus past and future are complexly infolded in the structure of authentic concern, marked by anxiety and resoluteness.

Heidegger develops this analysis by describing *Dasein*'s situation variously as 'fallen', 'existential', and 'factual', each of these terms corresponding to one of the *ecstases* of time. 'Fallenness' (*Verfallen*) pertains to the present, and is a mode of inauthenticity wherein the present is valued for its actuality (mere 'making present'), rather than for its possibilities. 'Facticity' (*Faktizität*) pertains to the past, and to our 'thrownness': we are already in a world and we inherit a past that remains contemporaneous. 'Existentiality' (*Existenzialität*) pertains to the future, and to the possibilities we choose through concern.

The inauthenticity consequent upon fallenness is manifest especially in gossip (*Gerede*), curiosity (*Neugier*), and ambiguity (*Zweideutigkeit*), and we might relate these to the three temporal *ecstases*, as their parody. Gossip is idle conversation repeating the shallow and conventional; it takes what is given and re-iterates it. Thus, through gossip we acquiesce in an inauthentic past. Curiosity is a superficial desire for novelty that fails to engage the future as a horizon of possibility. Ambiguity is a lack of resoluteness that comes from relinquishing a sense of the past and future, and is the mark of spurious presentness.

By contrast, the care-structure of authentic *Dasein* involves *angst*, and for Heidegger there is no freedom without guilt (*Schuld*). The very structure of concern inevitably entails guilt because choices always preclude alternative possibilities and are therefore a form of rejection, both of certain possibilities of one's own, and certain needs of others. Resoluteness then must carry *Dasein* through, to choose decisively and with its whole being, in the teeth of negativity, contingency and guilt.

In seeking authenticity by resisting alienation and the attendant distractions of the conventional and everyday, *Dasein* encounters things disclosing themselves anew in the immediacy of an original givenness, the Being in which they participate as beings, and to which we are to attend again as careful listeners. Thus in our engagements with a complex world, we might come into a clearing (*Lichtung*), a moment of illumination bearing in upon us with imperative and self-authenticating presentness. Heidegger argues that in the earliest speculations of Greek philosophy this 'standing presence' was caught in language, but the subsequent history of Western metaphysics records a gradual forgetting of that original transparency. Heidegger's attitude to the philosophers is therefore twofold: at once to show how their metaphysics promotes forgetfulness, and also to redeem through retrieval

(*Wiederholung*) the authentic elements of past thinking. But although *Dasein* dwells especially in language, explanation alone does not effect this retrieval or disclosure of Being. Rather, language must effect something of the difficult tracking process that departs from tried ways in order to break into clearing. Thus, as I pointed out earlier, Heidegger's style wrenches ordinary usage into a resonant strangeness, attempting to effect what it describes. Reflection itself then brightens into poetry, enabling us to recover from the roots of our most ordinary descriptions of things a surprising, fresh call upon our concern. As Heidegger elsewhere tells us, poetry (like art in general) achieves its end in letting the innermost reality of things shine forth: 'Poetry is the saying of the unconcealedness of what is.'[49] Yet, as we see, one consequence of this process is that its negative elements (Being is negatived in all its partial disclosures) are inseparable from anxiety. We belong, that is, but simultaneously know our alienation, the Flaw in the heart of things, the open wound in every presence.

It must now be evident to what degree Heidegger's thinking re-echoes St. Augustine's main themes.[50] The qualitative description of time, stressing the presentness of future and past and contrasting authentic engagement with aimless wandering amidst mere 'changeableness of times' is a central preoccupation in the writings of both. Also, they share a similar sense of anxiety accompanying the uncanny, authentic choosing of one's self, and both lament our alienation and fallenness amidst distractions and idle curiosity. Likewise, for both, authenticity is marked by a sense of illumination, which in turn enables a recovery of the past that informs future hopes and possibilities.

Nonetheless, the main, powerfully evident difference between these two thinkers is that Augustine is a theologian and Heidegger is both post-Enlightenment (his thinking is emphatically secular) and post-scientific (he claims that technology – or 'technicity' [*Technik*][51] – has destroyed an original harmony between the world and language). Consequently, I do not wish to suggest that Heidegger somehow seeks to revalidate the old doctrine of Original Sin. Rather, he grasps anew or retrieves something of what Original Sin intended, or pointed to, or disclosed about the fundamental predicament of persons within the dialectic of belonging and alienation, and he does so in a culture where the old doctrine has become, largely, an 'on hand' idea. Heidegger attempts, that is, to retrieve or restate for a post-Cartesian and secular age some viable understanding of the Flaw as an antidote to the unlimited Promethean aspirations of *Dasein* forgetful of Being.

For Heidegger, then, modern civilization is permeated by a dehumanising nihilism (loss of value, meaning, and so on), which he links directly to 'technicity', the culmination of Western doctrines of progress. It is as if in his own work the nihilistic consequences of a totalising sense of responsibility (man maker of meaning, colonising the world) are to be offset by a renewed emphasis on guilt, reminding us of our forgetfulness of Being. And yet, confoundingly, Heidegger chose to support a political party that developed the century's most horrifying example of totalitarian nihilism. How could this have been so?

It is impossible to push aside the issue of Heidegger's membership of the National Socialist Party from 1933–1945, and Heidegger himself insists on the links between politics and his philosophy.[52] In the *Spiegel* interview of 1966, he makes clear that in 1933 he was 'completely preoccupied with the questions that were developed in *Being and Time*', and these were 'fundamental questions of thought that touched also on national and social questions [though not im]mediately'.[53] Heidegger says he also believed the Nazis promised a 'new era' wherein 'technicity on the planetary level' (55) might be properly managed. In short, he insisted to the end on seeing National Socialism in the context of his own philosophical preoccupations. But his candour has been much questioned, and we need carefully to measure his explanations against the facts of his behaviour during the war, and the speeches and documents pronouncing his support for the Hitler regime.

As is now clear, Heidegger's enthusiasm for National Socialism was fired by strongly anti-democratic sentiment, and he became rector of the University of Freiburg in 1933 with a view to re-structuring the university in accord with the Führer-principle. In so doing, he wrote political informations against colleagues, and although he resigned as rector in 1934, he remained a dues-paying member of the party until 1945, and his services continued to be called upon. Heidegger indeed disagreed with official Nazi biologist and racist policies, and developed instead his own theory of Germany as a 'spiritual' nation. The degree to which he was anti-semitic is debatable, but I am inclined to agree with Ferry and Renaut that anti-semitism seems, from the evidence to date, not to have been a decisive element in Heidegger's National Socialism, however much tainted he was, if only by his support for the party throughout the war.[54] Certainly, his silence about the Holocaust after the war is, as Hannah Arendt and George Steiner say, all but unbearable.[55] However, my main concern here is to point to elements in *Being and Time* that might have disposed Heidegger towards the kind of thing National Socialism was. Even Farias, the most vigorous exposer of Heidegger's Nazi connection, allows that 'In no sense can we read National Socialism into *Being and Time*, but we can identify philosophical beliefs that foreshadow Heidegger's later convictions.'[56]

Herbert Marcuse spent four years (1928–32) studying with Heidegger, and concluded that *Being and Time* recommends 'a joyless existence, overshadowed by death and anxiety; human material for the authoritarian personality'.[57] In Marcuse's view, that is, Heideggerian guilt would open all too easily upon demagoguery and authoritarianism. And indeed (as we have seen with Augustine) guilt does look to authority for remission, a fact upon which, as Voltaire points out, the churches have never failed to capitalise. Yet anguish, contingency, and a sense of the Flaw remain fundamental experiences, and the problem is how to assess them responsibly. Here I am taking guilt and responsibility as polar opposites, each needing to be tempered by the other. The question then is not so much whether Heidegger should have developed a theory about guilt, as how he assessed our responsibility in relation to it, especially in the political arena.

As Paul Ricœur points out, Heidegger treats all Western history as virtually a history of metaphysics,[58] and one result is that Heidegger's thinking is seriously out of touch with the social realities of oppression, injustice, revolution and discontinuity that make for historical change. A further result of this all-consuming metaphysical preoccupation is that in *Being and Time* Heidegger sees 'authenticity' in terms of a mysterious disclosure disconnected from empirical, historical facts, yet calling nonetheless for resoluteness founded on tradition. And here a fundamental paradox begins to be evident, for despite his insistence that Dasein is always already guilty, Heidegger calls for an act of will and 'heroism' to counteract guilt in the name of authenticity. On the one hand, that is, guilt recalls us to our forgetfulness of Being, and is part of Heidegger's attack on the instrumental reason of a post-Cartesian, technological age. Guilt therefore reminds us of our Faustian limitations. On the other hand, the call to resoluteness reconfirms from another direction our Faustian self-determination, and remains as Heidegger's version of post-Enlightenment Neo-Pelagianism. Indeed, Heidegger came to believe that the German people would save the West through their unique self-assertion as a metaphysical people, endowed with a special language: all that was needed to vindicate the cause was a sustained, heroic act of revolutionary courage and will.[59]

Though with uneven success, Christendom attempted for well over a millennium to maintain some sort of balance between guilt and responsibility, and indeed this attempt became part of the process of describing what it means to be a person. But in Heidegger's politics something goes wierdly wrong in the balance, and this is especially evident in how, after *Being and Time*, Heidegger marked out the German people as having a unique, and therefore incommunicable (except to Germans) philosophical destiny, responsible for the salvation of Western civilization. Thus, for instance, Heidegger claimed a special solidarity with the Black Forest peasants and the Swabian soil (his work, he says, is 'intimately rooted in and related to the life of the peasants'),[60] and he tirelessly promoted this supposed pre-rational kinship between metaphysician and peasant as fundamental to the national spirit. In so doing, he held rationalism increasingly in disregard, invoking instead a pseudo-mysticism of blood and soil, with disturbing references to a 'historical mission' of the German people, who must 'once again will ourselves',[61] and so on. One result is the distinctly undemocratic bias that Heidegger never relinquished. Even in 1966, he tells his interviewer how he is unconvinced about the efficacy of democracy, and he clearly continued to feel that in 1933 National Socialism took a salutary turn towards restoring the people to their soil, and culture itself to authenticity. When we consider in this light the ideas in *Being and Time* on resolve in choosing not only one's self, but in choosing a hero, and on a people's past forming its destiny, we might see how short the step is to the *Rektoratsrede* of 1933, and the many turgid speeches and declarations welcoming the Nazi masters of Germany's destiny.

Guilt, I have suggested, craves authority, and so should be tempered by responsibility. But responsible, personal self-determination in turn needs to protect itself against a Promethean inflation of the ego by retaining a sense of its own inherent flaws and limitations. The way of such responsibility lies through a struggle for consensus in the midst of perplexities, entailing dialogue and a certain democratic trust in the efficacy – however limited and imperfect – of making our positions as clear as possible, and open to discussion. Without such conditions (or the will to bring them about) Heidegger's salutary retrieval of a sense of the Flaw appropriate for our times was all too easily tarnished and distorted by authoritarianism and obscurantism. Indeed, it is disturbing that Heidegger seems so little to have realised the meaning of his own Nazism. Rudolf Bultmann recalls talking with him after the war: '"Now you must," I said to him, "like Augustine write retractions [*Retractiones*] . . . in the final analysis for the truth of your thought." Heidegger's face became a stony mask. He left without saying anything further.'[62] It seems that Heidegger could not acknowledge the guilt consequent upon his version of acting responsibly, even though this responsibility putatively would compel us to a renewed sense of what guilt means in a world sunk in forgetfulness. Heidegger's thinking is thus immensely ambivalent, but it has also been immensely influential, and not least among the attendant paradoxes is the fact that this Nazi 'Mitlaufer' or 'fellow traveller' (as he was called by the denazification commission directed by the French), should have been appropriated so thoroughly after the war by philosophers on the left, especially in France.

These remarks have had a good deal to do both with dialectic and with equilibrium: in these latter pages, between guilt and responsibility, but especially, throughout, between belonging and alienation. My claim has been that the person is fundamentally constituted by an interplay between such opposites, taken up in a historical situation entailing a narrative of how we have come to be as we are. *Being and Time* provides one measure of this dialectic for our times, and as a way of understanding some further dimensions of this same dialectic as a historical phenomenon, we have noticed how *Secunda Pastorum* draws in its fashion upon the broadly Augustinian presuppositions of the culture governing its production, while disclosing also the contradictory blindness of that culture to its own un-Christian oppressiveness. Thus we can see how Augustinian guilt-culture calls out for the moral responsibility Voltaire demands. By contrast, in *Endgame* a nihilism consequent upon the assumption that human beings are guiltless and alone responsible for constructing meaning in an empty universe is revealed as a dead end.[63] *Endgame* calls out for a renewed sense of belonging, for participation in meaning not fabricated just by our own performance, and through which we might discover objective standards and norms. From the centre even of Beckett's most desperate bleakness comes a certain resistant sense of dignity and pathos, intimations of an unrelinquished solidarity against the homelessness of humankind. Although Beckett's world is not identifiable *tout court* with Heidegger's, they thus share a common ethos, as do St. Augustine and the author of *Secunda Pastorum*. And although the cultural circumstances of Augustine and Heidegger are distinct, they are joined nonetheless in a complex history from which, in part, emerges the category of the person as I am attempting to describe it, inseparable from the historical narrative of its development.

Throughout this chapter, I have used a number of paired contrasts to introduce such a description. These pairs include the fundamental experiences of belonging and alienation in a world that pre-possesses us and calls for engagement. The terms of this pre-possession involve, among other things, the experience of evil and the problem of a flawed existence in a flawed nature. Such a predicament cannot be explained, though calling everywhere for explanation. By finding ourselves within it, and by opening for discussion the claims implicit in what we take to be our most compelling experiences of belonging, we locate ourselves also as persons. Thus, in literature, philosophy, and the exercise of criticism we encounter the condition of our belonging and alienation, responsibility and guilt reproduced in a perpetual ambivalence, the simultaneous making present and absent that language effects. As Augustine and Heidegger alike say, retrieving the past is part of how we comprehend our fundamental belonging and imperfection, for thus we assess how prior achievements and constraints might still open up for us possible worlds worth striving for. Whether or not this striving wrests a degree of freedom from the world's necessities is then tested in the dynamic of the personal history each of us is to engage without quite knowing what it is to show us.

3

Validation

TESTING: THE PROBLEM OF COMMON EXPERIENCE

In Chapter 2 I mentioned that we ought not to treat in too cavalier a fashion the processes of empirical verification with which phenomenology and hermeneutics often take issue. But does it then make sense to say that a work of literature is testable? And if literature is not testable in any sense whatever, then does it not provide a merely private experience that falls short of being personal in the sense in which I have been using the term? Everything here of course hinges on how we are to use the word 'testable', but at least on this question phenomenologists and positivists agree that literature and criticism ought not to be confused with the hard sciences. In the previous chapter, I have outlined something of the case put by phenomenology against a strict objectivity; for the sake of clarity, let us now turn briefly to the positivist camp.

The term 'positivism' is often loosely used to indicate a trend in science and philosophy holding that if truth claims are not empirically verifiable they should be rejected.[1] Strict positivists consequently regard metaphysics as nonsense, and propose that scientific truth – which is the only kind – is value free. They hold that general, covering laws are the same for all sciences, and that these laws are confirmed by controlled tests. Historically, positivist attitudes might be traced to the ancient sceptics and medieval nominalists, but the trend assumes a distinctive modern form during the scientific revolution, especially through the methodological prescriptions of Francis Bacon (1561–1621). Auguste Comte (1798–1857) was then especially influential in the development of modern positivism by describing the course of history as a gradual emergence of science from an immature age of metaphysics, preceded by an age of religion. The positivist phase thus marks the development of mature thinking freed from empty speculation and superstition.

In the twentieth century, positivism is mainly associated with the Vienna Circle, which was concerned especially with logic and lin- guistics, thus giving rise to the descriptive label, 'logical positivism'. The Circle included such figures as Moritz Schlick, Rudolf Carnap, Otto Neurath, and Hans Reichenbach, with Ludwig Wittgenstein on the fringe (as ever), influential but not quite sufficiently partisan. Basically, these thinkers proposed that meaningful propositions deal either with matters of fact that are empirically verifiable, or with logical relations between concepts. Propositions about logical rela- tions (analytical propositions) provide no knowledge about facts, but are seen to be true by analysing the terms of which they consist, as is the case pre-eminently with logic and mathematics. Other kinds of propositions – such as those of religion and ethics – are, strictly speaking, nonsensical, even though they might have hortatory force. Logical positivism thus aims to show that if philosophical problems are not scientific they are meaningless, so that philosophy becomes a branch of science, constrained to clarify scientific propositions.

Today, the Vienna Circle's brand of positivism has been modi- fied in a number of ways, but the claim that science attains to objective truth confirmed by empirical tests and subsumable under general laws providing approximate descriptions of actual entities has remained dominant in explanations of how science works. This broad position is set out with thoroughness and clarity by Carl C. Hempel in *Aspects of Scientific Explanation*.[2] Hempel claims for instance that 'if a proposed explanation is to be sound, its constituents have to satisfy certain conditions of adequacy, which may be divided into logical and empirical conditions' (247). He then asserts that 'the explanans must contain general laws', and 'must have empirical content; i.e., it must be capable, at least in principle, of test by experiment or observation' (248). Hempel stresses that knowledge attained on this model is value-free, for although a scientist might choose to work on a problem for moral reasons, the resultant hypotheses are acceptable as scientific on the basis of how empirical evidence confirms them, and not because of any moral evaluation.[3] Clearly, from Hempel's point of view, literature and criticism are not scientific because opinions about a poem involve value judgements not subject to empirical tests or subsumable by known covering laws.

One way to attack Hempel's position is by pointing out that sci- entific frameworks are always governed by the historical character of perceived objects as well as by the observer's social situation. As we have seen, this kind of argument was broached by Dilthey in the nineteenth century and assumes a variety of forms in Heidegger's critique of post-Cartesian 'technicity'. A more recent, influential development is offered by Jürgen Habermas,[4] who argues that human sciences have different goals from positive sciences because drawing upon empathy and self-reflection to enable understanding. Consequently, the rules of positivist explanation and verification are not the only rules by which truth claims can be established.

By way of assessing some implications of this critique, I would like briefly to consider the influential contribution of Karl Popper, who was connected to the Vienna Circle, but as 'the Official Opposition' as Otto Neurath put it.[5] Popper was born in Vienna in 1902, and grew up in the climate of logical positivism; however, while contriving to maintain an objectivist view of science, he developed positions strongly critical of the Vienna Circle. As we have seen, for logical positivism, empirical verifiability is the key distinguishing factor between science and nonsense. Popper attacked this view on the grounds that general covering laws are not verifiable but are taken up because of their inherent convincing power, imaginative appeal, and so on. Indeed, far from being meaningless, metaphysical statements might be true, and although we cannot test them empirically we might still assess them critically. Against the sharp demarcation between science and metaphysical nonsense Popper set his famous principle of falsifiability: scientific theories are marked by being falsifiable, and unlike metaphysical statements, the general laws of science can be tested by systematic efforts to refute them. Refutation then leads either to abandonment or modification of the law in question, and knowledge proceeds in a tentative and piecemeal fashion, open-ended and unplanned, approximating to a truth we can never fully know.[6]

To develop his position, Popper assumes with the hermeneutic critics that all human observations are theory-infused. He points out that this is true even at the level of organic processes, which have a built-in capacity for adaptation and reaction to the environment. Then, as our abilities to adapt and solve problems become conscious through language we construct theories, some of which are testable in so far as we can attempt systematically to falsify them.

Although Popper's position at least allows us to treat literary texts as having a serious bearing on a common world, the fact remains that a critical evaluation is not a falsifiable proposition. The person who holds *King Lear* in contempt because it oscillates between

boredom and morbid sensationalism cannot be proved wrong in
the same sense as a person who disagrees that all the ping-pong balls
in this box are transfixed with nails. That is a simple distinction, but
it will help to clarify how, despite his useful critique of positivism,
Popper's principle of falsifiability still does not apply to literature.

Not surprisingly, Popper in turn has been attacked for not pushing the hermeneutic elements in his own arguments far enough
and, consequently, for failing to describe how scientists actually
proceed. In *The Structure of Scientific Revolutions*, Thomas Kuhn[7]
draws widely on the history of science to show that scientific
communities most often try to confirm existing theories rather
than falsify them, and that established practice guides the process
of 'normal science'. Kuhn's celebrated theory about paradigm shifts
(showing how the received view of a whole field can be transformed
and replaced by another, incommensurate one) has had widespread
effect outside his immediate subject. But Kuhn describes himself
surprised to find his position frequently taken to imply the extreme
hermeneutic claim that theory-choice is relativistic, and that 'might
makes right'. He has been careful subsequently to point out that
there are good reasons for choosing one theory over another, and
in the end he departs less drastically from the positivist model than
he is sometimes thought to do.[8]

More adventurously, Paul Feyerabend[9] attacks Popper and his
disciples the 'critical realists' (172) for self-righteous smugness.
Feyerabend claims that if falsification theory were strictly applied
nothing would get done, for science could not even begin. He
proposes that science is a lot 'more "sloppy" and "irrational" than
its methodological image' (174), and calls for a kind of pluralistic
anarchism. Feyerabend thus develops the side of Popper stressing
how all observations are shot through with theory, and at the same
time he questions the falsifiability principle, Popper's key guarantor
of objective testing. Feyerabend proposes rather that discoveries
come in unplanned ways, often as a result of following up seemingly
irrelevant notions, and through the sheer, pleasurable process of
play. He denies that there is any such thing as scientific method
(let alone 'normal science'), and welcomes a pluralism wherein
ideologies contend and standards are chosen by preferences for
certain options. Feyerabend's basic principle is, as he says, that
'anything goes' (296), for science is one among many ideologies
and hardly ever exists in a pure state.[10] He thus repeats Habermas'
position that there is not one privileged way of knowing, and with

such others as Richard Rorty and Bas van Fraassen, he is part of a broadly-based modern critique of positivism, stressing that science is a historically developed, specific kind of knowledge.[11]

It is easy to detect a Scylla and Charybdis in the argument so far: too strong an adherence to positivist principles falsifies the historical embeddedness and complexities of scientific practice; yet the hermeneutic position courts a relativism whereby it is easy to feel that nothing is certain, and that critical and methodological procedures are irrelevant. Exactly this opposition is the main subject of Richard Miller's *Fact and Method*,[12] which sets out to span the gap between the positivist and hermeneutic poles without surrendering certainty and well-foundedness. Miller's position is, as he says, 'a series of piecemeal defenses' (10) rather than an over-arching argument, but he does propose a set of basic criteria. Explanation, he claims, is 'an adequate description of underlying causes bringing about a phenomenon. Adequacy here is determined by rules that are specific to particular fields at particular times' (6). A cause centers on 'a diverse and stable core of cases' (6), and confirmation of a theory must be comparative as well as causal. Thus theories, causes and explanations evolve, and scientists at a given time rely on 'topic-specific truisms as their essential framework'.

For Miller, adequate theories and explanations are more contingent and historically conditioned than for positivism, but are rationally determinable nonetheless. Shrewdness, skill and connoisseurship combined with respect for evidence, sound reasoning and critical scrupulousness provide dependable explanations within specific fields of enquiry. Thus physics and chemistry by self-definition choose questions to which rigorous answers can be given (134). Questions that cannot be answered so rigorously are consigned to other fields – for instance, to geology or biology. History is by and large distinct from physics and chemistry because it does not have the privilege of confining its subject matter in the same way, and in the most influential aspects of Freud and Marx, theory takes the form of 'a repertoire of causal mechanisms' (137) rather than a set of propositions or general laws serving as premises for deductions. Miller thus posits a scale of questions framed in the context of field-specific maxims, and more or less susceptible of rigorous or experimentally testable answers. Thus, because history or music criticism are by and large not experimentally testable in the same manner as is the boiling point of water or the analgesic effect of morphine does not mean that these subjects are, somehow, immature science, or that they are contaminated by relativism or subjectivism in which anything goes. Rather, appropriate principles and ways of arguing, respectful of sound reasoning and encouraging comparison between theories, are worked out by the specialised communities in which there is a good deal of overlap and mutual influence. None of this is, in the end, value-free, but neither is reasoning constituted and determined by ideology – a point to which I will return in Chapter 6.

Through Miller, we might therefore begin to explore how Popper's thinking about our common biological capacities to react and adjust, merges with Feyerabend's claim that lay people are perfectly well able to make shrewd decisions about the applications of science, and with Habermas' reminder that science develops from ways of knowing shared by people in general. All of this is compatible with what I have been describing as 'personal': that is, with a kind of knowledge historically conditioned and requiring evaluation, held in tension between participation and distance, private and public, subjective and objective. In this sense, history, literary criticism, psychoanalysis, and so on, embody forms of reasoning and experience found also in the sciences, and, as Polanyi says, morphology or the recognition of characteristic shapes remains fundamental to science because it is fundamental to human cognition.[13] All of which leads us to the vexed issue of whether or not we can indeed describe a common world or common experience against which we might test our ideas and values. This is a matter of pressing concern to literary critics as well as philosophers of science, and one strong tendency among many theorists today is precisely to call in question the reliability of any such description.

As I have pointed out in Chapter 1, my own position is that things exist independently of us and we can come to know some of them imperfectly but sufficiently for purposes which might be highly practical. That the fabric of reality is immensely richer than our understanding of it is also one of the things we can come to know; indeed, one distinction of art is to show how this is the case. But even such a mild and apparently inoffensive stance is fraught with controversial implications. For one thing, it assumes that language is referential, and thus runs counter to that prevalent line of enquiry in modern linguistics that would shift attention away from the referential function of language and towards its internal dynamics. In Chapter 1, I pointed to Saussure's distinctions between *langue* and *parole,* signifier and signified, and his insistence that meaning emerges from within language by means of differences among signifiers. As we have also seen, deconstruction takes its impetus from Saussurian linguistics, and then undermines structuralism by pushing it to unforeseen conclusions. Thus Jacques Derrida[14] reproduces Saussure's distinction between signifier and signified within the distinction itself. Because the signified is a concept indicated by the signifier, it must in turn be a signifier describable by recourse to further signs. Language therefore operates through a perpetual slide wherein meaning is scattered along chains of signifiers, disseminated rather than centralised, caught in the 'trace' or flickering presence of the sign marked or undercut by its own internal difference and absence. Derrida's celebrated 'différance', combining the notions of difference and deferral, is meant to catch this sense of perpetually commuted and scattered meaning, and he is keen to deploy this key idea in the dismantling of binary oppositions through which terms appear to achieve clear sense. Derrida's point is that each term is contaminated by its opposite: the absence, as it were, that enables its presence.

The most important binary pair for Derrida is the one between speech and writing, which he uses to disclose the 'logocentric' excesses of Western metaphysics. Derrida claims that Western philosophy has always favoured speech, and, consequently, the immediacy and presence of meaning to a subject. But the effort by philosophers to suppress their own written discourse inevitably fails, for speech keeps turning into another version of writing in the same way as does the signified in the signifier/signified opposition. For instance, in the *Confessions* Rousseau attacks writing in order to show how civilization has artifically removed us from our natural origins. Yet writing remains Rousseau's way of making his case, and the result is a complex double bind by which the *Confessions* is both given and constituted. Deconstruction thus proceeds not simply by inverting a received sense, but by stressing the inter-involvements of apparently opposite terms. This is the case with speech and writing, metaphor and concept, literature and criticism, and so on.

There are two broad ways to take all this. The first, represented by Frederick Crews,[15] sees deconstruction as fostering irrationalism. By denying that propositions can be true, deconstruction stultifies its own discourse and reduces criticism to a futile and mandarin exercise, for 'if there is no stable object of enquiry, critical debate is pointless' (122). If indeed there is nothing outside the text as Derrida says, and if meaning is endlessly deferred (every concept or referential term being a repressed metaphor), then there is no recourse to evidence (170–71). Deconstruction thus also precludes the development of fruitful ideas, and is soon monotonous and hermetic, as well as irrationalist. Literary critics, Crews thinks, are abrogating their responsibility by subscribing to such theories.

Derrida's defender, Christopher Norris,[16] turns the tables on Crews' kind of argument by insisting that Derrida everywhere stresses 'the need to keep faith with enlightened reason . . . even while assaying that tradition's limits' (234); the irrationalism belongs rather to those who assume that Derrida is irrationalist without reading him carefully. According to Norris, Derrida attempts to dismantle the Enlightenment model only insofar as it treats philosophy 'as a locus of pure, disinterested enquiry' (236). Derrida does not call for an end to Western metaphysics, nor to 'the old mimetic regime' (53) because he realises there is no other ground on which to stand and that language 'is marked through and through by referential (or mimetic) assumptions' (54). Derrida merely would have us see that the 'classical ideas of this referential function have greatly simplified its nature' (54). Nor does Derrida deny the relevance of authorial intent: rather, as with Rousseau, an author's intention is often declared, but it is important to see how it is contained in a system that it does not dominate (243). In short, Derrida looks out especially for the signs of stress and omission, elision and marginal comment that indicate how difficult it is to reduce writing to a single or univocal truth.

Reassuring as Norris is, he ends up with a strangely tame Derrida – the lion with his teeth drawn. For of course deconstruction is right to remind us that meaning is not single, that there is more to literature than authorial intent, that there is no univocal, systematic and authoritative hermeneutic, and that we are encompassed by uncertainties and mysteries. But Derrida's sheer contrivance and ingenuity, his rhetorical pyrotechnics, dizzying obscurities and radical claims about undecidability, about there being nothing outside the text, his statements _sous rature_, and so on, lean decidedly towards the attenuation of referentiality and towards the undermining of appeals to evidence based on experience – in short, towards an extreme hermeneutic position that in fact results from Derrida's reading of Husserl and Heidegger.

Admittedly, Derrida is a subtle and complex thinker who is aware of the paradoxes in his own expression of the inexpressible, and he is often an amused ironiser of his own arguments. Partly for this reason, he elevates the principle of play, as he explains in the influential essay, 'Structure, Sign and Play in the Discourse of the Human Sciences',[17] describing the interminable pursuit of meaning through a text, 'the joyous affirmation of the play of the world . . . a world of signs without fault, without truth, and without origin'. By means of interpretation that 'affirms play', he suggests even that we might 'pass beyond man and humanism'. A similar sense of meaning unencumbered and unanchored by objective constraint is a key theme in such other playful intellects as Barthes, Lacan and Hartman,[18] and here too we might be reminded of Feyerabend for whom, as we have seen, science proceeds not by one method or single kind of enquiry, but through 'play' in which 'anything goes'. Yet if anything goes, nothing goes, and the limitations encroached upon by Feyerabend's anti-realist account of science are much like those entailed by Derrida's non-cognitive relativism. As A. D. Nuttall says of deconstruction in general, 'Without the ordinary restraints of objectivism, there is little for the first intelligences of Paris and Yale to do but play – with a sort of sub-Nietzschean hilarity, parsing and reparsing the texts.'[19] Nuttall's point is confirmed by Richard Rorty,[20] who claims that the later Derrida 'simply drops theory' in favour of 'fantasising' about his predecessors, 'playing with them, giving free rein to the trains of association they produce' (125). There is no message or method here; rather the achievement of a unique 'richness of texture' (129) allowing no distinction between fantasy and argument (133). This indeed is a wilder version of Derrida than the one Norris offers, but it points to a characteristic, unconfinable and solvent energy by which Derrida celebrates mainly the freedom to refuse any commitment whatsoever, including appeals to common experience and the assessment of evidence that assumes our descriptions refer to a common world.

At this point, the ancient concept of *mimesis* presses a claim. In the *Poetics*, Aristotle asserts that nature (*phusis*) is not static, but is a dynamic process. Through *mimesis*, that is, art reveals some significant aspect of this dynamism, which we recognise not just in the sense of comparing some original with what is represented as a likeness or copy, but by knowing in a new way a thing we already know. Through art, we discover the familiar anew, unencumbered by the jading habits of conventional description, and as part of the larger dynamism in which we also belong, so that we recognise the thing represented and ourselves together. As Gadamer says, this recognition of something revealed in ourselves and in the thing

represented is the 'presence' of the work.²¹ And here, as Aristotle
again insists, probability is a criterion. For art will not endure
unless it engages features recognisable as constituting powerful
attachments both between ourselves and the world, and between
one another, a point centrally confirmed by A. D. Nuttall's *A New
Mimesis*.²² As Heidegger says, art 'lets things be' in the presence of
a beholder whose recognition is awakened to surprise and wonder,
even across generations and a variety of cultures. Yet not all art is
equally durable in this way, for the needs of a particular, individual
receptivity might be more or less responsive to what is disclosed,
and the revelatory power of all art is not equivalent nor does it
exist somehow in a steady state. Likewise, the explanations and
responses people provide for what strikes them as significant will
vary with the standards they erect, and the assumptions about
nature, society, humankind, and so on, that they routinely make:
in short, in accordance with what kinds of persons they are.

It seems, then, we cannot be free of our historical embeddedness
and the theory-impregnated observations that bias our view of
the world even in the deepest recesses of our bodies, as Popper
says. We cannot stand outside ourselves in order to begin, and
the hermeneutic approach is correct to insist on how relevant
this fact is for the self-understanding of the positive sciences, as
Habermas points out. Still, we cannot be free either from the world
we inhabit and which constrains us, a shared reality that we can
know more or less adequately and in a variety of ways, and to
which we can appeal for evidence appropriate to the kinds of
questions we raise. Although it is arguable, as Derrida claims,
that words drive us to other words for fuller and more adequate
definitions, this principle does not obtain at the price of a common
reality, a resistant and independent world that different branches of
learning describe according to their special interests. The sciences
thus constitute a multicentric network of investigative procedures,
each with its own problems and critical vocabularies which are not,
however, mutually exclusive. For instance crystallography has a
bearing on microbiology, as does chemistry on physics, physics on
music, music on poetry, and so on. And although the processes of
verification set out by Hempel indeed cannot falsify the opinion of
our imagined reader of *King Lear*, yet they might be adduced to
prove by chemical analysis, say, that the Turin shroud does not date
from the time of Christ and should be valued differently by those
who believed it did. Analogously, no single method prescribes how

adjustments within or through such overlapping areas will affect the claims and procedures of any number of disciplines. But it is important that mutual adjustment and critical enquiry take place, and that we compare and choose among theories to assess fresh ideas. Within specific disciplines, a sense ('connoisseurship', Polanyi says) of the 'good reasons' Kuhn describes, such as 'accuracy, scope, simplicity, fruitfulness',[23] help to maintain the 'well-focused debate, high standards of reasoning, and even a degree of consensus'[24] Crews recommends. And as Miller points out, the defense of learning is piecemeal, not general, for no single model covers all the fields. Sovreignty among the disciplines is therefore important, as are the interpenetrations and common grounds we share as persons – as users of language, at once embodied, participating in the world yet distanced from it, negotiating and communicating through imagination, tact, and the skills and powers of discrimination that subtend and inform the articulations of reason. One distinguishing characteristic of literature is, precisely, its power to disclose this participatory element in knowing, so that we encounter afresh the strangeness and radiant potency subtending the familiar, and how, as users of language, our appropriations of the world are simultaneously disposals of ourselves, always already engaged in a project and in evaluation. Literature thus invites us to assess again and re-evaluate the personal values we might otherwise assume through habit or familiarity to be somehow 'natural'.

First and last, then, a work of art cannot be proven good or tested in the same way as the specific gravity of water or the Salk vaccine, but this does not preclude rationality. Rather, one attests the value of what is recognised, what is disclosed, what is significant, and criticism attempts to explore and mediate such personal evaluations as precede and exceed the critical explication itself. Thus, criticism has its own rhetorical and persuasive energy, but should be willing also to search the implications and understand rationally the sense of presence literature offers, and the standards entailed by affirming the excellence of certain works compared to others. This enquiry is conducted especially within the skilled communities who edit, promote, and argue about literature, and, as in other branches of learning, certain kinds of discrimination are acquired by practice. In this process the dangers of naive positivism and extreme indeterminacy can both be avoided, and within the broad area of concern that remains lies a variety of problems, issues, opportunities and points of engagement, both with other disciplines and with the common world upon which they bear. For instance, material bibliographers might draw on chemistry for evidence about dating and techniques of composition; compilers of concordances and stylistic analysts might find uses for computer science; biographers and critics might deploy the findings of historians. By such means a body of knowledge can be established, more or less well-founded, and engaged with the larger fabric of culture. Yet, fundamentally, the great works of imagination challenge us also to know familiar things anew and on such grounds to criticise whatever manipulative ideologies would confine our purview and constrain our hopes by suppressing or ignoring aspects of experience that art alone can adequately express. In such a context, criticism enables us to explore something of the complex pre-involvements out of which our standards and values arise. As an example of how this is so, and to conclude this section of the chapter, I would like to turn to Shakespeare's *The Tempest*, which is especially concerned with ways in which personal evaluations of justice and goodness compete for ascendancy within a society, thereby shaping it by setting norms and standards. In exploring these issues, Shakespeare also thematises the problem of a common world, and how our interpretations remain individual even though encountering a larger fabric of reality that puts them to the test.

As the play opens, Prospero explains to his daughter Miranda how his dukedom was usurped. He and his infant child were set adrift in a small boat, partly because his vision of himself as a learned magus had prevented him from attending to the problems of governing his dukedom and restraining the like of his usurping brother, Antonio. On the island where Prospero finds refuge, he revises his ideas about government, accommodating his magical knowledge to new circumstances and to the fact that his values are not self-evident to others. His power is continually tested by the primitive Caliban whose rapacious lust for the now grown-up Miranda would over-rule the law of reason and ceremony that Prospero holds necessary for civilized order. Protecting Miranda from Caliban requires constant vigilance and intervention.

When, partly by Prospero's magic, the usurpers are brought to the island, they too impose their own notions on their common world. Gonzalo thinks he has discovered a natural paradise, and describes an idyllic society living innocently close to nature. But for Antonio and Sebastian, the unregulated island merely renders the king, Alonzo, vulnerable and they plan to murder him. The very existence of their plan comments on the deficiencies of Gonzalo's idealising theories, just as his good nature shows up their nastiness. In turn, Caliban thinks the drunken jester and the butler, Trinculo and Stephano, worthy of obedience because they provide him with liquor, and Ferdinand's experience of the magically-produced masque convinces him that Prospero's insistence on holy ceremony is necessary for preserving order.

These contending evaluations mutually comment on, define and test one another, and each implies a standard of behaviour. The characters thus partly construct the worlds they inhabit, and Shakespeare flirts provocatively with the extreme hermeneutic position that they not only perceive physical reality differently, but perhaps even perceive different kinds of physical reality. The question of whether the storm initiating the action is real or illusory is never quite resolved, and the island shimmers uncertainly, at once definite (there are briars, furzes, pricking gorses) and yet haunted by spirits, strange musical sounds and illusions. Still, the play does not allow us to conclude that reality is just what we make of it, but presses the more intriguing and problematic notion that we interpret things differently according to the different personal evaluations and prejudices we bring to bear on what we perceive. Consequently, Gonzalo's idealism is generous and noble, but he is wordy and sentimental, screening out the hard facts that would modify his position. Antonio and Sebastian are practical and expedient, but also cruel and vindictive. Stephano and Trinculo are merry and carefree, but their coarseness and shallowness render them insensitive. Prospero is authoritative and bent on bringing about reconciliation, but the stress entailed by such an undertaking is evident in his irascibility, tetchiness and need to struggle against the pride that his own superior knowledge engenders. Thus *The Tempest* presents various motivations, projects, and understandings of the world, no single one fully embracing all the rest, and each commenting on the others to force a complex, intricate series of adjustments and judgements. Reality and illusion, verse and prose, music and noise, ideal and actual, theory and fact, character and circumstance, innocence and experience are presented in the process of world-shaping – the mutual shaping, that is, of the human and nature in the production of civilized order that is the play's theme.

At the end, Prospero renounces his magical power and participates, however churlishly, in the forgiveness to which he brings the others. The usurpers are exposed but forgiven, Miranda and

Ferdinand are betrothed and initiated into the mysteries of 'sanctimonious ceremonies' (IV,i,16), and Caliban at least claims to see the error of his ways (V,i,295–6). Prospero would lead them all to a reconciliation that he knows he cannot enforce: he knows – as his famous 'revels' (IV,i,146ff.) speech indicates – that we are moved at last not by proof or imposition, but by poetry, by the play's art that invites recognition just as Prospero invites the recognition of his own captive audience on the island. Paradoxically, the very power of mimesis is enhanced here by our appreciation of how tenuous is even the best case poetry presents, for at the end Antonio does not enter into the fellowship, and refuses what the others share. Even as Ferdinand and Miranda are discovered so charmingly playing chess after the betrothal, she accuses him of cheating (V,i,172).

Analogously and in a minor key, the preceding argument likewise depends on a reader recognising in the first place that *The Tempest* is a great and valuable work of imagination. For the patterning of episodes and various constellations of motivation and cross-motivation I have described do not in themselves constitute Shakespeare's greatness, and comparable structures might be found in many a soap-opera or comic-book. And so the piercing lyricism of the songs, the deep agonies of knowledge and love crossed with irascibility in Prospero's speeches, the resentments and terrors, lyrical and brutal complexities of Caliban, the enchantment, humour, whimsy, sadness, fierce wisdom and convincing power of the diverse visions of the island can only be pointed to. Their value cannot be proved or tested by controlled experiment or by falsification. Yet they bear upon the world we know and as we discuss the implications of that fact we too wait upon an affirmative response, as in the Epilogue to the play itself: 'Gentle breath of yours my sails / Must fill, or else my project fails.'

But if the present project is not entirely in the way of failing, I want to conclude that the hermeneutic position outlined in the last chapter should stop short of privatising experience and denying the constraints of a real world, outside ourselves. Persons find an identity in the face of such constraints and in a shared effort to negotiate them. Yet because of the world's immense complexity and our embodied condition, we proceed by trial and error, by the assumption of values upon which we wager, and standards we strive to fulfill. Literature especially enables us to explore some of the complex pre-involvements out of which such standards arise, and criticism, among other things, should promote our clarification and assessment of the values by which we live our lives, and which also govern (and are produced by) our concern for literature. In this process, theory-comparison, dialogue, and mutual testing all have a part to play, remaining open to scrupulous argument and the appeal to evidence. As I have said, literature cannot be tested in the scientific manner described by Hempel, but it can show us that persons need to recognise values and set standards that are publicly and communally debatable, and that have a bearing on a common world, not-ourselves.

REPEATABILITY: ON THE PATTERNS OF INTENT AND DESIRE

One criterion of scientific verifiability is whether or not an experimental test can be repeated. Analogously, it is sometimes argued that one way in which the value of a literary work is tested is by its being read over and over and thus withstanding the trial of time. What used to be called 'a classic' is then simply a book that stays alive, that keeps its staying power through cultural change. Although 'repeatability' in this, second, sense is clearly not the same as the repeatability of a controlled scientific experiment, again we should avoid concluding that the consensus according Dante, Shakespeare and Goethe the status of classics is produced with no bearing at all on a common world. But let us now try to sharpen the focus and ask more specifically about what is *repeated* when we read a literary work.

There has been a substantial amount of commentary on the general subject of the repetition of motifs within a literary text, which critics tend to see as either a unifying device highlighting sameness, or as a way of projecting and showing up differences.[25] There is general agreement that the opposed principles of sameness and difference are also interdependent, but there is a good deal of disagreement about whether literary repetition foregrounds the work's unity or its heterogeneity. Recently, J. Hillis Miller[26] suggests that the two kinds of repetition (he calls them 'grounded' and 'ungrounded') mutually subvert one another and thus force us to acknowledge the work's open-endedness. In this context it is possible to argue that reading or re-reading a work is again a form of repetition involving the paradoxical interplay of sameness and difference: each reader has a different experience of the text, and yet the work itself is the same.

I do not want to enter into this debate directly, but rather at an oblique angle, by raising the question of what kinds of value a literary text might promote, and one way to do this is by adding to the distinction between sameness and difference a further distinction between desirable and undesirable repeatability. This further distinction pertains to the representation in works of literature of values that strike us as substantively good, and which we want to promulgate. That is, a literary work might make present again a certain good, perhaps the product of a quite different cultural phase, yet still relevant to us. Alternatively, a great work might offer a compelling warning about oppression and cruelty based on experiences now past but all too reproducible in our present circumstances, in which case, the warning itself is given a form that we affirm as salutary. Yet, in great literature these substantive goods and salutary warnings are highly complex, often grapsed indirectly or through contradiction and paradox. But even such complexity might strike us as true to life and valuable, as distinct, say, from contrived and tedious. My point is that a desire to affirm – and so to repeat – a certain good as valuable to our lives is a necessary presupposition of critical reading, the subtlety and complexity of such an affirmation notwithstanding. In short, literature that does not teach us how to live is merely a distraction, and in the modified form I have described, the idea of repeatability constitutes one way of testing what we take to be a worthwhile book.

A well-known example of what I mean by 'desirable repeatability' is provided by Marx's admiration of ancient Greek art, though Marx deplored the slavery upon which that society was based:

> A man cannot become a child again, or he becomes childish. But does he not find joy in the child's naiveté, and must he himself not strive to reproduce its truth at a higher stage? . . . The Greeks were normal children. The charm of their art for us is not in contradiction to the undeveloped stage of society on which it grew. [It] is its result, rather, and is inextricably bound up, rather, with the fact that the unripe social conditions under which it rose, and could alone arise, can never return.[27]

That is, a certain potentiality for communion between the human and nature, celebrating the body's harmony and the mind's sense of form, had been shaped 'in an unconsciously artistic way' in Greek mythology, and then reproduced in Greek art. This unselfconscious innocence and communion are not recoverable directly in modern society, but are recoverable – that is, repeatable – on a higher plane as an element in a culture that has passed beyond the brutalities of a slave economy. Analogously, we might point to how the intricate tapestry of interlacements throughout medieval Romance embodies a complex understanding of how we give one another being by selfless dedication within the delicate elaboration of the civilized. Uniquely in the Romances love is explored as a personal value we might still prize, even if (among other things) we learn also of the oppressiveness of feudal codes, of savageries perpetrated in the name of honour, and the like. Or again, with Dickens we might discover the humanising effect of an individual kindness and the strength and dignity of those whose imagination is nurtured to inform judgement, even as we are invited to recoil from the enslaving horrors of the industrial revolution.

'Desirable repeatability', then, is the recovery of a certain good from the literature of past times, and in this sense the thing to be repeated is a utopian fragment, an energiser of present hopes and aspirations. Thus, we might say, the future of the past is desirable repeatability, the utopian element that works of imagination are especially fitted to engage. However, as we also see in the above examples, evaluating a repeatable good is intimately bound up with the imperfections and cruelties of history's nightmare, the experience of negative contrast that desire always and immediately produces.[28] One special distinction of literature is to give us a sense of how the good and what distorts it are engendered together, so that our response to the utopian becomes part and parcel of a critical recollection whereby we learn also about the mechanisms that thwart us, and how these also are the substance of history's narrative. As I have said, this very interdependence has a bearing on the general notion of testability, and how subtle and indirect are the impingements of literature upon a common world. The relationship is not univocal, and the validations a critic might pursue are, rather, tentative and discriminating negotiations, neither wholly private nor wholly objective in the positivist sense. With this in mind, let us briefly consider Chaucer's Pardoner.

'The Pardoner's Tale'[29] is a satire against corrupt ecclesiastical practice. This is already suggested in the General Prologue to *The Canterbury Tales* through the Pardoner's close association with the Summoner, who should by rights be prosecuting him for abuse of office.[30] By contrast, as the Pardoner sings 'Come hider, love, to me', the Summoner in reply 'bar to hym a stif burdoun' (672–3). The two are singing the same tune, which is Chaucer's way of pointing out how both are abusing their spiritual trust. Moreover, the General Prologue presents the Pardoner as sexually disturbed. His beardlessness and carefully-tended hair derive from current satires about fops and suggest effeminacy; his high voice and glaring eyes suggest eunuchry and shamelesness; the references to goats and hares suggest lechery and hermaphroditism.[31] To this engaging mix the narrator adds his own opinion: 'I trowe he were a geldyng or a mare' (691). 'Gelding' again indicates eunuchry, but 'mare' is less clear, perhaps suggesting homosexuality. Thus, when the Summoner bears 'a stif burdoun', the pun adds to the sense of sexual disturbance,[32] and the 'unnatural' abuses of ecclesiastical office practiced by these two are presented metaphorically in terms of an 'unnatural' sexuality.

Responding to such clues, one critic suggests that the Pardoner typifies the *eunuchus non Dei*,[33] whose condition reverses that recommended in Matthew 19:12, approving of those who become eunuchs for the kingdom of heaven's sake. The Pardoner's physical attributes here again are a way of representing his spiritual sterility. Yet we might object that it is not clear that the Pardoner really is a eunuch:[34] rather, as we see, he is described in terms suggesting hermaphroditism, effeminacy, and homosexuality, as well as eunuchry. Also, the narrator's surmise ('I trow') is carefully indefinite, as is the phrase, 'a gelding *or* a mare', where the meaning of 'mare' is also unclear. Chaucer's imprecision even seems calculated to *prevent* us from reducing out a direct or plain allegorical sense, and in this resistance to classification we might also feel the Pardoner emerging as a memorable individual. Indeed, as the tale develops we come to know him as a dangerous, tormented, vulnerable and horrifying person who in the end eludes us, but whose presence is disturbingly immediate. The degree to which Chaucer is the master of this combined effect becomes especially evident when the Pardoner introjects into his tale a moralising sermon so clearly different in style from the tale proper that we are forced to ponder what the contrast means.[35] To clarify this, let me reconstruct briefly the order of events.

The Pardoner begins by confessing to the group how he preaches sensational sermons promising that his false relics will cure diseases and remit sins. His self-disclosure itself is sensational and is a kind of performance. Although it is shot through with apparent self-loathing ('Thus spitte I out my venym under hewe / Of hoolynesse, to semen hooly and trewe' [421–22], and so on), the general effect of bravado and exhibitionism makes it difficult to be sure if all this is the anguished revelation of a compulsive sinner, or the brilliant manipulation of his audience by a hardened and cynical one.

The Pardoner then tells a tale about three revellers, but has no sooner begun than he digresses into a sermon against gluttony, gambling and swearing: that is, against revelry in general. The sermon is replete with learned allusions – to Seneca, John of Salisbury, various legends of the ancient world, and several books of the bible – and is charged with rhetorical overkill ('O wombe! O bely! O stynkyng cod, / Fulfilled of dong and of corrupcioun' [534–35]). Again it is a display, listing vices, citing authorities, and denouncing sins with a fine excess of passionate indignation. But then the Pardoner gets back to his tale of the three revellers in the tavern, who set out on a drunken quest to slay Death. Soon they meet an old man who directs them up a 'croked wey' (781) to a grove of trees where, surprisingly, they find treasure. The youngest of the three is then sent to town for bread and wine, and when he is gone the others plan to murder him. Meanwhile, the youngest plans to murder them by poisoning the wine, but when he returns he is killed by his companions who then drink the wine, so that in the end all three are dead. At this point the Pardoner launches into his professional sales pitch, pressing his audience to buy the relics he has already admitted are false. He is rudely treated by the host, and the Knight effects an uneasy peace.

As is often noticed, the tale proper is compressed, rhetorically plain, and sinister. The mysterious old man is in some sense a *memento mori*, but does not yield to any single interpretation, and remains unsettling and enigmatic.[36] The rioters (like the old man, un-named) are ironically destroyed from within by death which they hoped to discover and destroy as an external enemy. The main sins in the sermon against revelry are here addressed again, but now they are shown taking a grip on people's lives which are terminated in unexpected ways. The contrast between sermon and tale thus corresponds roughly to the contrast between outside and inside. It is easy to denounce sin by classifying it and fulminating against it, and the Pardoner well knows his sermon is a display of just such official indignation, expertly performed but contemptibly deficient in its power to grapple with the 'inside' workings of sin.

Chaucer's calculated indefiniteness in the tale proper is therefore of signal importance. The old man, the boy, the crooked way, the treasure, the bread and wine, all hover on the edge of allegory, but interpretations along such lines inevitably shade into a less generalisable sense of the undifferentiated and anomalous. The effect here duplicates exactly the calculated uncertainty about the Pardoner's sexuality and motivations. Instead of conceptual clarity we have the sense of something ambivalent, subtle, interior, not speakable directly and yet present: in short, the impress of an individual person as distinct from a type.

Here, then, we might come to know more fully the content of what I am calling 'undesirable repeatability'. In an 'external' sense, indeed the same old patterns of gluttony, swearing and murder keep on recurring, and it is easy to warn against them and denounce them. It is much more difficult to catch the deepseated sense of an individual's thwartedness, the confused mixture of desire and loathing in a person whose actions might be classified after the event, but whose innermost compulsions easily escape us. Chaucer's great achievement in 'The Pardoner's Tale' is to give us an immediate, disturbing sense of the Flaw in the heart of things, the anomaly of unmaking that cancels being and is not susceptible to direct description. Not surprisingly, the Pardoner tells so many lies (words of unmaking) that in the end we do not know sufficiently who he is to gauge the compulsions that drive him to go on repeating the same, desperate performance. 'I wol yow nat deceyve' (918) he assures his audience. Well, yes and no, for here we meet again the old conundrum of the Cretan who declares all Cretans liars: we cannot form an opinion on the matter that is not immediately undermined. Correspondingly, undesirable repeatability undermines what it would affirm, and we go on reading Chaucer's tale because he has found a way to show us with what powerful indirection the mechanisms of such repetition can operate. The Pardoner's own ideology produces alienation engendering resentment and defensiveness fueled in turn by the ideological categories against which the resentment is directed. This circle rapidly assumes the power of the zero, annihilating its products. Just so, the Pardoner's need to belong is undermined by a sense of hypocrisy caused by his loathing of the need itself. The value of Chaucer's art is to convince us of this, and such value is inseparable from a sense that Chaucer here shows us something of how we really are.

At this point, the question of what, in a work of literature, is repeated and tested anew by our own experience and circumstances comes to include the author's intent, as I have indicated even by the locution 'Chaucer here shows us'. Yet the notion of authorial intent is extremely vexed, and has been called in question especially by recent post-structuralist attacks on the idea of a stable subject. One influential essay on the topic is Foucault's 'What is an author?'[37]

Basically, Foucault claims that no single authorial presence unifies a text: indeed, the convention of attributing a text to an author appeared at a certain moment in history. Foucault then is at pains to point out that 'today's writing has freed itself from the dimension of expression. Referring only to itself, but without being restricted to the confines of its interiority, writing is identified with its own unfolded exteriority'. This means that the writing subject 'constantly disappears', and Foucault concludes that 'we must entirely reverse the traditional idea of the author', who is not 'an indefinite source of significations which fill a work' but is rather 'a certain functional principle by which, in our culture, one limits, excludes, and chooses'. Foucault maintains that discourse is always about peformance and power (Chaucer's Pardoner would agree) and as a way of revealing the arbitrary and ideological basis of what passes for meaning and truth, he stresses how the writing subject is dispersed through the text. This position is consistent with the view that reading is a repetition foregrounding difference.

Based on arguments in the previous section of this chapter, my claim at this point is, simply, that a degree of inferrable intention is legitimate on the grounds that it is a part of our everyday personal experience and communication with others. Without inferrable intent, we would not relate to one another as persons at all. Just so, without inferrable intent no text would have a discussable meaning, and there would be no effective comparison of points of view, and no choice of standards with any bearing on the world: in short, there would be no personal knowledge. Authorial intent might therefore be defended roughly as one would defend the efficacy of paraphrase. That is, literature is not confined to the paraphrasable and indeed we value literature for the ways in which it exceeds paraphrase. Yet this excess subsumes the paraphrase and does not negate it. Just so, a work of literature is not confined to an author's intent, but this intent is part of what constitutes it. At the very least, critics should be willing to offer clear paraphrase as a basic means of mediating a text to less expert readers (experimental texts that defy paraphrase can be shown to assume traditions of conventional meaning upon which they are parasitic, as Gombrich points out is the case with painting).[38] Critics should therefore try to assess what meanings are compatible with an author's probable or declared intent, without losing sight of the fact that literature is also much more than the author intends. As I have suggested, well-founded arguments occupy a position between relativist irrationalism and naive objectivism, and in this spirit I have suggested that Chaucer's general satiric intent in 'The Pardoner's Tale' can be inferred, and is part of what we encounter in our repeated readings.

At this point it might be useful to consider another, trickier example, where the author's intent is highly elusive. Shakespeare's *Henry V*[39] is in large part a jingoistic celebration of England's invasion of France, and of the victory at Agincourt. The war is both the occasion and symbol of national unification under the 'mirror of all Christian kings' from whose reign the House of Tudor established its claim to the throne.[40]

As is often noticed, the play is full of epic effects. There is a great deal of heroic rhetoric, martial enthusiasm, formal eulogy, catalogues of notable warriors slain, elaborate concern for genealogy, celebrations of destiny, and a set of formal prologues by the chorus to evoke epic panoramas the stage cannot contain. ('Can this cockpit hold / The vasty fields of France?': no, but we are to 'make imaginary puissance' [Prologue, 11–12; 25]). Henry's exalted set- pieces fairly swell with heroic enthusiasm:

> 'Once more unto the breach, dear friends, once more;
> Or close the wall up with our English dead!'
>
> (III,i,1–2)

> 'This day is called the Feast of Crispian:
> He that outlives this day, and comes safe home,
> Will stand a-tiptoe when this day is named,
> And rouse him at the name of Crispian.'
>
> (IV,iii,40–43)

It is hard not to be stirred by the sheer volume and energy of these cascading and emblazoned speeches.

Notoriously, however, the play admits a countervailing reading, and to some critics Henry V is a model Machiavellian, a ruthless and manipulating schemer.[41] This is the king who insists that the war be conducted 'justly and religiously' (I,ii,10), and who attends to the Archbishop of Canterbury's explication of the Salic

law upon which the English claim to France is based. The Archbishop's speech is long, circumstantial, studded with proper names,
presented formally and without interruption. On the one hand, it
is an epic genealogy affirming Henry's inherited right, formally
supported by legal and ecclesiastical sanction. On the other, it
is protracted, complex, and all but impossible to follow, so that
it might equally seem merely to disguise Henry's warmongering
intent under the forms of ceremony. After all, the Archbishop had
just before confided to the Bishop of Ely that a proposal of war
would help to relieve an outstanding church debt. We are scarcely
reassured when the king accepts the bishop's intricate account with
unseemly alacrity, and then launches into a speech promising to
repay the Dauphin's insulting gift of tennis balls with a vengeance
that will leave France with 'many a thousand widows' (I,ii,284),
and worse. This is the king who orders the throats of prisoners
to be cut, and who has Bardolph executed for a trivial theft, who
offers Harfleur the alternatives of surrender without resistance or
of having English soldiers mow down 'Your fresh fair virgins and
your flow'ring infants' (III,iii,13–14), spitting naked children on
pikes and dashing out the brains of old men. This is the king
who talks himself out of responsibility for his men whom he visits
incognito and who present him with a view of the inglorious side
of war. 'Every subject's duty is the king's,' Henry concludes, 'but
every subject's soul is his own' (IV,i,176).[42] Admittedly, Henry
is perplexed and ruminates about the gap between 'Ceremony'
(IV,i,244) and his own frailty, as well he might, but he soon pushes
all that aside in a stirring public invocation of the 'God of battles'
(IV,i,289). In short, it is as if the play as epic (the larger-than-life
panorama of patriotic heroism outreaching 'this unworthy scaffold'
[Prologue, 10]) and the play as drama (the lively exchange between
individuals, the sense of conflict, mixed motives and split loyalties)
are sharply and deliberately in counterpoint.[43] Although the epic
heroism offers to absorb what the drama presents, the reverse is
just as feasible, for the drama convincingly gives us Henry the
machiavel, the hard as stone and ruthless politician in quest of
power and possessions.

Critics disagree about how to take all this. Either Shakespeare
intends to celebrate the Tudor myth, or to show it up as a sham.
Or perhaps he no longer believed in the cause he found himself
having to promote. One critic even concludes that the two positions
are intended to be irreconcilable, and that the play is like the trick

drawing of a rabbit/duck, which we can see one way and then the other, but not both ways simultaneously.[44] Yet, whichever of these critical positions we might adopt, the fact remains that Shakespeare's general satiric intent is more difficult to infer than Chaucer's, despite the complexity of the poetry in both cases. Personally, I find it improbable that Shakespeare did not intend to produce the serious qualifications the play offers of Henry's heroism, even though the author's exact stance remains elusive, and there is a suspicious excess of apparently wholehearted jingoism. The portrait of Henry therefore presents us with a rich and provocative undecidability, which shades then into an uncertainty wherein Shakespeare's own motivations are not beyond reproach. Still, the case here is basically not much different from that which obtains in everyday exchanges between people. The wellsprings of intent are finally inaccessible even to ourselves, but often they are sufficiently plain to permit some rational exchange without grievous misunderstanding. So it is with Shakespeare's Henry. He exceeds our descriptions of what motivates him and how Shakespeare intended us to regard him. But it seems sensible neither to deny authorial intent a bearing, nor to claim that it is simply determinative. Our certainty on such matters might vary from author to author and work to work, and readers through the ages will probably continue to find surprising new dimensions and kinds of significance in the great books. Such 'hermeneutic potential' exceeds an author's control, and although Shakespeare's intentions are not negligible, it is hard to say in what sense he would recognise as 'intended' the subtleties and extensive consequences of his splendid language proposed by generations of interpreters. In short, like all of us to some degree, Shakespeare knew more than he said and said more than he knew.

Authorial intent, then, has a bearing on the common world within which personal values are maintained and tested. But I do not want to leave this topic without considering briefly the structuralist claim that a culture coheres because certain underlying, unconscious codes are repeated through its rituals, art and customs, and these are more significant than any supposed reference to an external, commonly accessible world, or individual declaration of intent. Claude Lévi-Strauss even holds that in describing the basic patterns discoverable in a body of myth we make contact with the most universal thinking processess of the human mind. In a more piecemeal fashion, however, such patterns tell us about how kinship systems, rituals, cooking practices, and so on, bind whole communities together.

For instance, in his analysis of face-painting among the Caduveo Indians, Lévi-Strauss suggests that symmetrical designs lying across an oblique axis are a way of expressing and resolving in imaginative form the difficulties of a caste system that other, neighbouring Indians had resolved by means of a more effective social order. Thus we are to see Caduveo art as 'the phantasm of a society ardently and insatiably seeking a means of expressing symbolically the institutions it might have, if its interests and superstitions did not stand in the way'.[45] The real meaning of the face painting is the significance of its underlying structure, which is repeated in a variety of manifestations throughout the community.

The best known application of Lévi-Strauss's principles to a literary text occurs in his essay, 'The Structural Study of Myth', in which he analyses the Oedipus story.[46] The analysis deploys a four-column chart and Lévi-Strauss suggests that when we read across from left to right, working down, we learn the story; when we read from top to bottom, working across, we learn the structure, the true meaning of the myth in all its versions. This meaning has to do with a belief that human beings are autochthonous, which contradicts the fact that all humans are born 'from the union of man and woman'. Thus, the myth counterpoints situations where blood relations are over-rated, to others where they are underrated, thereby expressing the tragic intensity of 'the attempt to escape autochthony' and 'the impossibility to succeed in it'. As with other kinds of symbolism, ritual and artefacture, the Oedipus myth mediates contradictions of which the story-teller or artist is likely to be unconscious.

Another example of this kind of analysis that will help us to a broad assessment of the idea of repeatability in relation to structuralism is Edmund Leach's 'Fishing for Men on the Edge of the Wilderness'.[47] Leach acknowledges his debt to Lévi-Strauss, but applies the master's principles to his own 'personal style of biblical exegesis' (579).

Leach holds that 'all the New Testament fishermen stories can be treated as component elements in the same myth/dream story' (595). For instance, Jesus enlists two pairs of brothers, Peter and Andrew, James and John. This can be understood in terms of the Graeco-Roman myth of the Dioscuroi or Gemini, who are Leda's sons Castor and Pollux, one begotten by a mortal father, Tyndareus, and the other by Zeus. Both children eventually become immortal because of their love for one another. The strange title of James and John, 'Sons of Thunder', is related to the Dioscuroi ('Sons of God'), and also to the thunder god, Zeus. Moreover, the Dioscuroi protect sailors and appear as white birds stilling the waters; just so, in the baptism story the Holy Spirit descends as a dove. In this context, the water is a symbolic boundary between secular and sacred, a dividing line between opposites and also a means of ritual initiation by which the boundary is crossed. All this in turn has a bearing on Jesus' combined divinity and humanity.

Yet it might be objected against both Lévi-Strauss and Leach that these various underlying codes or basic units (mythemes) are described at the expense of the stories. Clearly, detecting structural patterns is important to interpretation because the uncovering of deepseated contradictions and conflicts helps us to recognise hidden ways in which consciousness is shaped. But detecting the codes within a story entails treating it as self-referential: the story is, in the end, about itself and its own codes. However, as Cedric Watts correctly points out, Sophocles, Seneca and Cocteau give us significantly different versions of the Oedipus myth. 'We can again reverse Lévi-Strauss and say that since some versions of the myth are replete with significance while others are not, the scholar should not pursue the unattainable goal of analysing every variant but should concentrate on the best versions.'[48] These 'best versions', as we see, will call upon our response to mimetic force, and how it impinges on and energises our sense of the world in a manner unaccounted for by a structural analysis alone. Thus we may be said to 'test' the work against our experience, which again in turn is open to debate and modification.

These observations apply also as a corrective to Edmund Leach's argument about Jesus' baptism. James and John are different characters from Castor and Pollux, as Zeus is different from the God of Abraham, Isaac, and Jacob, the 'Father' to whom Jesus owes his allegiance. Besides, the whole orientation to experience in the gospel, energised by Jesus the eschatological prophet, is distinctly different from the cyclical polytheism of Greek and Roman mythology. This difference directly influences decisions people have made and continue to make about how they must act in order to be saved. The 'Dioscuroi code' obscures this distinction, even while revealing structural parallels between various myths concerned with human beings as paradoxically divine and mortal. We might just as readily find the 'Dioscuroi code' in the rhyme about those other famous twins:

> Tweedle-dum and Tweedle-dee
> Resolved to have a battle,
> For Tweedle-dum, said Tweedle-dee,
> Has spoiled my nice new rattle.

The twins in contention over the rattling thunder-god are present here too, but the rhyme does not mean the same thing as the Gospel of Mark, or Plutarch.

In this section I have been dealing with repetition mainly in the context of value, and how we might test our claims about the merits of a work of literature. I have introduced the notion of desirable and undesirable repeatability to suggest how the vision of a good inherited from the past as a model for the future is complexly bound up with the thwarting distortions of history. In the midst of this complexity which we inhabit as persons, we might reasonably expect to infer to some degree, and in an interpersonal way, an author's intent as one element of what is repeated in a work, just as we might detect structures that operate unconsciously. But structure and intent do not account for a literary work, even though they are not irrelevant. Rather, as we have seen, a work's mimetic force, its power to re-engage us in surprising ways with features of the world in which we already belong, can only be encountered and recognised. 'That,' we say of a compelling poem, 'is how things are.' The statement invites contradiction and discussion. And insofar as our prejudgements and biases cause us to be mistaken, we might come to know by clarifying something of that mistakenness how we have been entrapped all along in the kind of repetition that would in the end unmake and dissolve us. Such entrapment indeed is entailed by our condition as historical creatures, which is to say, as persons caught in the paradoxical and contradictory play of presence and absence, repetition and making new.

So far in this account of repeatability, however, I have managed to avoid the entire question of the relationship between literature and psychoanalysis. Like structuralism, psychoanalysis appeals to the determining patterns of the unconscious, and casts a sceptical eye upon intentionality and the claims of the apparent subject. Also, psychoanalysis holds itself to be therapeutic, but whether or not the results of psychotherapy can be empirically tested is debated these days with increasing vehemence. My own, general position is simply that psychoanalysis is testable in many of the same ways as literature, and indeed literature and criticism are a kind of psychoanalysis. But I would like to consider this position more carefully.

EMERGENCE: LITERATURE AS PSYCHOANALYSIS

Among other things, structuralism teaches us that deepset patterns of conviction and prejudice are inherited, giving us a sense of identity even as they blind us to all that such identity precludes. Moreover, as we have seen, these patterns can remain absent from the purview of consciousness, so that we encounter them only in the repetitions by which they are made manifest, though we do not recognise them there. The maxim that those who cannot remember the past are condemned to repeat it thus applies equally well to history and to the etiology of the neurosis as Freud understood it. Indeed, an interplay of repetition and remembering is basic to the psychoanalytic view of how repression causes us to forget certain traumas which afterwards declare themselves as pathological compulsions. Analysis then must disclose both the deep structures enabling a stable ego to emerge, and the traumatic events hindering that emergence in a particular case. Repetitions constituting a patient's symptoms are thus the product of unconscious causes, and Freud's view of the psyche is highly structuralist. He claimed also that his methods are therapeutic and that psychoanalysis is a science.

Today, Freud's scientific claims have been so widely attacked that some of his defenders contrive a kind of Pyrrhic victory by claiming that the master misunderstood his own position on this matter. For instance, Jürgen Habermas maintains that Freud laboured under a 'scientistic self-misunderstanding'[49] and we should cease trying to validate his theories by empirical means appropriate to the natural sciences. Understandably, Freud's attackers are keen to insist that his scientific claims should be taken seriously and it is not enough to claim that he misunderstood. Thus, Adolf Grunbaum points out that although Freud's early 'Project for a Scientific Psychology' was abandoned, Freud nonetheless continued to think in terms analogous to neurobiological models depicting psychic energy in terms of space, force, and so on.[50] Grunbaum concludes that Freud everywhere stressed the *scientificity* of his clinical theory, and this legacy has died hard even among Freud's revisionist followers. As Frederick Crews points out, even the liberal Erik Erikson repeatedly refers to psychoanalysis as a science and is convinced that proper forms of verification will eventually be discovered.[51] This optimism is repeated by Seymour Fisher and Roger P. Greenberg, and even the heretical Jacques Lacan looks forward to a 'grounding that must assure our discipline its place among the sciences'.[52] Grunbaum himself, though attacking Freud most powerfully on the grounds that claims made for psychoanalysis largely fail to meet modern standards of inductivism, stops short of denying that all Freud's positions should be dismissed.[53] Even Grunbaum thus leaves the way open for future verifications, and to this degree does not entirely part company with the hopefuls who see psychoanalysis as a science in the making. Crews (an admirer of Grunbaum), however, asserts more vehemently that the 'Freudian research tradition has failed to yield a single authenticated discovery',[54] and considering the hundred years it has had to prove itself, Crews finds this record disheartening, to say the least.

Attacks on the kinds and quality of verification offered by psychoanalysis have come to constitute a powerful negative critique.[55] It is often pointed out, for instance, that clinical interviews are highly vulnerable to contamination by suggestion, and key notions such as resistance, substitution, distortion and so on, allow that a patient's evidence can be taken at face value, or to mean the opposite, or some other displaced meaning, so that, as George Steiner points out, psychoanalysis has all the cogency of 'demonology and exorcism during the sixteenth and seventeenth centuries'.[56] In other words, there is no end to the evasions and denials a psychoanalyst can discover or fabricate. Again, Freud considered repression the cornerstone of his theory,[57] but in so doing he requires us to accept that a traumatic event occurring in infancy and driven into the unconscious is a main cause of symptoms appearing in adult life. But there is no adequate explanation of this protracted latency, nor of the means by which reliable access can be gained to the putative childhood trauma. Even though Fisher and Greenberg review such evidence from a pro-Freudian standpoint, they doubt 'whether the therapy exists as a clearly definable set of operations'.[58] However, they also maintain that there is some support for Freud's theories of male homosexuality, and the anal and oral character traits, among other points.

Recently, Richard Miller has formulated a position claiming that in practice most analysts 'are inclined toward a dogmatic denial that their field has foundations': in other words, psychoanalysis does not provide deductive premises for explanation in the manner of the 'hard' sciences, as Habermas says. Yet Miller is also among those who argue that psychoanalysis might turn out to be a field with foundations, and he thinks that some researchers should continue to investigate this possibility. Meanwhile, he describes a set of 'core' positions through which psychoanalysis offers a 'description of a repertoire of mechanisms'[59] giving 'approximately true descriptions of causes, that are justified in light of the data'.[60] He argues that judging Freud in terms of dogmatic statements made at different points in his career distorts the best (and truest) that Freud has to offer. Specifically against Grunbaum, Miller claims that some psychoanalytically-oriented therapies are well-founded.

In a recent book, Anthony Storr[61] agrees broadly with Miller's position on the therapeutic value of various short-term treatments, but he argues for a more thoroughgoing hermeneutic position than Miller's. Storr claims that psychoanalysis is 'a hermeneutic system', a way of looking at human nature' (10), and 'is not and could never have been, a science in the sense in which physics or chemistry are sciences' (9). He goes on to conclude that even if every specific idea of Freud's were found wrong, we are still in Freud's debt because he transformed the way we listen to and treat the mentally disturbed and criminal, and even one another's emotional needs (127). In short, the varieties of psychotherapy developed under Freud's influence provide singular and distinctive means for distressed and alienated people to deal with emotional problems through the mediation of a skilled, sympathetic listener (114ff). The therapeutic situation and the quality, subtlety and discernment of the analyst are therefore frequently more significant than the dogmatic propositions by which the analyst's position might be described. In the case of the Wolf Man (the only case of Freud's with a long-term follow-up) Sergei Pankejeff was never convinced about the etiology of his neurosis offered by Freud, but nonetheless declared Freud a genius who immensely influenced his life (106).

Storr's hermeneutic emphasis, stressing the advantages of relatively short-term therapy and focusing on object relations (that is, attributing problems to a variety of interpersonal relationships rather than to traumatic and unconscious repressions in early childhood), overlaps extensively with the interpretations of psychoanalysis offered by Jürgen Habermas and Paul Ricœur. Both of these philosophers agree about Freud's 'scientistic self-misunderstanding', and both advocate a hermeneutic approach privileging the patient's self-reflection and insight as criteria for judging the therapy.

For Ricœur,[62] a psychoanalytic relationship is essentially verbal and is concerned with meanings that can be 'deciphered, translated, and interpreted' (248). The aim is to restore to language a capability of speaking the subject's desires, thus overcoming the traumatic blocks that have replaced a free expression of emotion with compulsions to repeat. Remembering, says Ricœur, must replace repetition (253), and in bringing about this result, memory constructs a narrative, recovering for the patient a story recognised as coherent and adequate to the facts of the case and to what we know of ordinary life. Psychoanalysis thus has an investigative side and a therapeutic side: that is, a set of relations having to do with meaning, and a set having to do with force (255). The investigative side has a strong affinity with textual interpretation (the psyche is a complex text to be deciphered); the therapeutic side is concerned with working through the analysis towards self-understanding.[63]

Clearly, Ricœur's 'investigative' emphasis is a suggestive means of rapprochement between psychoanalytic concerns and literature, but it is worth noticing at this point the kinds of attack mounted by the empiricist camp on the hermeneutic model in general. For instance, Grunbaum[64] denies (among other things) that the patient enjoys a privileged cognitive position, and points out that Freud emphasises the opposite. 'Frequently there is an epistemic asymmetry between doctor and analysand' (26), says Grunbaum, because the doctor's inferences need not be less warrantable than the patient's memories. Moreover, we often have only inferential access to our own deepseated motivations and feelings (31). Against Ricœur, Grunbaum points out how a 'narrative criterion' that aspires to be true is at odds with the claim that psychoanalytic 'facts' are not observable in the same way as scientific facts. Psychoanalytic explanations are causal, and therefore are not satisfied by the criterion of a 'coherent story' alone, but by causal imputations that can be validated (54).

With these various opinions in mind, and to establish a position for the purposes of the present argument, I would like to return briefly to the hermeneutically inclined analyst, Anthony Storr and the empiricist literary critic, Frederick Crews. At one point, Storr describes the Oedipus complex as a kind of extended metaphor. He points out that we can notice generally in our society how small boys are vulnerable to taunts about their size and weakness, and are likely to experience rivalry with their fathers. By contrast, girls often consider themselves inferior and despised in a world where men hold power, and thus feel that their ability to produce babies is an equaliser. This 'metaphoric extension',[65] Storr says, gets us closer to 'what Freud was getting at' in proposing that boys want to kill their fathers and marry their mothers, whereas girls feel their inferiority (which they blame on their mothers' lack of a penis) and then desire to be impregnated by their fathers.

For Crews, however, this kind of 'metaphoric extension' is an evasion. No one, he says, challenges 'the watered-down, conversational apprehension' of Freudian terms; the point is that these terms have a 'technical meaning' within psychoanalysis, and must be judged and tested accordingly. Repression is, once more, a key example. For Freud, it is an 'unconsciously compelled and traumatic forgetting' that occurs in early childhood and can cause disturbances in adult life.[66] However, an alternative and fairly widespread use of the term takes it to mean that a consistent denial or refusal to face certain emotional or physical needs can cause a great deal of suffering and anguish. Deeply ingrained habits of defense against our emotional lives will cause us to fall ill, or to express the problem somehow indirectly and symbolically by unusual behaviour. This second kind of explanation is closer to everyday experience, but Crews would regard it as a soft interpretation of a term that has a much more precise sense in Freud. So it is also with the Oedipus complex, which, in Crews' view, describes, precisely, a traumatic and repressed early experience. Turning the theory into an extended metaphor diminishes its specifically Freudian element, and by such means psychoanalysis as a whole can easily be reduced to a quasi-literary or quasi-religious exploration of the self that masquerades nonetheless as scientific.

Still, we might argue that stressing the interpretive or hermeneutic side of psychoanalysis need not divorce the theory entirely from empirical considerations. As we have seen, the validations we seek for the kinds of experience offered by literary texts also rest on an appeal to the varieties of ordinary experience, including our capacity for recognition, and so on. Literature and criticism enable us to know ourselves and our world anew, more adequately, and ever to discover fresh or unacknowledged dimensions of our emotional lives as well as to grasp something of our place in the culture we inhabit. Such a process involves the investigation of complex structures, modes of adaptation and habits of perceiving that overlap considerably with the processes of psychoanalysis, as Ricœur says. And here Miller's description of a psychoanalytic 'core' carefully feels out a position accepting *tout court* neither the hermeneutic argument nor Grunbaum's. For Miller, this 'core' consists of a rough consensus based on working practice, and permitting a few generic hypotheses, which he lists as follows: (1) if defenses against one's inner life are entrenched, great suffering can result; (2) distinctive processes of threat and inner defense are the origins of certain typical problems; (3) dreams, transference phenomena and association provide useful data; (4) acute symptom relief precedes the hard work of analysis.[67]

Storr would likely agree that therapies conducted from within some such a 'core' are frequently helpful to patients,[68] and even Crews would allow something of the kind. But Crews would then likely point also to the 'watered down' content of this purported 'core': much of it comes close to general knowledge, and certainly much of it overlaps with the kinds of truth literature and philosophy perennially reveal. In short, Miller's 'core' allows a degree of well-foundedness to certain therapeutic procedures, and also has a place for Ricœur's emphasis on the 'investigative' element of psychoanalysis, and for Storr's treatment of its doctrines as extended metaphors. As Ricœur says, deciphering the psyche has much in common with interpreting a text, and the main psychoanalytic concepts are also understood as ways of classifying and making available for discussion certain common emotional states and difficulties. The fact that many different kinds of therapy seem to be equally effective, which is to say, more effective than no therapy at all, suggests that the therapist's discernment, care and understanding of the relationship between individual persons and their culture can be salutary. The kinds of symptom relief brought about, say, by brainwashing or consultations with gazers into crystal balls will not serve equally well because, by comparison with alternative means of explaining and producing a satisfying acculturisation, these others perform poorly. Which is to say, the 'core' of psychoanalysis helps to explain the therapeutic effectiveness in an approximate way, and is confirmed by the kinds of investigation of emergent knowledge and the vicissitudes of the apparent self explored also by literature. Certainly, psychoanalysis should go on seeking to justify its therapeutic practices as Miller advises, but as a hermeneutic enquiry, it overlaps extensively with the kinds of discernment and critical assessment through which, as we have seen, literature and criticism also promote the development of a sense of personal identity and of a humane culture. The deeply linguistic orientation of psychoanalysis is the main site of this overlap.

At this point, I would like to turn briefly to the heretical Freudian, Jacques Lacan, whose thinking goes furthest in developing Freud both in the direction of the linguistic theory informing much recent literary criticism.[69] Controversial and difficult though he is, Lacan provides some useful guidelines for understanding Freud in terms of the processes of an emergent, personal knowledge produced also by literature.

For Lacan,[70] one consequence of human prematuration at birth is that infants are physically uncoordinated and helpless, but spend a lot of time gazing and hearing. In this condition, they experience the body as fragmented, but through seeing other people they also imagine the body as a totality. Every human subject thus becomes aware of a unified, external form of a body even while experiencing internal fragmentation and chaos. This is Lacan's celebrated theory of the mirror stage that occurs at approximately six months of age, when an infant apprehends others as it would an image of itself in a mirror: that is, as a satisfying unity to which it aspires. Mirror images of the integrated self are subsequently developed in various ways through encounters with other persons and things, but the mother is especially significant because a child's earliest feelings of fusion and unity are centered on her.

Although the period of separation from the mother is traumatic, Lacan reminds us that this separation must occur for a child to recognise its cultural dependency and become socially adjusted. This process is what is meant by castration (separation in its various forms) and by the Father (mediator of the Law, the cultural order), who bears the phallus (symbolic agent of separation). Thus, each human infant develops from an early stage of bodily fragmentation, through the *imaginary* identifications and misrecognitions of the mirror stage, and into separation and the *symbolic* order of culture, marked by absence and difference. Emergence from the 'imaginary' to the 'symbolic' occurs especially with the acquisition of language, the key agent of human acculturisation, for the child acquires language at the same time as it experiences separation from the mother and from the 'full' imaginary union that she represents. Metaphoric identifications of the mirror stage are then replaced by a metonymic process whereby words mark the difference or gap between desire and its object. Basically, words signify a lack, or difference, and it is easy to see how Lacan draws here on Saussure's ideas about the differential structure of language.

Lacan also draws a distinction between what he calls the 'objet petit a' (*autre* with a small a) representing our myriad identifications with things in the effort to unify ourselves and ground desire, and the Other (*Autre* with a capital A) which eludes description because language cannot grasp it any more than language can grasp the subject which is, as we see, defined by difference and separation. This unconscious Other is neither subjective nor objective, but leaves its trace in our experience by means of the gaps and strange dissonances through which the unconscious breaks into discourse, and which Lacan designates the 'real'. The ego then is basically the way a subject presents itself to itself within the threefold imbroglio of imaginary, symbolic and real, and Lacan distinguishes between our conscious construct of ourselves (the *moi*) and the *je* that actually speaks but remains occluded and anterior to *moi*. One task of psychoanalysis is to bring *je* to recognise what a fictional construct *moi* is, and thereby to 'achieve a dealienation of the subject'.[71]

The structure of language, in all this, is also the structure of the unconscious because we are acculturised by insertion into a language that always means more than we know, and precludes us from saying all that we want. Lacan's own notoriously oblique and enigmatic style foregrounds the difficulty of expressing in language his celebrated claim that the unconscious is structured like a language. Consequently, as with Heidegger, Lacan combines philosophical self-reflexiveness and metaphoric verve to produce a sense of emergent consciousness shot through with ambiguity, ambivalence, and fugitive illumination.

At this point, we return to the general relationship between psychoanalysis and hermeneutics, for Lacan's originality in interpreting Freud through modern linguistics leads him also to Ricœur's position that deciphering a text is like deciphering the psyche ('Commenting on a text is like doing an analysis').[72] Moreover, Lacan tells us that an ideal Faculty of psychoanalysis would teach (among other things) 'that supreme pinnacle of the aesthetics of language, poetics', on the grounds that the search for inferences requires 'a profound assimilation' of a language, and especially the kind 'concretely realised in its poetic texts'.[73] That is, one must be able to respond to fine shifts and valences expressed through metaphor and symbol, tone and diction, and to how the subject always says more than is consciously intended, as does a poem. Thus, in one description of the mirror stage Lacan reminds us (rather in the manner of Storr) that he is 'developing a metaphor', and that his schematising coarsens and simplifies a more encompassing, more accurate discourse which, like poetry, 'discloses being'.[74]

For Lacan, then, analysis finds people already taken up and immersed in a language through which they can be brought to recognise an authentic subjectivity, which is also their history.[75] All this smacks of Heidegger, in whom indeed Lacan is entirely steeped. As Anthony Wilden says, 'in making his often implicit rapprochement between Freud and Heidegger, Lacan perhaps leaves too much unsaid, so much of his work is imbued with a Heideggerean viewpoint'.[76] For instance, as Wilden goes on to point out, there is a strong affinity between Heidegger's view of the 'they self' (everyone is the other, and no one is himself') and Lacan's view of the alienated subject misrecognising itself in the other.[77] But as Mark Taylor also claims, Lacan explores Heidegger through Freud's *fort/da* in order to correct Heidegger by emphasising the absence (*fort*) upon which *da* depends. Lacan says 'There can be no *fort* without *da*, one might say, without *Dasein*. But, contrary to the whole tendency of the phenomenology of *Daseinanalyse*, there is no *Dasein* with the *fort*.'[78] For Lacan, fragmentation and cleavage thus subtend the partial unities we experience and desire, so that presence is always also the presence of an absence.

Nonetheless, Lacan often cites Heidegger directly,[79] and frequently seems to be citing him without noticing. For instance, when he says in a seminar, 'I am showing you the paths for the realisation of being, not the realisation of being, but only its paths',[80] or when he talks of providing a 'glimpse' into a 'dimension of being',[81] or of the psychoanalyst as a mediator between the 'man of care and the subject of absolute knowledge', where 'care' is *souci*, the usual French translation of the Heideggerean *Sorge*, we feel the very idiom of *Being and Time*.[82] This is the case also when Lacan defines his project as a reaction to the *cogito*,[83] complaining against the objectification of humans in the modern world[84] and insisting that the subject is spoken rather than speaking.[85] Likewise, Lacan's insistence on recognition as the key to authenticating an analysis is consistent with Heidegger's thoughts on the disclosure of Being

A crucial moment occurs, Lacan tells us, with the 'sticking of language', or at the 'clicking-point' where a subject has 'the feeling of truth'.[86] Admittedly, such recognitions are also misrecognitions, falling short of a full presence of the subject to itself. But as we have seen in an earlier chapter, the experience of the Flaw – Lacan's *coupure, béance, manque à être* – is deeply ingrained also in Heidegger, and not surprisingly Lacan praises St. Augustine enthusiastically for having known much that modern linguists think themselves to be discovering. Like Augustine, Lacan holds himself to be centrally concerned with illumination, recognition, and the experience of the Fall, all of which are fundamental to human language and culture.[87]

Lacan thus enfolds us again in the hermeneutic position, assuring us that psychoanalysis is like reading a text, and that his schemes and attempts to systematise are ways of investigating the subtle and complex processes of consciousness emergent through language. As T. S. Eliot says, there is indeed a sense in which words can disclose 'a network of tentacular roots reaching down to the deepest terrors and desires'.[88] Poetry reveals something of this, as psychoanalysis also claims to do, especially on the 'investigative' side, as Ricœur says, so that poetry and criticism might even become one touchstone against which the 'myth' or 'allegory' of psychoanalysis can in part be measured. To assess further how this is so, I would like to consider T. S. Eliot's *Four Quartets*, a set of poems very much concerned with the struggles and gratifications of emergent knowledge within a troubled cultural phase especially preoccupied with fragmentation, absence, and the loss of self.

Eliot offers a compelling exploration of the psyche's complex structures and elusive energies. He writes about memory and repetition, difference and sameness, dreaming and reality, about how a fragmented self seeks its own image in the world's fugitive radiances, haunted and informed beyond its own knowing by the unconscious that is also language speaking through us. Thus, insofar as we might find *Four Quartets* a compelling statement about how by such means we come to know one another and the world, we might find ourselves willing also to accord Lacan a comparable kind and quality of discernment on a comparable set of issues. Yet, one immediately imagines various contending positions (*Four Quartets* is Eliot's weakest poem, and Lacan is more convincing; *Four Quartets* is Eliot's best poem, and really shows up Lacan's needless obscurities; neither Lacan nor Eliot has much to say that is worthwhile; Eliot and Lacan are too different to compare). But here literary critics are on familiar ground, as various opinions reflect different receptivities. As we have seen, this does not mean that in literary criticism anything goes. Criteria of adequacy are implicit in the practice of criticism as a whole, and through the study of literature we hope to produce (among other things) careful reasoners whose critical judgements have a bearing on decisions they make in the world, and on their self-understanding. And so I would like to propose a reading of *Four Quartets* stressing how Eliot's subject is the process of emergent knowledge, and my claim then is that by some such means we can come better to grasp the 'investigative' aims of psychoanalysis, as well as the extensive overlap between its 'core' concerns and that domain of personal and cultural concern which is literature. Thus I do not propose to read Eliot from a psychoanalytic viewpoint, but rather to assess the claims of psychoanalysis from a literary viewpoint, with a view to suggesting some common processes of their validation.

Throughout his life, Eliot's thinking and sensibility continued to be moulded by F. H. Bradley.[89] The main idea in Bradley's *Appearance and Reality* is that we live in a world of appearances, and knowledge is relative. Human consciousness divides and classifies, and we come to know an ordered world through our particular 'finite centre' (199–200). But there is also a 'general condition before distinctions and relations have been developed, and where as yet neither any subject nor object exists' (406). This non-relational, original condition of immediate experience is perpetually displaced as we go on locating ourselves in space and time, coming to know a variety of objects and other people. Thus emerges our individual point of view and with it the world of appearances which is private and relative. What we call true and real in ordinary experience is, in the end, a convention agreed upon by those whose points of view happen to coincide. The original and enduring wholeness without subject and object, division and fragmentation, Bradley calls the Absolute, which we posit even though our limited and partial meanings do not encompass it.

Bradley's idealism is distinct from Heidegger's ontological phenomenology and Lacan's discourse of the Other, but the three share a similar post-Hegelian concern for the subject's contingency Certainly, for Eliot the experience of a fragmented self and of how individual experience is tenuous and haunted by illusion, was a lifelong preoccupation. We can trace it in his enthusiasm for such as Charles Maurras, Irving Babbitt and T. E. Hulme: everywhere, that is, Eliot sought consolation from thinkers for whom structure and discipline represented a bulwark against the chaos always ready to swallow or dissolve the perilously unstable centre of the apparent self. And yet Eliot was quite aware that new knowledge, especially the kind afforded by poetry, is a quest for disclosure that courts the very invading chaos against which traditional order and custom protect us. This quest, with its attendant dissolutions, recognitions, and sense of tentative emergence, is especially thematised in *Four Quartets*,[90] and suggests how we should approach the poem's structure.

Critics have found various kinds of internal order in *Four Quartets*, but with a degree of arbitrariness, rather as one might find patterns in a carpet. For instance, each *Quartet* might centre on one of the elements: 'Burnt Norton' is centered on air; 'East Coker' on earth; 'The Dry Salvages' on water; 'Little Gidding' on fire.[91] Or it might be possible to read the whole sequence as a meditation on time,[92] and perhaps we can detect, with Hugh Kenner, a dominant principle whereby two terms are opposed, then falsely reconciled, and finally reconciled truly in a way that opens up into a metaphysical conception.[93] For instance, in 'Burnt Norton' Kenner finds a basic opposition between light and dark falsely reconciled in the flickering light of the third movement, and then truly reconciled in a spiritual dark night. Donald Davie takes Kenner a step further by suggesting that 'The Dry Salvages' (which he thinks otherwise unaccountably weak) strikes a false note on purpose, and is the example of false reconciliation in the larger structure.[94] And perhaps, with Denis Donoghue, we can detect a 'camouflage of different voices',[95] even though other critics like to feel that *Four Quartets* is the most personal and directly confessional of Eliot's poems.

Certainly, as Donaghue says, we can distinguish between the speculative thinker of 'Burnt Norton I' ('Time present and time past / Are both perhaps present in time future'); the quizzical literary man of 'East Coker V' ('That was a way of putting it – not very satisfactory'); the casual interlocutor of 'The Dry Salvages I' ('I do not know much about gods; but I think that the river / Is a strong brown god'); the cryptic lyricist of 'Little Gidding II' ('Dust in the air suspended / Marks the place where a story ended'); the banal purveyor of nostrums of 'East Coker II' ('There is, it seems to us, / At best, only a limited value / In the knowledge derived from experience'). And because we can hear such different registers, we might be tempted to hear different speakers. But we could just as readily hear one voice in a variety of modes, for none is quite distinct enough to crystallise into a separate persona. Once again we are given intimations of an ordering principle that in the end proves too tenuous to control the discourse firmly. That is, no single scheme explains everything, but each of those mentioned has some value and gives us a place to begin, a way of looking at the text that carries a degree of explanatory force.

My own proposal for the five movements of each quartet is based on what I take to be the entire poem's most striking achievement, namely the convincing subtlety with which it presents the emergence of new knowledge. Movement I then deals with revelation (some new thing) disturbing the order of time, and leaving us with a moment of fusion. Movement II consists of two sub-sections: the first is a lyrical presentation of the cryptic nature of emergent knowledge, and the second analyses the difficulty of describing such a thing. Movement III deals with darkness impeding further knowledge and compares this darkness to a wise ignorance that is a precondition of learning. Movement IV is a lyric about uncertainty and waiting. Movement V recapitulates, and in so doing draws our attention to how the poem exemplifies the kind of emergence it describes.

According to this scheme, the relativity of order and tenuousness of the self are central to Eliot's concern and his poem invites but also frustrates our pattern-finding. This helps to explain the poem's unusual but distinctive combination of tentativeness and directness, plainness and elusiveness, public declaration and private reminiscence, rhythmic certainty and shifting tone.

The same principle applies to Eliot's imagery, which presents the complex enfoldings of identification, misrecognition and desire that characterise the processes of understanding. Among other things, the poem repeatedly describes gardens, roses, the underworld (a kind of dark descent), clouds (or other kinds of shadow), mechanisms of several kinds, circles, music, and various types of light. The same image might be pleasantly surprising or convey an upsetting strangeness; it might bring clarity and a sense of belonging, but also evoke a deadening entrapment and alienation. We might become aware also of how an image develops the theme of the movement where it occurs, and then recall its relationship to a matching movement in another *Quartet* so that the puzzling interpenetrations of memory are evoked, at once asymmetrical with the present yet continuous with it. Or the rhythm and tone might modify the sense of an image, inviting us to assimilate it to matching voices elsewhere in the poem. At last, we are left meditating a potentially endless process of interpretation and discovery, of re-gathering and emergence, of the self remaking itself in the image of a multivalent past which is also its present, in the prospect of an imagined, proleptic unity. The familiar strangeness of all this is the ground also, Eliot would have us learn, of religious wonder: 'The hint half guessed, the gift half understood, is Incarnation.'

Let us consider an example or two in more detail, beginning with the opening of 'Burnt Norton I', where we are led by the bird into a garden filled with invisible presences. These are partly memories (the presence of the past) combined with speculation about what might have been (the past as absence). The intimation of lost happiness (the sense of a radical flaw) blends here with hope of recovery (the intimation of possibility) so that in this special moment, past and future enlarge the present with a poignant but bittersweet sense of promise. And though it is illusory, the moment is not just subjective, for it is occasioned by an actual drained-out concrete pool seeming to be filled with water, which is in fact sunlight. Seeing and interpretation mingle here to produce a startling synthesis evoking both a mood and a cluster of meanings associated with the lost garden of mythology. Then a cloud passes:

> Go, said the bird, for the leaves are full of children,
> Hidden excitedly, containing laughter.
> Go, go, go, said the bird: human kind
> Cannot bear very much reality.

The bird speaks imperatively, 'Go', and the repetition helps to remind us that of course birds do not talk, but that its song resembles human words of our own making, for thus we find ourselves through nature's otherness. The delicate excitement in the intervening lines, 'for the leaves are full of children, / Hidden excitedly, containing laughter', suggests a game of hide and seek, and also a sense of lost innocence, uncertainly poised, like the birdsong, between illusion and reality. The sombre tone and rhythm of the conclusion, 'human kind / Cannot bear very much reality', bring us back to the ordinary, which enabled and yet was transformed by the disorienting, visionary moment. All this belongs with the general theme of the first movement, stressing the paradoxical fusions of past and present, loss and hope, recognition and misrecognition constituting our knowledge of the world.

Gardens occur throughout *Four Quartets*, and so does hidden laughter. For instance, in 'East Coker III' we hear of

> The wild thyme unseen and the wild strawberry,
> The laughter in the garden, echoed ecstasy
> Not lost, but requiring, pointing to the agony
> Of death and birth.

These lines recall 'Burnt Norton I', and again deal with the fugitive and half-hidden, the mixed sense of recognition and pain, knowledge offered and withdrawn. The garden now has a touch of wildness, and 'ecstasy' stands in contrast to the promise of suffering with which it is also bound up. As I have said, the third movements compare two kinds of darkness: one – the alienating kind – preventing knowledge, and the other preparing us for it by reminding us of how reality is more than we know – always Other. The negative ignorance of the first part of movement III has been vacant and oppressive, but is now compared to a darkness of waiting, which will be alleviated by the garden ecstasy described in these lines. The 'agony / Of death and birth' therefore indicates the pain of going down into a fructifying darkness, which will be a kind of birth of new insight, a return to lost innocence. The touch of wild freedom suggested by these lines is a measure of the anxiety that journeying into darkness always produces. The imagery thus is adapted to the movement in which it belongs, even as it evokes and develops the gentler, speculative mood of 'Burnt Norton I', inviting us to understand both the contraries and their enfoldment in one another.

The garden occurs again in 'Little Gidding V', as the poem comes full circle, and we learn of 'children in the apple tree', who are 'Not known, because not looked for / But heard, half-heard, in the stillness'. Eliot is aware here of looking back to the beginning ('And the end of our exploring / Will be to arrive where we started') but the secret life of things continues to be 'Not known' because we keep on encountering it from within our partial assimilations of experience, our fragile self-consciousness. Still, we are unsettled by the very knowledge that we do not know, and then by things half-heard promising a fuller, richer understanding. In a way, the poem throughout has tried to give us a sense of this mysterious beckoning and, in the fifth movements, Eliot draws our attention specifically to how the poetry itself merges with the subject it describes. Consequently, this fifth movement opens with an extended meditation on the exact use of words ('And every phrase / And sentence that is right'). Eliot's design here (the fifth movements we recall thematise the poem) might even awaken us in retrospect to a wordplay in 'Burnt Norton I': 'for the leaves were full of children'. The word 'leaves' might suggest not only the garden, but also the leaves of a book – this book – also full of fugitive echoes. In such a manner, past experience might gather new meaning as the manifold of our knowing remains open to transformation in the future. For 'We are born with the dead: / See, they return, and bring us with them' Thus 'history is a pattern / Of timeless moments' where the present is also the past as well as knowledge of our future death, the final otherness that (as Lacan says) has the last word.

The cluster of images on the underworld reveals the same fusions of enfoldment and emergence. Conventionally, underworld journeys are rites of passage. In epic literature, they occur in a perilous place between life and death, where the hero meets his ancestors and learns his future. In the underworld, past, present and future thus meet in a moment of revelation. For Eliot, this theme is closely connected to the mystical dark night, where a devastating experience of absence precedes revelation, and indeed seems to be its prior condition or even its very substance, unrecognised. In both cases, darkness and deprivation represent one precondition of conscious knowledge. Thus, in 'Burnt Norton III' we are told: 'Descend lower, descend only / Into the world of perpetual solitude / World not world, but that which is not world'. This descent is necessary for recovering the lost garden and thereby knowing again the hidden centres of desire, but it is disorienting and painful, as the poem goes on to say. Something of this confusion is caught here by the repetitions of 'world' causing us to puzzle out the sense. There is a clear echo of John's gospel, reminding us that Jesus, the Logos, is not of this world. Thus, Eliot's line suggests that the descent leads us to unworldliness (we too, like Jesus, are to be in this world but not of it), and that such a condition is real, even though 'not-world'. The deliberately smudged meaning and play of sound confusing the sense of these simple monosyllables itself suggests departure from the familiar which 'descent' entails. This also is the 'way of ignorance' of 'East Coker III'; the 'way of dispossession' where 'what you do not know is the only thing you know'. Again, Eliot's subject is the process of discovery through an interplay of absence and presence, conscious intent and unconscious recovery of that which being lost to consciousness makes consciousness what it is.

There are many allusions to the underworld in *Four Quartets*, and the motif is developed through references to clouds, or to other things that obscure the light, such as shadows, fog, ash, and dust. Eliot repeatedly suggests how half-light is comforting because it prevents us from being overwhelmed by the full glare of reality; thus, even understanding that our knowledge is foggy is an illumination. Indeed, the more in the dark we find ourselves to be, the closer we are to light. This paradox is central also to the Christian mystics to whom Eliot alludes in *Four Quartets*, and who have in common a preoccupation with how revelation pierces the cloud of unknowing.

However, another kind of movement in human affairs also symbolises a fullness in counterpoint to the journey of descent. This movement is circular, but of such a kind that we remain aware of a still point at the centre. Circumference and centre define each other, and thus also represent a pattern of knowing. Here motion without a centre is meaningless, but the attempt to be centered with no context, no sphere of operation, as it were, is an empty dream. Thus Eliot asks us to think about the 'still point of the turning world' and the light issuing from there, or the 'evening circle in the winter gaslight', the 'circulation of the lymph', the 'bedded axle tree', and the movement of the poem itself, arriving where it started. This return to the beginning entails a new kind of consciousness because when the circle is complete we 'know the place for the first time'. But such emergent consciousness does not cancel what we know, for it enables us to see a familiar world in a new way. In so doing it entails also an engagement with the mystery that religion addresses, for religion is rooted in our intimations of an infinite surprisingness that makes all things new. This then is Eliot's theme: it helps to explain the structure of *Four Quartets* and the processes by which the articulate points beyond itself to a reality that is always more than we know, and where the conscious, controlling ego is subtended by a deeply fissured and ambivalent subjectivity that we might come partly to recognise but not encompass.

Insofar as Lacan's concern is the labour of emergent consciousness which is also a labour of language through the flaws and misrecognitions, fusions and longings, anxieties and entrapments of history and the psyche, we might come to recognise the dimensions in ourselves that he addresses by having a poem such as Eliot's partly show it to us. Thus we might discover in Lacan, as we do also in Eliot, something of the complex poise of a perilous selfhood, repeating itself despite itself, discontinuous, fluid, haunted by a lost plenitude, and, in the fusions of the fleeing present, caught up by intimations of desire. That too is the world we inhabit, and in assaying it with tact and concern, in knowing it critically and humanely, we might impart a salutary understanding both to others and ourselves. This is not to evade the burden of proof that falls upon psychoanalysis to validate its therapeutic claims and to provide evidence for the causal mechanisms it describes and which separate it from literary discourse. Rather, the present argument affirms that the investigative element in psychoanalysis overlaps extensively with the practices of literature and criticism in exploring what it means to be a person. As we have come to recognise (misrecognise) and value it, the sense we have of a modern identity is in turn a product of a culture that has given us both Freud and the *Four Quartets*, and which enables us better to know thereby the uncertain and riven labours of our emergent consciousness. Such labours are pre-eminently a work of language, and through them we might touch again in order to know in a new way the roots of certain terrors and anxieties, fugitive recognitions and longings. The process does not stay still, as our necessary misrecognitions open the gaps between word and body, present and past, and as we attempt then to re-gather from memory the lineaments of a viable possibility wherein the satisfaction of each would be satisfying to all. The culture that has produced such understandings by teaching us to listen to and interrogate the poets has offered us also that body of knowledge we label broadly as psychoanalysis. The main concern of both is how emergent knowledge entails a perilous subjectivity, the very contingency of which we might value as one inalienable hallmark of the personal.

Thus we return to the general concern of this chapter, namely the means by which we attempt to validate our personal beliefs. On the one hand, we cannot stand outside our own historicity and containment by the unconscious, but this does not mean that we should surrender the appeal to evidence and the pursuit of objectivity. Persons are interlocutors who act in accord with values and standards which are debatable, and which have a bearing on a common world. Also, they are prepossessed by the unconscious body and by the unconscious or latent meanings inhabiting language itself. In such a context, persons are at once contingent and also seekers of coherence, of a narrative that can make some sense of a life and of the perplexing world in which it finds itself, and against which it is continually tested. Yet this process of testing and of making sense is never complete, but, rather, completion is sought through an emergent knowledge, bearing utopian intimations in contention with all from the past that would stultify and mechanise, reducing the process to a mere routine of 'undesirable repeatability' emptied of hope and meaning. Throughout, my fundamental contention has been that literature and criticism provide access to this process in all its resilient tentativeness and vulnerable tenacity.

4

Imagination

IMAGINATION AND THE DIVISIONS OF TIME

As we see, Lacan interprets imagination as part of the search for a unified self. Yet this sought-after unity remains outside us and we ourselves discordant, asymmetrical, rent even by the desire driving us to quench ourselves, thus, in the other. Ambiguity, oscillation and tension characterise imagination's pursuit, relieved now and then by a sense of fusion but deflected always in a nemesis of misrecognition re-iterating the incessantly exigent 'Who am I?'

Lacan's theory of the mirror itself represents metaphorically the interplay of union and separation, identity and difference that he would have us understand, so that here imagination is grasped, as always, by an act of imagination. The felt change of consciousness which occurs when a set of particulars brightens into a new pattern or formal radiance *is* imagination in act, and explanations of it depend on us recognising a process so familiar that it enables us to grasp the explanation itself. And yet, language can be used more or less imaginatively, and for practical purposes we distinguish between metaphoric and literal meanings. The codes, conventions and clichés of everyday speech are usually considered inimical to imagination and must be startled into new life, disclosing fresh dimensions of experience. The pragmatist Richard Rorty and the Neo-Romantic Owen Barfield[1] agree that what we call literal is a dead metaphor, and that new linguistic tools – live metaphors – are forged on the basis of old, sedimented meanings. Imagination in this view (I will have more to say about it by and by) is therefore especially active in producing metaphors, but is implicit in all language because the literal is a metaphor that has become commonplace.

The strong associations between this general line of thinking and Romanticism partly explain why nowadays imagination is a topic frequently eschewed, for it appears too readily linked with such other Romantic notions as personal freedom, individual self-consciousness, and creative subjectivity. For the Romantics, in short, imagination helps to forge and express a unified personality, and this runs counter to assurances from structuralists and post-structuralists alike that subjectivity is contingent and consciousness is not free but produced by social conditions. Lacan asks, 'Is the *one* anterior to discontinuity?' and immediately provides an answer: 'I do not think so, and everything that I have taught in recent years has tended to exclude this need for a closed *one.*'[2] That is, our notions of personal identity always rest on misrecognition, and do not indicate a single, synthesising centre. Yet, Lacan's barred subject, like Derrida's subject *sous rature*, does not dispense with subjectivity altogether, for then neither writer could even begin to offer evidence or argument for the position he seeks to describe. On exactly this point, J. Hillis Miller distinguishes himself from Harold Bloom who, according to Miller, believes in an intrinsic self; for Miller, what we call the self is 'a kind of locus where language takes place',[3] and the play within language is of first importance. Miller's use of 'locus' here suggests that the self is a kind of grid or receiving station, even though he goes on to recommend that persons make ethical choices, which he maintains they are free to do. In short, personal subjectivity is not obliterated even when taken to be primarily a constructed and contingent thing, rather than a self-identical whole.

Marx's emphasis on the priority of social structures to consciousness[4] can epitomise the widespread, modern critique of Romantic creative individualism, and Marx's position finds confirmation among a variety of structuralists who also are keen to assimilate individuality to the codes that produce it. The combined force of Marx and Lévi-Strauss is clear for instance in Louis Althusser, who is sometimes described as a structuralist Marxist.[5] Althusser again argues for the priority of social determinants to individual consciousness and confirms his position by appealing to Lacan: just as the mirror gives us a misleading image of ourselves as unified, so society gives us an illusory sense of personal autonomy. It is to the advantage of the ruling class that we see ourselves as free and self-determining, and this illusion Althusser describes as Ideology.

However, we should be careful not to confine an emphasis on the decentered subject to recent theorists such as Lacan, Althusser and Miller. The search for a unified self through the interminable chains of signification and weavings of desire is as familiar in Augustine and Bonaventure as in Lacan and Derrida, as Lacan himself notices.[6] 'Our heart is restless, until it reposes in Thee', says Augustine, for whom the world is full of signs that never satisfy but promise the One Source who is not wholly present to us making our pilgrimage through 'changeableness of times'.[7] For Augustine, the imagination is equivalent to what he calls 'visio spiritualis' or 'spiritual vision' standing between the 'intellectual vision' of angels or pure spirits and the 'corporeal vision' of animals.[8] Spiritual vision proceeds by the agency of signs that give rise also to our experience of time, through which we might imperfectly glimpse a design of providence. Here again imagination is both enticement and delusion, recognition and misidentification. It is a synthesis confirming our lack of transparency to ourselves, and yet is laden with meaning, a certain luminous inchoation that promises yet fuller recognitions and deeper understandings, as a result of which, in the fullness of time, we will be made whole.

A major difference between the medieval theologian and the modern post-structuralist lies, however, in the fact that for the theologian *Logos* is an antecedent unity from which we derive being and with which we can hope to be re-united. For Lacan and Althusser such hope is empty because God is yet another desired object in which we misrecognise ourselves and by which we merely confirm our alienation. Still, imagination is depicted by both camps alike as ambivalent and insecure, and these characteristics are no less evident among the Romantics, who, we remind ourselves, stood in reaction against Descartes' reassuringly clear theory of the subject as a spiritual or 'thinking substance' set over and against a world of 'extended substance'. Not surprisingly, Descartes' watertight 'ego' sprang leaks almost immediately and his disciple, Malebranche, quickly deemed the self after all a perplexing, uncertain entity.[9] Hume continued the critique that proceeded from Malebranche through Locke, by assimilating the self to sense impressions which we retain in a weaker form as ideas, and which, as they in turn weaken, we call imagination.[10] Kant's reaction to Hume led then to a proposal that we construct phenomena by our own configurating activity, by means of a synthesis already at work in perception and prior to understanding. Kant names this process 'productive imagination' to distinguish it from 'reproductive imagination'[11] which occurs when we conjure up an image in our minds (for instance, think of your foot in your shoe or of a green dragon). And so Kant returns to something broadly analogous to the Augustinian 'visio spiritualis' or the Platonist 'phantasia', placing imagination ambivalently between understanding and the senses, spirit and body. Despite various internal differences, this entire tradition thus reaffirms the tentativeness and insecurities of the quest through imagination for personal wholeness. A similar sense of the perilous path towards selfhood is evident also in Coleridge, the chief philosopher of the imagination in Romantic England.

It is well known, Coleridge responded enthusiastically to Kant, though also looking over Kant's shoulder to Tetens' *Philosophische Versuche*, on which Kant himself had drawn.[12] For Coleridge, the capacity of human beings to 'superintend the works which they are themselves carrying on in their own minds'[13] is the key to imagination, but the mind arrives at self-experience only by encountering an object and becomes 'a subject by the act of constructing itself objectively to itself'.[14] Thus we 'understand' ourselves in and through objects which in turn are partly products of thinking, and Coleridge calls this synthesis 'primary imagination'. In a much-cited passage, he defines it as 'the living power and prime agent of all human perception, and as a repetition in the finite mind of the eternal act of creation in the infinite I Am'.[15] Imagination here is at once creative and finite, and in coming to know its power we participate in Reason, a kind of spiritual unconscious which could be described as nature's inner power of significance. But Reason itself has two aspects, for although it is superindividual and we participate in it as we do in Being, it is also the principle enabling logic and analytical detachment.[16] The paradox with which I began this section therefore recurs, for we are to grasp Reason by analogy with the process whereby the classified parts inhere in an organic whole, just as the whole informs the parts. Grasping this principle is itself an act of imagination, and is irreducible.

Coleridge's 'primary imagination', then, is so instinct with 'thinking' that we are usually unconscious of how it links us with and yet detaches us from nature. But when we consciously invent fictive images we deploy 'secondary imagination'. This is at one with primary imagination insofar as both draw on what we might call the creative unconscious, but is distinguished from Fancy, which is a mere juxtaposition of similarities – a superficial, aggregative pursuit that does not synthesise the parts into a containing whole. Weak poetry is thus fanciful rather than imaginative: it does not forge metaphors to make useful or compelling new meanings.

Clearly, Coleridge does not regard the self as a pre-established

essence set over against an extended material world. Rather, subjects become conscious through objects which, in turn, subjects
help to produce by active configuration, and this, as I have been
arguing, is part of what is entailed by the idea of the person.
Nonetheless, Coleridge does strongly privilege self-consciousness
and the notion that the mind can 'find itself' through imagination
and thereby come to know its innermost unity with the powers
and energies of sustaining nature. Coleridge's world and that of
the post-structuralists could not, therefore, be mistaken for long,
even though the path from Coleridge to Derrida through phenomenology is marked by continuity as well as contrast. And, as we
have seen, among phenomenologists the status of the subject and
the structure of perception receive intense scrutiny. For instance,
Maurice Merleau-Ponty points out in a broadly Kantian way that
perceiving is always perceiving something, and all perception is
imbued with a degree of general significance. But Merleau-Ponty
then goes on to suggest that because 'perception' entails active
interpretation there is no need to introduce a further occult power
into the transaction. The word 'imagination' consequently should
describe our deliberately produced fictions.[17]

Yet Coleridge is not so easily shaken off, and is already alert to
this objection when he describes how pure thought and simple
percepts are outside our normal experience.[18] Perceptions are (as
Merleau-Ponty says) thought-imbued, just as concepts, however
rarefied, are shot through by traces of the concrete and perceptual.
Coleridge points out that we repeatedly distinguish what we do not
separate, and ordinary thought could not proceed otherwise. Just
so, in analysing an act of cognition we can distinguish between
what proceeds from our thinking and configurating activity, and
what impinges upon us. Indeed, Merleau-Ponty finds himself doing
just this when he analyses perception as a single power uniting two
forces (active and passive) which is precisely what Coleridge also
does.

As we have seen, such dialectic between self and world remains
fundamental to the way in which persons become aware, through
language, of their mutual understandings and separations. In their
several ways, these various theorists of the imagination thus continue to acknowledge this basic aspect of the personal. For instance,
Merleau-Ponty retains subjectivity because (as he points out) he
would otherwise be unable to describe a human engagement with a
world that resists us and is always more than we know. At the same

time, he reconfirms a further basic element of what it means to be a person by striving to show how elementary events preceding reflection are already invested with meaning or latent evaluation, so that the philosopher's task is 'to make reflection emulate the unreflective life of consciousness' [19] in which a world is first given to us. There is no question of somehow solving the problem (or 'mystery' as he calls it) of perception, but only of describing its basic forms closely, which in turn (and yet again) entails an act of imagination as the philosopher re-evokes the process of our coming-to-know. Through his words we 'recognise' (24) and thus consciously recover the latent dimensions of our own thinking, for 'consciousness must be faced with its own unreflective life in things', and also 'awakened to its own history which it was forgetting'(31).

For Merleau-Ponty, then, subjectivity remains a central concern. He describes how concepts can modify perception, how consciousness needs to 'forget its own phenomena thus enabling "things" to be constituted' (58), and how tentative is the unfolding of ourselves, exploring the world's body which always also contains or prepossesses us. Consequently, for Merleau-Ponty speech does not somehow describe thought, but rather embodies it, making it present: 'the spoken word is a gesture, and its meaning, a world' (184). Just so, imagination is not a copy or representation, but an act of embodied consciousness, at once a probing and interrogating process, and also the capacity to make present an absence by picturing something that is not in fact before us ('an absence of the object which tries to pass as its presence').[20]

At this point, where Merleau-Ponty's theory of imagination engages the paradoxical interplay between participation and separation characteristic of the human use of language in general, he echoes Sartre directly (though elsewhere criticising him), for Sartre also says that imagination is an irreducible act of consciousness (it is impossible, he claims, to describe the contents of a mental image). According to Sartre, imagination pre-eminently makes present an absence, and this fact is of signal importance because it is central to freedom that we can hold the world at a distance, imagining a certain non-existent that enables choice. The mental image is nebulous, but by calling upon action it signals our freedom.[21]

In short, despite anti-Romantic attacks on privileged consciousness and creative individuality, it is difficult to dislodge subjectivity from human thinking. In the myriad, irreducibly complex adjustments, *gestalten*, negotiations of feeling and skills of adaptation by which persons adjust to one another and explore our world, the sense of a self as agent having a degree of identity and continuity, remains. Its shaping activity, even through the untellable complexities and powerful constraints operative upon it, remains importunate. The fact is that in meeting another we encounter a subjectivity akin to our own, and in negotiating the world we are active interpreters, makers of tools, choosers of directions. For so it is to be a person, and 'imagination' describes in its fashion this many-sided and perpetual encounter and adaptation, interrogation and synthesis. In such a context, our claims for imagination might also be quite modest, for it describes a limited and contingent power, taking into account our incompleteness and tentativeness, our uncertain engagements and perennial restlessness: 'the best in this kind are but shadows'.

We might now propose that imagination comprises three main elements. The first is a configurating and synthesising activity at work in perception, by which a thing becomes an object (that which I know and can talk about, and apprehend as full of potential significance). The second is the capacity to produce a fictional world, in some ways an alternative to the one we live in, and which then also lets us interpret our familiar world in a new way. The third is the power to make present an absence and thus to hold out alternatives enabling choice and action. In a sense, the power of negation evident in the third element is operative in the other two as well, for the self we know in the object (first element) is never fully present, and our fictional worlds (second element) are not actual worlds. All three elements are therefore taken up together in a dialectic of presence and absence, and are enfolded upon one another much as is our experience of past, present and future time. Thus, a critique of imagination will disclose how imagination engages the dynamic of our temporal embededness which is basic to our condition as historical persons. Imagination's role in perception then is analogous to the presence of the past, in the sense that it deals with the givenness of a world and of history (Heidegger's 'factuality'). Imagination as fiction belongs especially in the present, where we recognise most intensely the production of new effects and fresh metaphors, at once constrained by history and yet novel, present yet figurative (Heidegger's 'fallenness', marked by ambiguity). Imagination as negation belongs with the presence of the future because it is concerned especially with openness and possibility (Heidegger's 'existentiality'). In all three, bodily immediacy and disembodied distance are fused, and imagination, like language itself, emerges from an interplay of presence and absence, the tension of 'is and not-yet' within which the personal is constituted.

Let us now look briefly at two poems that take quite different initial approaches to the relationship between imagination and the constraints upon our subjectivity. The first is Coleridge's 'Frost at Midnight', and the second, Yeats's 'Sailing to Byzantium'.

Coleridge begins with a meditation on nature which also attempts to catch and discover imagination in the making. Thus, in the formation of frost crystals the speaker recognises his own mental activity. The crystals are formed outside the cottage where he sits, inside, before his dwindling fire. Our attention then is called to the fact that the frost also has its own inside, the 'secret ministry' shaping the crystals. This 'secret' agency is at work in nature and in the speaker's musing solitude alike, but the speaker comes to know this only through an opposition between himself and nature, inside and outside, fire and frost.

He tells us then how he is alone, 'in solitude, which suits / Abstruser musings: save at my side / My cradled infant slumbers peacefully'. The word 'save' is initially corrective, informing us that he is not really as alone as he seems. But because the baby is asleep, the correction re-confirms the solitude after all, and the imaginative reverie cuts the speaker off from those around him (the 'inmates of my cottage'), even as it enhances his sense of belonging in nature's mystery. Self-consciousness once again emerges by means of a polarity (solitude/community), which is developed further when we realise that the baby might also be the child within, an original unselfconscious merging of the human and natural dormant in all of us. As if then to confirm the liabilities of adult consciousness as an agent of division even as it works to transcend division, the meditation becomes increasingly vexed as the speaker tries to catch in words the strange, silent calmness of pre-conscious life. But in the effort to penetrate into the 'secret' he finds himself paradoxically driven further outside, to 'This populous village / Sea, and hill, and wood / With all the numberless goings-on of life.' Here again the 'extreme silentness' is caught imaginatively by an appeal to sounds evoked to confirm their absence, and the speaker's attention returns then to the inside, focusing upon the fire, where a film of soot flutters in the embers. The uneasy yet lively motion of the film seems to him to catch the fluttering of his own thinking, sustained by a more fundamental energy, itself burnt low. Just as the outside is wintry, so the speaker's 'inside' energy is depleted, but, as the poem goes on to suggest, the flame of creative imagination promises to burn again more brightly.

As we turn to the second section, the contrasts between inside and outside, fire and frost sustaining the 'dim sympathies' between the speaker and nature, extend to embrace a further polarity between present and past. It is as if meditating on the film has awakened the slumbering child within, for the bars of the grate recall by association the school window bars, and the small boy's expectation of a visiting stranger who would rescue him from the imprisonment of his formal education. Yet the boy whose reverie is an escape from the tedious enervation of school also dreams of his own 'sweet birthplace', thereby in turn evoking the pleasure of 'things to come' and the hope that a 'stranger's face' will appear. Thus, the speaker's memory of childhood does not provide much solace, but itself stands as a metaphor for his present vexation: the boy merely imagines a yet more remote origin to awaken hope for a more enlivening future. It seems that in making present an absent past he inevitably rediscovers the present in that past, for such is the interwovenness of things that are distinct but not separate.

As we might expect, the speaker now follows the small boy's example by leaping from memory to anticipate the future: 'But *thou*, my babe! shalt wander like a breeze / By lakes and sandy shores'. His own child is to learn through nature's sounds and shapes the 'intelligible and eternal language' of the 'Great universal Teacher'. However, this anticipation again reproduces the present perplexities of imagination at work, for nature even here mirrors itself to the child's innocent eye ('the clouds, / Which image in their bulk both lakes and shores / And mountain crags'), and the 'sounds intelligible' are also a 'language' to be interpreted.[22] Even when projected onto the future, the discovery of unity in diversity reproduces and mirrors imagination's present condition.

The happy vision of reconciliation, integration and acceptance described in the final section has been lost by the speaker, and yet the child who receives it as a matter of course will know what the speaker already has achieved by dint of imaginative labour, as the section quietly indicates by pointing us back into the body of the poem. 'Smokes' describes the future sun-thaw, but also recalls the fire in the grate and the fluttering film, just as 'the secret ministry of frost' echoes the opening meditation. Likewise, the inhering of opposites in a single organic process that will make 'all seasons sweet' for the child is a figure for the poem itself, duplicated by the imagery all the way through, and culminating in the final lines. These lines are a figure for all the rest, and depict various phenomena as manifestations of a single substance, water, for the smoke here is in fact steam rising from the thaw, and the drops and icicles are also water in other forms. In analogous fashion, the opposites to be synthesized in the child's future are already brought together by the process of imagination in the poem itself.

'Frost at Midnight' attends especially to the processes of an individual, creative mind, and the speaker remains a privileged consciousness gathering itself into meaning. But it is worth noticing how this emphasis is qualified by certain complex elisions and misidentifications that induce anxieties and indicate uncertainty and tentativeness. For instance, the owlet's cry of line 2 deepens the silence it seems to break, just as the speaker shrinks from the threat of solitude he apparently cherishes. The words 'extreme silentness' ending the sentence are followed by 'Sea and hill, and wood / This populous village! Sea and hill and wood / With all the numberless goings-on of life, / Inaudible as dreams.' The repetitions suggest an attempt to remind himself that the village is really there, even while he marvels at his distance from it. And, as we have seen, the words on the sleeping child initially suggest that the speaker is not alone because the child is nearby, but then the fact that the child is sleeping (as are the villagers) increases the sense of exclusion. Thus, there is a kind of clinging to things that would prevent solitude, and the speaker is not really at one with himself or with nature, but is more like the film – tenuous, opaque and erratic. The 'stern preceptor' and the 'Fixed' regimen of study remain in the adult as conditions of an anxious alienation that offers to repair itself only by utopian imagining. Moreover, imagination seeking for solace in the past or future finds itself inevitably returned to a present perplexity, perennially a stranger to itself.[23]

For Coleridge, then, imagination is a restorative power, but it is also complex and ambivalent. Thus, in its fashion, imagination mirrors our condition as persons taken up by language enabling a degree of mutual recognition and creative autonomy, even while confirming our individual separateness as we are called to make plans and voice our aspirations within the care-structure of time. Like Coleridge, Yeats was fascinated by the interplay of subjectivity and objectivity, and even proposed that history oscillates between these poles, in two-thousand year cycles.[24] Thus Christianity intro-duced a subjective phase which, in the twentieth century, is already almost transformed into its opposite. Personalism and individual-ism, that is, have been in the ascendent and are now yielding to history's use of individuals for a trans-personal purpose. But Yeats also tells us that there are no purely subjective or objective human types, for people always conjoin the physical and spiritual to some degree. 'Sailing to Byzantium' applies this theory to the creative process, depicted as a manifestation of contrary forces moving through us and not just at our disposal. In short, although Yeats puts less stress on subjective autonomy than does Coleridge, he can no more dispense with the person as subject than Coleridge can dispense with the necessary encounters between a creative subject and the resistance of an obdurate and fragmenting world.

The 'aged man', the speaker, acknowledges in the first section that the 'sensual music' of his youth is now inaccessible. But the intensity of the young depends on a submersion in nature's pre-personal, physical energies, such as produce also the 'mackerel-crowded seas' and the generic kinds, 'Fish, flesh and fowl': the young are 'caught' in that sensuality, and are compelled by it. The speaker says that he would not return to such a state, and in the next two sections he describes his own condition. Initially, he sees himself as an effigy, a wretchedly diminished physical specimen, a 'tattered coat upon a stick'. This grotesquerie is part of the price of passing beyond physical passion, and the sense of loss is relieved only if 'Soul clap its hands and sing'. That is, an old man must not depend on the body, but on spiritual force whereby the soul can thrive by 'studying / Monuments of its own magnificence'. Therefore he has sailed to Byzantium, symbolising an achievement of form both splendid and static, and where the 'sages standing in God's holy fire' will cultivate his spirit and teach him to sing.

In a passage written to accompany a BBC reading of 'Sailing to Byzantium' (but unused in the event) Yeats explains that Byzantium was 'the centre of European civilization and the source of its spir-itual philosophy, so I symbolise the search for the spiritual life by a journey to that city'.[25] Consequently, in the 'holy city' things are highly patterned, and the splendid abstractions, however gratifying to consciousnes, are removed from sensual immediacy. But here again we recognise loss as well as gain, and the concluding lines of section 3 are carefully ambivalent:

Consume my heart away; sick with desire
And fastened to a dying animal
It knows not what it is; and gather me
Into the artifice of eternity.

He wants his heart to be consumed because physical desire is painful, and yet suffering comes also from loss of the heart's passion and resentment that his dying body still clings. The 'artifice of eternity' is a release, but the words 'It knows not what it is' convey mixed feelings of nostaligia, contempt and anticipation marking the phase of transition.

The final section then takes us forward to the imagined end: 'Once out of nature I shall never take / My bodily form from any natural thing.' He will assume the same artificial perfection as the golden birds set before the 'lords and ladies of Byzantium' to sing 'Of what is past, or passing, or to come', and this final transition is the complementary opposite of the passionate unselfconsciousness of section 1, where the lovers are caught up in the brief moment. Here, instead, time is arrested, and past, present and future coalesce in a static and splendid immobility. But now the birds have lost their vitality: gold and emerald do not live and breathe, and spiritual existence is confined by its own laws that regulate consciousness as remorselessly as the young are driven by blind passion.

'Sailing to Byzantium' is a masterpiece of symmetrical organisation, suggesting that psychological experience is not just what an individual makes of it, but also what given conditions enable an individual to experience. Still, the 'aged man' is not merely a discontinuous set of mental states, but a person struggling with the present through reference to a past and aspiration to a future. Thus, the first section evokes the past to explain the present and the middle two sections turn self-reflexively on the present, discovering pain, longing, and paradox, which are then put into perspective by imagining the future. Yet the aspiration expressed at the opening of section 4, 'Once out of nature', is in fact not realised because the artefact of 'gold and gold enamelling' draws on nature for its own kind of embodied splendor, however different this is from the physical splendors of the young. Again, the sages who step out from the 'holy fire' to instruct the soul are said to 'perne in a gyre'. These strange-sounding words suggest a mysterious, transcendent design, but spinning gyres are also Yeats's symbol for the cycles of history. Thus, like the bird on the golden bough that sings 'Of what is past or passing, or to come', the sages do not entirely step outside history or beyond sensuality, nor does the soul they instruct. The 'birds in the trees' of section 1 sing of 'Whatever is begotten, born, and dies', imparting a sense of concreteness in contrast to the song in section 4, about 'past or passing, or to come'. Nonetheless, both songs are about time, and both depict an embodied condition striving to find itself in language and through imagination.

In contrast to Coleridge, Yeats indeed de-emphasises the autonomous, creative subject, and attempts to place subjectivity and objectivity together in some larger structure. But his depiction of this larger, containing process is itself imagined. Analogously, Coleridge's poem foregrounds the creative subject, but turns out to be less than fully confident about the solitary individualism the poem offers to celebrate, so that the imagining self of 'Frost at Midnight' is also fragile and contingent. Moreover, as both poets show, it seems that the necessary involvement of sign-making with our experience of time entails that the synthesising and configurating activity we know broadly as imagination (and which reflection discovers to be already active in the production of signs) will itself have a temporal structure. Imagination then will express the force of desire orientated to the future, and will do so within the constraints of language received from the past and tested in the perpetually uncertain present formation of our self-conscious but unconstituted selves. The synthesising process by which a remembered and re-narratised past releases through the labyrinths of present ambiguity and exigency a possible freedom is, we might conclude, one way of describing imaginative activity that reconfirms the notion of the personal for which I have been arguing throughout.

All of this leads me to a final consideration, namely, the relationship between imagination and politics. For clearly the emphasis on individual self-creation in Romantic theories of imagination might easily occlude the political, or regard it mainly as a forum for individual self-realisation. Indeed, it can be argued that one main challenge inherited from Romanticism by the twentieth century is how to reconcile the personal freedoms of self-determination proclaimed by the Romantics with the fact that the self is socially formed. I will deal further with this question in a later chapter on the relationship between persons and the social community, but to conclude this section, I would like to turn briefly to George Eliot.

Felix Holt, The Radical (1866)[26] was written about the first Reform Bill, at a time when the second was pending. It is the first of Eliot's novels to focus on the problems of urban, industrial England,[27] and the main setting is Treby Magna, a rural town undergoing the process of industrialisation. Coal mining and a tape factory have already made an impact on the town, which has also been designated a polling place. Felix Holt, a proudly poor artisan (he repairs watches) declares himself a Radical and in support of reforms to improve the lot of working people. The official Radical candidate, Harold Transome, has returned from abroad with a fortune to repair the run-down family estate presided over by his imperious, lonely mother who is advised by the unscrupulous lawyer Matthew Jermyn. Harold's declaration of the Radical cause scandalises his mother and the neighbouring Dubarry family who provide the Tory candidate. Garston, manager of the mine, stands as a Whig, and the miners and townspeople are drawn half-comprehendingly into the turmoil of opinions and rumours.

By an elaborate plot device, Eliot contrives to have Esther, the daughter of a local Dissenting minister, Rufus Lyon, emerge as the rightful heir to the Transome estate. Esther then is courted by Harold, but at last decides to renounce her claim to the estate and marry Felix. This choice is at the heart of George Eliot's concern, and Esther's decision is said to be based mainly on feeling. She comes to realise how 'the best life' is 'that where one bears and does everything because of some great and strong feeling – so that this and that in one's circumstances don't signify' (356). Later, she worries that 'her best feeling . . . had been called forth just where the conditions were hardest' (550), but in the end she saves herself by accepting the necessary sacrifices.

The narrator makes clear that choices such as Esther's are part of an organic process and can unify a whole life:

> It is only in that freshness of our time that the choice is possible which gives unity to life, and makes the memory a temple where all relics and all votive offerings, all worship and all grateful joy, are an unbroken history sanctified by one religion. (551)

The stress here falls on 'unity', unbroken', and 'one', suggesting that a choice of love made with spring-like spontaneity can knit a life together and make it whole. The religious sentiment – 'temple', 'votive offerings', 'relics', 'worship', and so on – is Romantic and natural, and the notion of a hallowed memory nurturing us in later life is distinctly Wordsworthian. In short, Esther falls in love for the right Romantic reasons, and the novel contrives to suggest that as it is in love, so it should be in politics.

Felix explicitly voices this opinion in a pre-election speech. He points out that the steam engine 'will help to change most things' (400), and when he applies this example to political reform, he concludes that the force working the engines 'must come out of human nature – out of men's passions, feelings, desires. Whether the engines will do good work or bad depends on these feelings' (400). The intensity here matches Felix's opinion that everyone should have an interest in politics: 'I despise every man who has not – or, having it, doesn't try to rouse it in other men' (146). Initially, Esther was preoccupied with dreams of being a fine lady, and her affectations provoked Felix's rebuke, so that in coming to love him, she discovers not only her own deepest feelings, but also how these entail a political commitment. Her rejection of Harold Transome is at once an affair of the heart and the rejection of an outmoded feudal politics.

Eliot works hard to show the necessary interpenetrations of the personal and political: as the narrator says in a famous sentence, 'there is no private life which has not been determined by a wider public life' (129). Still, at the centre of this interrelationship is the strong feeling that binds humans organically to nature, time, and others, through sympathy and mutual affection. Basically, Eliot draws heavily for these ideas upon the early Romantics, and especially on the Wordsworthian primary imagination.[28] As a young woman, she discovered her 'own feelings expressed' in Wordsworth, and according to Cross she retained this admiration until she died.[29] Barbara Hardy suggests that although there is no systematic account of imagination in Eliot, the key emphases throughout the novels on imaginative extension of the self and on the feelings enabling it draws basically on Wordsworth and Coleridge.[30] Thus in *Felix Holt* the willful and desolate Mrs. Transome as a young woman had laughed at the *Lyrical Ballads*, preferring to indulge her taste for 'the lighter parts of dangerous French authors' (104). This error of taste symbolises and anticipates the disastrous choices that at last cut her off so painfully from human society.

Some of the best things in *Felix Holt* deal with how mutuality emerges from a development of one's natural feelings in relation to a nurturing past, and how isolation is caused by rejecting such a development. For instance, the Transome household exemplifies a painful series of alienations wherein egotism and the will to dominance replace sympathy and love. It is rumored that Mrs. Transome wished her first-born, imbecile son dead (82), so that her favourite, Harold, would inherit the estate. When the first son does die, she is indeed relieved, but when she learns that Harold is returning from abroad with a child of his own, she tears up the letter in a rage (100). Death here brings pleasure, and new life a sense of frustration and resentment. Moreover, the past to Mrs. Transome is a nightmare, mainly because she must conceal from Harold that the lawyer, Jermyn, is his father, but also because her will to dominate has prevented the cultivation of any nurturing relationship. Consequently, she remains 'still young and ardent in her terrors; the passions of the past were living in her dread' (438). Her failure of imaginative sympathy turns memory into anxiety, and the present is experienced merely as alienation. 'What dreary future was there after this dreary past?' (595), she asks herself, looking out into the night where 'the black boundary of trees and the long line of the river seemed only part of the loneliness and monotony' (596). The trees and river mark her separation, and her failure in sustaining a human relationship is also a failure of relationship to nature: she pays a heavy price for having laughed at Wordsworth. Even the moment when she attempts to confide in her loyal servant Denner, is immediately frustrated:

> I believe you are the creature in the world that loves me best, Denner; you will never understand what I suffered. It's no use telling you. There's no folly in you and no heartache. You are made of iron. You have never had any trouble. (487)

The initial move here towards confessional intimacy is quickly checked by the slightly deprecatory and self-dramatising implication of 'creature', for Mrs. Transome is aware rather of the pathos of being reduced to confiding in a servant – an inferior 'creature' – than of the servant's love that she professes to appreciate. The confidence itself then takes the form of a series of negatives disavowing the utility of confiding, and this disavowal at last is justified by the conclusion that Denner has no capacity for feeling ('You are made of iron', and so on). Yet there is also a good deal of pathos in the scene as a whole, and the torment, imperious dignity and loss of meaning experienced by Mrs. Transome combine to make her the most impressively rendered character in the book. Her son, Harold, and erstwhile lover, Jermyn, are both marked by similar failures of feeling and imaginative sympathy, and as Esther is to discover, there is a price to pay for inheriting Transome Court.

By contrast, there is an immediate, strong sympathy between Felix Holt and the dissenting minister, Rufus Lyon, even despite the head-on collision between Mr. Lyon's religious convictions and Felix's anti-religious ones. The point here is that difference and mutuality are compatible, and there is a distinction between an energetic bridging of differences and the kind of disrelationship experienced by Mrs. Transome. Again, strength of feeling and imaginative sympathy are crucial. Mr. Lyon is a 'man of sensitive fibre' (344) because he had once loved Esther's mother, whom he found abandoned and wandering after Esther's father had died. 'His love was the first love of a fresh young heart full of wonder and worship' (168), and he sacrificed a great deal for it. Although her mother died when Esther was still a child, the memory of those early years sustains Mr. Lyon, and is central to the bond between him and Esther, though he has never disclosed that he is not her father. Basically, Esther 'recognised the purity of his character, and a quickness of intellect in him which responded to her own liveliness' (161), and their relationship thrives. However, Mr. Lyon eventually must confess to having kept the secret, and he does so in trepidation:

Esther listened to her mother's story, and to the outpouring of her step-father's long pent-up experience. The rays of the morning sun which fell athwart the books, the sense of the beginning day, had deepened the solemnity more than night would have done. All knowledge which alters our lives penetrates us more when it comes in the early morning: the day that has to be travelled with something new and perhaps forever sad in its light, is an image of the life that spreads beyond. But at night the time of rest is near. (354)

This is the obverse of Mrs. Transome's frustrated confession to Denner, and the emphasis now is on hope, sustaining imagination, and mutual presence. The result is 'a new sympathy in which Esther felt herself exalted' (354), and Mr. Lyon experiences 'a surprise and joy that were almost painful in their intensity' (355). At the end, Esther chooses this Romantic, organicist kind of relationship instead of Transome Court, and although she and Felix also must overcome differences, they are depicted as sharing a common, vital sympathy.

The main problem in *Felix Holt* arises from whether or not such a lovingly evoked Romantic organicism rooted in imaginative sympathy is convincing as a model for political reform in the social circumstances the novel also carefully describes. Despite his fine rhetoric calling for power for the working man, Felix argues against universal suffrage and ends up with a position confirming the traditional ruling class that the novel otherwise depicts as moribund and devitalised.[31] At the end of the book, Felix settles for obscurity, indeed welcoming it as the best expression of his political opinions, so that we might after all think George Eliot's description of him as 'the Radical' is tinged with irony.[32]

The difficulty here of reconciling the Romantic and political is duplicated and clarified within the novel by Eliot's treatment of time. As we have seen, memory can nurture the present and promote hope, or it can weigh us down with guilt and anxiety. Our life choices, and especially those involving deep feeling, are crucial to how we will come to know ourselves and one another through time. But time in *Felix Holt* is also imagined as a kind of fatal mechanism, and there is a great deal in the novel about how our past, through no fault or design of our own, sets the tracks along which our lives must run.

Thus we are told how Harold 'was trusting in his own skill to shape the success of his own morrows, ignorant of what many yesterdays had determined for him beforehand' (277). Ironically, the facts of Harold's birth confound him all the more completely because he insists on being 'master of my own actions' (117). At one point, he describes events affecting Felix as 'fatalities' (435), and Esther jokingly says about her anxiously-dropped stitches, 'Those blunders have a design in them' (502). The narrator muses on the 'irony of the human lot' (517), and Harold on the fact that a woman 'would not find me a tragic hero' (540), though later he feels upon him the yoke of a 'mighty resistless destiny' (587).[33]

There is a great deal of this kind of thing throughout the novel, reminding us that people's freedom of self-determination is limited because choices are constrained by circumstance which imposes its own design. Tragedy requires that we should feel the simultaneous grandeur and helplessness of human beings caught in the dense and imponderable meshes of such a predicament. But *Felix Holt* is less about tragedy's encounter with metaphysics than about social reform, and Eliot produces a strong sense that social destiny is inherited and individual psychology is deeply, even irreparably shaped by it. The whole idea of effecting political reform by way of a mutual extension of personal sympathy and imaginative identification with others is therefore drastically limited, and, despite his fine rhetoric, Felix also capitulates to this inevitable consequence. As Cross says of Eliot:

> her roots were down in the pre-railroad, pre-telegraphic period
> – the days of fine old leisure – but the fruit was formed during
> an era of extraordinary activity in scientific and mechanical
> discovery. Her genius was the outcome of these conditions.[34]

Basically, that is, Eliot was strongly drawn to Romanticism and to educating the primary imagination, but she needed to adapt this concern to a technological and urban society. And although in *Felix Holt* she presents a strongly imagined view of the conflict between the personal and political, she does not equally effectively imagine a synthesis whereby the laws governing society and the freedoms of imagination are mutually sustaining. As inheritors of the problem to which she gives such thoughtful consideration, we might better understand, by reading her, the necessary involvement of imagination with politics in the development of an adequate theory of the person, whose identity is irreducibly social, the facts of a limited creative autonomy notwithstanding.

In this section, I have been dealing with imagination in general, and how it relates to the idea of the person. My main claim is that persons as agents are called to some degree of active interpretation, and experience some degree of identity, continuity and autonomy. Yet no person is fully autonomous, and the play of imagination therefore is taken up within the play of presence and absence that marks the dialectic of participation and alienation of individuals in culture at large. I would like now to consider two further dimensions of this topic: first, how fantasy thematises imagination's ambivalent self-presence; second, how imagination relates to ideas.

FANTASY

In fantasy, imagination thematises its own ambiguity, and one hallmark of fantasy is the hesitation it elicits concerning our belief or disbelief in the strange or uncanny worlds it describes. The most influential account of this hesitation is by Tsvetan Todorov, the Bulgarian-born disciple of Roland Barthes and student of Russian Formalism.Todorov believes that modern linguistics has brought literary criticism to a unique self-awareness, and that academic literary theory 'is born . . . only with the twentieth century'.[35] Todorov firmly distinguishes between theory and exegesis, but claims that exegesis always presupposes theory (however unconsciously), and without exegesis theory is sterile (7). According to Todorov, Western criticism has favoured exegesis, and the time has come to right the balance by developing the theoretical pole. To this end, he turns to structuralism, on the grounds that 'the object of poetics is not the sum of empirical phenomena (literary works) but an abstract structure (literature)' (10).

The most concise introduction to Todorov's thinking is his *Introduction to Poetics*. Basically, he argues that literature is inseparable from human sign-making and cultural symbolism in general, and he sees 'poetics' as playing 'an eminently *transitional* role, even a transitory one' (72) in the emergence of a general theory of discourse. In so doing, Todorov attempts to place himself historically, interpreting his special concern as 'the site we have reserved for the *other* since the Renaissance' (xxxi). By this means, he tells us he is reaching towards such large questions as tolerance, xenophobia, colonialism, and 'assimilation of the other and identification with the other' (xxxii).

Todorov's reassurance about his historical concern is partly a defence against the standard accusation that structuralists ignore history. Yet his own writing is characteristically abstract, and the approach to fantasy in his well-known book, *The Fantastic: A Structural Approach to a Literary Genre*,[36] is very much what the subtitle declares it to be. Todorov's key argument is that fantasy produces an effect of combined hesitation and wonder (24) occasioned by the intrusion into our familiar world of an extraordinary event that cannot be explained adequately by the laws of that familiar world (25). The fantastic lasts only as long as the hesitation between belief in supernatural intervention on the one hand, and incredulity on the other. If the reader decides that the laws of the familiar world do after all offer a sufficient explanation, then the strange event can be described as uncanny. An example is Jan Potocki's *Saragossa Manuscript*, where '"the miracles" are explained rationally at the end of the narrative' (44), as is the case also with many detective novels. If supernatural laws are invoked, then the event is marvellous, as in the *Arabian Nights* (54). But fantasy takes its life precisely from an uncertainty poised between these alternatives.

According to Freud, the uncanny is a sense of dangerous and horrifying transgression linked to guilt and taboo, but caused by the projection of hidden desires and anxieties onto the environment and onto others.[37] If we find we cannot explain the uncanny by natural means, it might also strike us as supernatural. The important point for Todorov is that fantasy evokes the unsettling limit-experience Freud describes, but without reducing it to the natural (that ghost was nothing but the shadow cast by a shirt on the clothesline), nor by uncritically seeking out the supernatural (that ghost was your father returned from purgatory).All of this in turn reflects Heidegger's account of the uncanny as a sense of homelessness accompanied by anxiety, a primordial intuition of 'nothing' that marks Dasein's fundamental Being-in-the-world, 'even though in an everyday way' such experience of nothingness is 'covered up'.[38] Like Freud and Heidegger, Todorov would have us learn how anxiety arises from the unsayable or concealed elements subtending and threatening our sense of normality and certainty.

As Rosemary Jackson points out, by dissolving familiar structures in this way, fantasy also replaces presence by absence,and subverts 'that most cherished of human unities, the unity of "character"', the stable self.[39] In short, by enlivening readers to the strangeness of ordinary things, fantasy thematises the ambivalent, configurating process of imagination, and challenges the unity of personal identity. Todorov concludes that, in so doing, fantasy does not speak differently from literature in general: rather, it speaks 'at a different intensity, this intensity being at its maximum in the fantastic' (93), which then 'represents the quintessence of literature, insofar as the questioning of the limit between real and unreal, proper to all literature, is its explicit centre' (168).

Todorov's observations confirm the arguments developed in the first part of this chapter, describing imagination's presence to itself in the making of fictive worlds, which in turn are embedded in the care-structure of time wherein persons make plans and commitments. At one point Todorov even explicitly aligns his threefold structure (uncanny-fantasy-marvellous) with the divisions of time. Because the marvellous refers to something unknown, 'never seen as yet, still to come' (42), it pertains to the future. By contrast, the uncanny refers us to previous experience for an explanation of strange events, and so pertains to the past. But when we encounter the fantastic, 'the hesitation which characterises it cannot be situated, by and large, except in the present' (42). As Jackson says, fantasy draws attention to 'the *process* of representation' by 'foregrounding its own signifying practice',[40] and in so doing, involves us in ambivalence, the hallmark of Heidegger's 'presentness' and of the anxiety inevitably accompanying our personal involvement in human culture, where a sense of simultaneous belonging and of radical flaw marks our deployment of (and by) language itself.

Two questions now press for consideration. The first is the place and function of representation in fantasy, and the second is the problem of desire and wish-fulfilment. As is often pointed out, fantasy needs to present a convincing sense of the familiar and ordinary, so that the crucial interruption of the 'uncanny-marvellous' can be registered in a manner compelling enough to cause hesitation and wonder. Fantasy therefore depends on an initial acceptance of the conventions of realistic representation.[41] Appropriately, as Todorov and Sartre point out, fantasy comes into its own in the nineteenth century, the great age of 'realistic' fiction, and is partly a reaction against commonplace nineteenth-century positivist and utilitarian biases about everyday language and the world of solid things.[42] That most celebrated of Victorian fantasies, *Alice in Wonderland*, is all about the bizarre arbitrariness of authority, codes of social behaviour and rules of argument. The Red Queen's fierce and tetchy authority, like the White Queen's abstract imperiousness, are conditions of the adult world to which Alice must adjust as she grows up. Humpty Dumpty's disquisition on words and the white sheep's attention to the particular sense represent how fragile language is and also the pedantic narrowness with which it is confirmed as common sense. The point is that our everyday assumptions turn out on examination to be just as fantastic as this fantastic adventure into the 'uncanny-marvellous', and the best-known writers on fairy tales and fantasy all point this out.

For example, George MacDonald, who draws on German Romanticism to develop his own theory of fantasy,[43] argues that imagination is nourished by facts to which it initially submits but then shows to be strange and mysterious (2), opening upon 'infinite lands of uncertainty lying all about the sphere hollowed out of the dark by the glimmering lamp of our knowledge'(29). MacDonald's theory has a theological dimension, for he wants to awaken us to a sense of God's goodness in a world full of sorrow and pain. The world must be governed by a finer plan than we know from what we take to be the facts, and imagination is the key to this better, desirable scheme of things. Fantasy thus helps to fill out what we do not know, and our resort to it indicates how 'We live by faith, and not by sight' (28). MacDonald's 'faith' and Todorov's 'hesitation' are therefore akin in that both find the key to fantasy in the power of imagination to awaken us to a sense of wonder making the familiar strange and the strange familiar. This theory is by and large repeated by MacDonald's more famous disciple, J. R. R. Tolkien, who again stresses in his essay 'On Fairy Stories'[44] how fantasy depends on the realistic representation of familiar facts. Like MacDonald and W. H. Auden (and, most recently, George Steiner), Tolkien holds that we can make alternative worlds because of a sense that 'we are made' and confined to a painful condition from which we long to escape to something better. Fantasy gives us a glimpse of this better state, in response to our deep desires.

In a penetrating analysis, Lynette Hunter divides recent theories of fantasy into two types, the first having to do with games and the second with desire.[45] Johannes Huizinga exemplifies the games approach, and his key idea is that fantasy is not to be confused with real life, but is neutral, just as games are. Tolkien exemplifies the desire approach because he holds that the main achievement of fantasy is to activate longing in a pure form. Hunter, however, is keen to point out the problems inherent in both approaches. In fact, games are not so conveniently separate from real life as Huizinga says, and values deriving from non-games activities are frequently manifest in the games themselves. Likewise, Tolkien attempts to justify the secondary world of fantasy in terms of desire, but warns that fantasy must not be escapist, or supplant the real world with a private one. Yet desire is always conditioned by our experience of the primary world and the secondary world always to some extent does supplant the primary one, which is much less stable and certain than Tolkien implies. Hunter maintains that Huizinga and Tolkien prefer to overlook these difficulties, and can do so because they share an underlying, typically nineteenth-century faith in the representative function of language that many of today's critics find unacceptable.

These observations are especially helpful for revealing the theological elements in the MacDonald-Tolkien accounts, and how these elements are latent also in the authoritarian canons of 'realism' to which fantasy is bound even while declaring its independence. Still, we had better stop short of pushing such salutary arguments as Hunter's all the way into the chasm of non-referentiality, where language is denied any access at all to a world of substantive existents. And here, however improbably, G. K. Chesterton affords a useful corrective. Although he too has a theological agenda and his thinking derives from George MacDonald, Chesterton has a quick eye for easy or sentimental evasions.

With characteristic breeziness, Chesterton reminds us that we cannot say how an egg turns into a chicken any more than we can say how a bear could turn into a prince,[46] and the fact that fairy tales make rivers run with wine reminds us 'for one wild moment' that they run with water (54). In short, such reflections force us to see what an 'eccentric privilege' life is, and, especially, how man is 'the Great Might-Not-Have-Been' (64). Realisation of this perilous condition causes anxiety, but also provokes action. Our world is full of pain but is also our home, at once an ogre's castle and our own cottage. Can we then 'hate it enough to change it, and yet love it enough to think it worth changing?' (72).

Chesterton's account overlaps with Tolkien's and MacDonald's, but he concentrates on contingency ('the Great Might-Not-Have-Been'), and on the resultant anxiety and call to concern, as Heidegger would say. His argument thus opens up easily upon the theories of Sartre, Todorov, and the hesitation-and-ambivalence school in general. In so doing, it calls our attention especially to the uncertainty of language and of the self which is historically-produced and sustained in ambivalence, though called perpetually to interpret, evaluate and act decisively. All of which returns us to some of the main positions of the present study. With this in mind, let us consider a novel by George MacDonald.

At the Back of the North Wind[47] is the story of Diamond, a child of poor parents in the city of London. His father is a coachman, who names his son for a favourite horse. The two Diamonds share a bond of affection all the more poignant as we gradually discover that the child is frail and ill. His bouts of sickness are not described directly, but rather we infer them from his series of close encounters with the North Wind. These encounters are described from the boy's perspective, which is far different from that of outside observers. And so, as Diamond discourses with the mysterious North Wind, he learns also to love and work with the splendid, long-suffering horse, his namesake. From time immemorial, the human condition has been described as poised, thus, between beast and angel, matter and spirit. But between these two poles we also find imagination and dream, strangely irradiated with gleams and fragments of some occluded condition which is our true destiny, prevented by the carapaces of alienation and suffering, the inherited flaw that is history's nightmare, our bondage to physical labour and illness.

Throughout the novel, there is a good deal about suffering. Diamond is ill, and dies at the end. The crossing-sweeper, Nanny, is confined in a children's hospital, and when Diamond's father falls sick, the family goes without food. The plight of London's homeless and unemployed, as well as the condition of its bullies, drunks, and 'deserving poor' are constantly before us. This is part of a real world, the oppressive actuality of Diamond's everyday existence, which in turn is MacDonald's industrial England. Still, there is happiness in the child's life as the family manages on the coachman's wages and Diamond sleeps in the loft above the stable, where the north wind comes whistling through a knot-hole.

At this point, we cross the threshold, for Diamond encounters North Wind as a beautiful woman. She comforts him and carries him nestled in her hair; he is enchanted by her beauty and power, and amazed to find that 'Nobody is cold' with her (18). People are cold only when they are 'without'; that is, when they do not know North Wind's inside, or true nature, but only her negative, external manifestations.

MacDonald handles the threshold phase ingeniously, first describing the wind as loud and angry and 'whistling shrill' (13). These terms depict the natural phenomenon, but also personify it, so that even such conventional terms prepare us for the lady's appearance. Also, the knot-hole is described as a window, with some play on the antique meaning of window as the wind's eye. The knot-hole thus is the North Wind's window through which she sees out of her house into Diamond's, so that the threshold between worlds is crossed in two directions. Not surprisingly, the boy is amazed, fearful, and entranced. Moreover, North Wind assumes many forms: she is tiny enough to hide behind a primrose and powerful enough to sink a ship. She can be a wolf or a tiger or a girl or a majestic lady. She is chaos among the elements, and also the safe, motionless centre. Yet her power is limited (78), and only by passing through her cold, seated figure can Diamond arrive at the country of delight and promise at her back. Here of course she is also death, and by venturing through her into the country at the other side and then returning, Diamond brings into his own, waking world a sense of joy and freedom from anxiety. But although he has a salutary effect on everyone he meets, people sometimes think he is simple-minded. Rather, we are meant to realise that he has a fuller knowledge of the principles governing the world than is normally available, and that such knowledge transforms his understanding of the novel's 'real' world, so that he appears foolish to those who judge him by its standards.

A story like this can easily collapse into banality (as this one does frequently enough), but MacDonald knows the hazards, and has an expert feel for the ambiguity and hesitation which, in fantasy, betoken imagination's presence to itself on the border between reality and make-believe.[48] Diamond might, after all, be suffering from hallucinations caused by his illness, and the uneasy boundaries between dreams, hallucinations and waking reality are kept before us throughout. At first, he awakens and thinks what a curious dream he has had, but then his memory brightens 'until it did not look altogether like a dream' (26), and he falls into doubt. The story presents us also with dreams within dreams (69,178), and at one point Diamond admits that Nanny has been dreaming, but assures her that her dreams 'are something more as well' (225). At the end, when he asks the narrator '*Could* it be all dreaming, do you think, sir?' the judicious reply is 'I daren't say, Diamond'(286). Here, the world of dreams itself becomes a kind of window opening in one direction onto a naturalistic explanation of Diamond's uncanny experiences, and, in the other, onto a marvellous, higher vision of how the world is governed. Throughout, the point of hesitation remains carefully enigmatic, for otherwise the poignancy of the best passages would be lost, and MacDonald works hard to provoke us. Thus, the question of Diamond's illness and the fact that he may have 'a tile loose' (142) keep modifying our assessment of events. Also there are frequent reflections on the peculiarities and uncertainties of naming, and how naming a thing is different from knowing it (16). Personal identity is also subjected to question ('Well, which me is me?' [57]), and there is even a passage on Diamond's 'unconscious influence' (264) on those around him. Also, amidst the wonderful events is a series of reflections on the even more wonderful strangeness of ordinary perception. 'I don't know what I know' (119), the narrator tells us, and 'the most wonderful thing in the world is how people come to understand anything' (22). In short, the ordinary things are marvellous and also poignantly contingent, as we come to realise by seeing 'inside' them through imagination. Yet imagination does not give us conceptual clarity, and especially when it focuses on its own operations it cannot avoid encountering its own imperfections.

MacDonald's best effects are in creating the simultaneous sense of wonder and hesitation Todorov describes, but he does not always manage to do so, and sometimes indulges in flat-footed moralising and sentimentality. A good deal throughout the novel remains coarse and over-simplified, so that the best effects of the fantastic as 'uncanny-marvellous' can be gauged also in contradistinction to the not-infrequent lapses. Something of the difficulty can be felt in North Wind's sinking a ship in which men, women and children are drowned and only a few survive. The incident exemplifies that strictest of hard facts, namely, the suffering of innocent people. When the burden of this problem confirms our doubt about a benign providence while activating our desire for a solution, the writing remains complex, reproducing a strong sense of imagination's ambiguities. Thus Diamond struggles with the possibility that the world might simply be cruel: 'I can't believe that. I don't believe it. I won't believe it. That would kill me' (59). But MacDonald himself sometimes cannot stand the strain, and later in the novel he provides a tiresome explanation: among the survivors was a Mr. Evans, who had behaved like a cad to a certain Miss Coleman, who happens to be the daughter of the Coleman family who hired Diamond's father as a coachman. The shipwreck has now taught Mr. Evans an improving lesson, for he finds his way back to Miss Coleman, and there is a suggestion that the drownings might provide other, similarly improving lessons. At times MacDonald's novelistic nerve cracks even more entirely, as when the narrator comes straight at us with the advice that some reactions to suffering come from 'not having faith enough in God' (238), and so on.

At the Back of the North Wind, then, is often flawed, but MacDonald does nonetheless give us passages that create a heart-rending desire for the overcoming of alienation and a simultaneous, painful awareness of the kinds of frailty, contingency and uncertain identity, that mark our condition as persons. These are the special achievements of fantasy in which, as we have seen, imagination examines its own presence to itself, discovering its inherent ambiguity and the uncertainty of the borders between reality and illusion. This ambiguous self-presence is also inevitably to some degree the presence of a past made up of facts establishing us as contingent creatures in a 'real' world. Just so, present ambivalence opens likewise upon a future, the not-yet of our unfulfilled desires. MacDonald knows this well enough, and his narrator tells us that fairyland is only glimpsed, and 'I am always *going* to see it so some time' (21). When he arrives at the back of the North Wind for the first time, Diamond finds himself in a happy place that is also somehow sad, and where people 'looked as if they were waiting to be gladder some day' (90). Later, he learns this place is only a picture of the place he will at last visit (278). In such passages, MacDonald keeps us alive to a presence only glimpsed, so that the reassurances of joy and happiness are at last restrained by a pervasive melancholy.[49] In our contingency and necessary bewilderment, it seems that no imagined happiness brings us finally home to ourselves and out of hesitation into certainty. For certainty affords clear understanding, but our perennial experience is of an uneasy dialectic between images that disclose our participation in the world, and the ideas by which we would understand such disclosure. I would like now to consider this dialectic in more detail.

IMAGES AND IDEAS

Aristotle tells us that a metaphor is 'the application of the name of a thing to something else',[50] and as Gilbert Ryle points out, this description treats metaphor as a category mistake – a sort of deliberate error. 'I will speak daggers to her', says Hamlet (III,2,404), who talks also of the sepulchre's 'ponderous and marble jaws' (I,4,50), and of 'unpacking my heart with words' (II,2,592). We all know that words are different from daggers, that a sepulchre cannot properly be said to have jaws, and that a heart is not a suitcase. Yet these deliberate errors – or category mistakes – enable us to shape experience in new ways and produce new dimensions of meaning. Words are indeed weapons that can wound; death has a predatory aspect; the heart can conceal pain and longing, shut up within. As Paul Ricoeur says,[51] metaphors have a predicative function that remakes a common reality. Yet this remaking in turn calls for reflective understanding, for the kind of clarity provided by concepts. Thus, the dialectic between belonging and separation, participation and distance which lies at the heart of our personal concerns, is reproduced also in the play between metaphor and concept, image and idea.

But where does such a process begin? As we have seen in the opening section of this chapter, one theory maintains that all language is originally poetic and that literal meanings are, more or less, metaphors that have settled into common usage. Rousseau and Shelley present this theory in high Romantic dress, and we have seen it re-echoed in Richard Rorty and Owen Barfield. Jacques Derrida, however, asks us to be wary, on the grounds that definitions of metaphor such as Aristotle's always assume a pre-established literal sense, the 'name that belongs to something else'. In short, it is impossible to argue for the priority of metaphor because the very idea of a metaphor is grasped through the notion of a literal meaning always already in existence. As I have pointed out earlier, Derrida's special interest is, as Norris says, to explore the 'mutual crossings and involvements'[52] of such apparent opposites as metaphoric and literal, and to dismantle arguments giving priority to one pole or the other. In Derrida's writings, this process often involves discovering how certain key concepts in a line of argument are themselves contaminated by metaphor, so that the stability of the commonly-accepted meaning is undermined from within. Derrida's main conclusion is that meaning does not come to rest or achieve full presence, but that the tension between rhetoric and logic, metaphoric and literal, image and idea, inevitably involves us in *aporias* that destabilise our certainties and push our enquiry ever further afield.

As I have also mentioned, one of Derrida's main examples is Rousseau. In the *Essay on the Origin of Languages*,[53] Rousseau argues that speech is the natural form of language, and the development of civilization precipitates a fall from an original, natural mode of communication into the authoritarianism and indirection of writing. As elsewhere in Rousseau, nature and culture are opposed, and we are enjoined to work towards recovering an original state of innocence from which we are departed.

In Derrida's opinion, Rousseau's argument shares a predominant bias of Western philosophy since Plato, aligning speech with self-presence, truth, and a mystique of origins. Derrida contrives to disclose the latent authoritarianism and prejudice of this general position, and thus argues that Rousseau's case against writing is itself made in writing ('he valorises and disqualifies writing at the same time' [141–2]). As Derrida says, the 'already-thereness of instruments and of concepts cannot be undone or re-invented' (139), and nature, like all our ideas, is given to us already imperfect.

Yet Derrida acknowledges that Rousseau is aware of the difficulties: for instance, he understood how we 'are dispossessed of the longed-for presence in the gesture of language by which we attempt to seize it' (141). Nonetheless, Rousseau persisted, and on the one hand, therefore, admits that the 'spoken plenitude' (270) of language loses itself in the act of articulation; on the other, he tries to affirm the origin of speech to a self-present subject. To negotiate this difficulty, he turns to metaphor, arguing that if metaphoric language comes first and in the beginning is only poetry, then conceptual language must come after. But to maintain this position, Rousseau needs to avoid the complications attendant upon the Aristotelian definition, and to do so he stresses the link between language and subjective affect. Even though metaphor is an inadequate description of an object or event, says Rousseau, it expresses a subject's passion. For instance, if a savage says, 'I see giants' when in fact he sees men, the signifier will be metaphoric (which is to say, figurative and inadequate) but the expression of fear will be truly designated. Rousseau concludes:

> The illusory image presented by passion is the first to appear, and the language that corresponded to it was also the first invented. It subsequently became metaphorical when the enlightened spirit, recognising its first error, used the expressions only with those passions that had produced them. (276)

Yet Derrida insists that we 'must also turn these relationships inside out', for although the speaker lacks 'the truth of the object', he 'speaks himself fully' and has 'a relationship of truth and literalness with that which he expresses' (277). The 'enlightened spirit' (277) might indeed clarify the object by means of a more adequate literal sense, but this does not mean the first speaker's meaning was not also literal, though mistaken (275). Rousseau thus does not succeed in recapturing 'the instantaneity of a full language' (279) because metaphor at all points still requires the literal. As Derrida says, 'Metaphoricity is the logic of contamination and the contamination of logic',[54] and although images and ideas might be distinct, they also merge in a constant, dynamic exchange, each unsettling and re-defining the other's domain. Rousseau's 'instantaneity' is illusory because, as Derrida explains, 'language cannot be truly born except by the disruption and fracture of that happy plenitude, in the very instant that this instantaneity is wrested from its fictive immediacy and put back into movement' (280). In short, language never comes to rest because the word and the world's body do not perfectly coincide: 'is' is perpetually what also has been and what is not-yet. And so, in turn, Derrida's texts must somehow attempt to produce a sense of their own incapacity to stabilise what *they* mean.

Of course, Derrida is aware of this difficulty, and understands that he cannot simply jettison such traditional notions as authorial intent, metaphysical abstraction, and the referentiality of language. Rather, as Terry Eagleton says, 'The strength and weakness of deconstruction is that it seeks to position itself at the extreme limit of the thinkable',[55] and we have seen how Richard Rorty points to the unpredictability of Derrida's writings as one technique for approaching such a limit. According to Rorty, Derrida has increasingly dropped theory 'in favour of fantasizing', and 'Falling back on private fantasy is the only solution to the self-referential problem which such theorizing encounters'.[56]

Earlier, I attempted also to indicate how stultifying to the idea of the person is a theory that would deprive language of access to a common world, and here again we are left with the prospect of an elaborate playfulness refusing to depart from its own self-ironising processes. It seems that too eager an insistence on proceeding modestly because we always mean more and less than we say, might end up pitching us into a self-reflexiveness inhibiting us from proceeding at all. And yet Derrida is correct to insist that the metaphoric and literal interpenetrate: indeed, metaphors need to be clarified and understood, and understanding needs affective energy and participation in what is being said. But neither pole can claim priority, and neither can be reduced to its opposite. Criticism therefore should be especially aware of its mediating function, discovering at once through the struggle for clarity the need for affective engagement that precludes clarity, and how through such a dialectic the complex symbolic narrative of history and culture develops. Today (as Geoffrey Hartman among others proclaims), criticism is likely to foreground its own metaphoricity, yet criticism is usurped from within if interpretive clarity yields excessively to rhetorical indirection. Rather, the distinction and progressive tension between images and ideas as well as their interdependence is the very subject of critical enquiry as cultural hermeneusis, and remains a fruitful approach to culture as a dialectic of presence and absence, bodies and language, within which persons might seek a degree of liberation without distorting some necessary part of what it means, in the first place, to be a person.

Renaissance literature is especially interesting in this context, because during that period, and especially with the Scientific Revolution, strong attacks were mounted on metaphor and on literary imagery generally, in the name of conceptual thinking conducted with mathematical rigour. At the same time, old authoritarian ideas were being challenged by Renaissance Humanists in the name of an expanded imaginative vision. The terms of this debate have a strikingly modern ring, and the tale is cautionary.

As is generally known, during the Renaissance a strong English empirical tradition in philosophy, extending from Bacon through Hobbes to Locke, insisted so firmly on the exact description of things that it held imagination gravely in suspicion as a distorter of clear knowledge. It is less well understood how the transmission of European Humanism into England contributed to this new philosophical climate, and to the crisis of confidence that still marks the course of modern culture, having to do with the separation of science and metaphysics, and with the uncertain cognitive status of images in relation to ideas.

Italian Humanism [57] is especially associated with Marsilio Ficino (1433–99) founder of the Platonic Academy in Florence, and with his mercurial disciple, Pico della Mirandola (1463–94), who challenged the learned world with his 900 theses and *Oration on the Dignity of Man* (1486). The *Oration* is a soaring display, full of a sense of impassioned discovery and aspiration to master all knowledge. Indeed, Pico comes close to suggesting that he had already done just that: 'I have ranged through all the masters of philosophy, investigated all books, and come to know all schools.' [58] Consequently, he proposes a synthesis of the best and highest of human wisdom, and sets his sights on bringing 'into the open the miracles concealed in the recesses of the world . . . even so does the *magus* wed earth to heaven, that is, he weds lower things to the endowments and powers of higher things' (249).

Pico felt that the ancient philosophers, with whose names he so lovingly and showily studs his *Oration*, harboured a secret wisdom now made available through the free play and synthesising imaginative designs of the thinkers of a new age, such as himself. Here is the famous passage in which he describes God's first address to humanity:

The nature of all other beings is limited and constrained within the bounds of laws prescribed by Us. Thou, constrained by no limits, in accordance with thine own free will, in whose hand We have placed thee, shalt ordain for thyself the limits of thy nature. We have set thee at the world's center that thou mayest from thence more easily observe whatever is in the world. We have made thee neither of heaven nor of earth, neither mortal nor immortal, so that with freedom of choice and with honor, as though the maker and molder of thyself, thou mayest fashion thyself in whatever shape thou shalt prefer. Thou shalt have the power to degenerate into the lower forms of life, which are brutish. Thou shalt have the power, out of thy soul's judgement, to be reborn into the higher forms, which are divine. (225)

Alone among the hierarchies, among the specifically formed and determined degrees of angels, animals, and vegetative life, the human being is a 'chameleon', a 'self-transforming nature' free to make of itself what it wishes, a glorious lord of creation, a 'Proteus' in whom lie the 'germs of every way of life' (225) to be cultivated and brought to maturity according to its own pleasure. This extraordinary picture of the human as self-creating rather than as the interpreter of an already ordained scheme of things, as synthesiser and pattern-maker rather than analyst and classifier, has the effect of re-casting established ideas in the mould of an imaginative, creative play.

It is clear that the Spanish Humanist Juan Luis Vives had read Pico's *Oration*.[59] We can see this from his little treatise *A Fable About Man* (Louvain, 1518), which takes over the central conception of the human creature's ability to choose a place in the hierarchies and even to become Godlike. Vives describes how Jupiter entertains the other Gods by creating the world as a stage on which the master-player is man. Although man has something in him of Jupiter's own immortality, he wears a mask of flesh to play his part which, as in Pico, is undetermined and open to free-ranging, imaginative interpretation. At the height of his power, man is free even to transform himself into Jupiter's nature, and is able to act almost as his own providence:

From religion and memory, foreknowledge is almost obtained, with the prophecy of the future, evidently a spark of that divine and immense science which perceives all future events as if they were present.[60]

The spirit of Pico's Florentine Humanism thus passes into Vives' *Fable*,[61] unmodified except for the depiction of man as the master-player at a game of perpetual, imaginatively free making-up.

Vives' treatise *Against the Pseudodialecticians*[62] is also relevant here because it shows how well he knew the philosophical consequences of such a depiction of imaginative freedom. As is clear even in the brief passages already cited, Vives, like Pico, relies heavily on rhetoric rather than logic – on images rather than ideas – to communicate a sense of what distinctively constitutes the human. Both authors assume that attempts to classify the place of human beings in nature has led merely to logic chopping, which is what Vives means by 'Pseudodialecticians'. Human freedom within the cosmic hierarchies is thus analogous to freedom from certain scholastic habits of mind attempting to construct a systematic, clear order of ideas and subjects for human thought to explore. According to Vives, such academic systems are not just misguided, but perverse, and he scoffs at their inflexible arbitrariness and garrulous ignorance disguised as 'new feats of verbal legerdemain' (56–9). In short, too intricate a pursuit of the exact definition soon leads to abstract confusions which become especially misleading and destructive when applied, for instance, to the basic truths of faith:

> although the Nicene Creed and the consensus of the whole Church deny that there is more than one God . . . these men still, in their invincible disputations, strenuously maintain that there are three Gods, three uncreated, omnipotent, external, and immense creators, and this over loud protests of all the Church Fathers and the resistance of Christian piety, and in spite of all the angels and of God Himself, while the very devils wonder at their impudent temerity. (83)

Vives is deft here in defending his orthodoxy: academics, he maintains, constitute the real threat to plain, old-fashioned truth because they are so over-developed technically, and so proud of their expertise that they refuse the general consensus. The new Humanism is thus presented as wanting basically to return to old-fashioned orthodoxy, but, as we shall see, as with other Humanists, Vives' appeal to consensus and common sense is a stalking horse that conceals a more radical assault on received authority in the name of imaginative freedom.

These brief observations can serve to suggest a series of strong tendencies characteristic of Humanism's attitude to literary language, which can be summarised as follows:

1. an optimistic conviction about the creative power of human imagination and will.
2. rhetorical persuasion of the reader, the important thing being to awaken a change of attitude.
3. an attack on obscurantist jargon which would divide and classify human action, rather than affirm its synthesising, creative freedom.
4. a persuasion that common sense and usage tell us enough about language for us to behave morally; demands for too much consistency lead only to undesirable deviations from well-tried truths, the *consensus gentium*.

These tendencies are all clear in Vives' *Against the Pseudodialecticians*, and yet we ought to notice how, in some respects, his arguments are unsatisfactory. For instance, his general case against philosophy is that of any person of bluff but narrow common sense against any kind of specialist vocabulary. In our own day, mathematicians often do not understand learned papers by one another, and most of us do not understand the working vocabularies of our medical doctors. Yet we would not be without our mathematicians and doctors, despite what appears to be their obscurantism. Besides, the Humanists themselves were far from being as populist as they suggest, for they were an elite international club of Latin-speaking specialists who spent a great deal of time writing congratulatory notices to one another. Finally, Vives' confident suggestion that we should be content with the plain sense of the Nicene Creed stands in uneasy relationship to his own teachings stressing the flexibility of language. On the one hand, then, we cannot follow Vives' main argument all the way without abjuring exact definitions; on the other, exact definitions constitute the 'consensus' on which Vives himself relies. I shall return to this point by and by.

Meanwhile, let us turn briefly to Erasmus' *Praise of Folly*,[63] for its famous irony and fun are intimated by Vives' arguments against the pseudodialecticians. Basically, the *Praise of Folly* is an extended pronouncement, or *declamatio*, by Folly herself: she shows us how full the world is of her devotees, and how she is necessary to make the world go round. What could be more foolish, after all, than the process of human generation: 'So if you owe your existence to wedlock, you owe the fact of wedlock to madness.' 'Thus,' Folly continues, 'from that amusement of mine, drunken and absurd as it is, spring haughty philosophers and their present-day successors who are popularly called monks, kings in their purple, pious priests and thrice-holy pontiffs' (76–7). Without Folly, there would be no human world at all, a fact that makes human pretension all the more amusing, all the more foolish. The touch here is playful, and yet the comedy swiftly veers into satire as monks, kings, priests and pontiffs are revealed as Folly's malicious, inadvertent worshippers, prey to their own vanity and duped, mainly, by taking themselves too seriously. But the satire is then itself refracted when we recall it is Folly who speaks, and so we must not heed a word that she says. Under the multiple refractions of such irony, Erasmus protects himself from accusations of irreverence, and indeed Folly sees life as a play wherein we do best if we assume many masks:

> To destroy the illusion is to ruin the whole play, for it's really the characterization and make-up which hold the audience's eye. Now, what else is the whole life of man but a sort of play? Actors come on wearing their different masks and all play their parts until the producer orders them off the stage, and he can often tell the same man to appear in different costume, so that now he plays a king in purple and now a humble slave in rags. It's all a sort of pretence, but it's the only way to act out this farce. (104)

Join in, participate in the illusion, the metaphoric indirections, and accept the nonsense, for 'this is the way to play the comedy of life' (105). The metaphor of theatrical disguise and the emphasis on performance help to confirm how imaginative language best teaches Folly's lesson that a clever exhibition is the most important thing. Even so, the concluding section of her declamation is not at all frivolous in recommending Christ's 'divine foolishness' as a means of leading us away from worldliness towards 'the supreme mind which alone they call the *summum bonum*' (204). In the world's eyes, this 'transformation' may be foolish indeed, but it is also wisdom. And it is the same transformation of the synthesising, imaginatively free-ranging mind into God as is described in Pico's *Oration* and Vives' *Fable*.

At this point it is worth mentioning a difficulty noticed frequently by readers of the *Praise of Folly*, arising from the fact that Erasmus does not consistently succeed in masking his own moralising intent when Folly speaks, so that the wit and irony spill over into straightforward social commentary. I do not wish to dwell on this issue, other than to say how it makes clear that, despite Folly's insistence on the imaginary and illusory, Erasmus himself remains a conventional moralist. He is free to take such lighthearted, elegant pleasure in Folly, precisely because he believes something clear and certain. For practical purposes he was prepared to admit a consensus[64] that he called the 'philosophia Christi', a kind of openness to the plain teachings of Christ in the spirit of shared, common truth.[65] No less than Vives, Erasmus singles out the hidebound, pedantic logicians for distorting these generally-accepted Christian truths by obscurantist games, elitist institutions and sterile word-mongering.[66] Indeed, for Erasmus, word-mongering, power-mongering, and war-mongering are closely allied. The vested interests of the ruling elite, he held, are protected by an obscurantism enabling the free exercise of power, which leads inevitably to war.[67] Erasmus therefore holds that the destruction of Christendom (guaranteed by protracted war) would be a consequence of abused language, and he did not hesitate to lay this charge squarely at the door of philosophers who refused to acknowledge the primacy of rhetoric and *bonae litterae* for a humane education.[68]

It follows that, despite the emphasis on imaginative transformation and on the free play of metaphor, improvised meaning and corrective wit, imagination for Erasmus preserves a fairly strict cognitive function within the objective order of 'Christendom'. His attacks on the logicians, equating their abstract language with elitism and then with violence, do warn us effectively against one possible distortion of learning, and insofar as Erasmus shows how imagination humanises by teaching us to avoid extremes of conceptual rigour, we can be thankful. But, as with Vives, Erasmus' method is less than thoroughgoing, for he still assumes the basic ideas and definitions of an ancient faith as the very bastion of a corporate and public truth to which he is devoted. It seems that however firmly imagination insists upon freedom (the play of metaphor), it does not achieve the kind of humanising effect Erasmus desires if it is entirely divorced from the ideas (or literal sense) that an adequate abstract language provides. The *Praise of Folly* offers little explicit awareness that this is the case. But into the elegant fretwork building of Erasmian wit and imagination, Martin Luther brought a flaming torch.

Luther, quite simply, insisted upon a rigorous interpretation of the critical issue which Erasmus, like Vives and many Humanists, was content to fudge: if words, the mirror of human intelligence, are indeed metaphoric, illusory and fickle, we cannot discover through them any reliable body of authority, or any objective hierarchy serving as a ladder for our creative spirits to mount towards God. Why, Luther might ask, should Pico's vision of a stable chain of being not be yet another fiction of the free-ranging imagination he extols? Reason is a whore, Luther roughly concludes – seductive, unreliable, exploitable. Our will is not free to effect any self-transformation into God, and Christ is in us by a gift of grace, unmediated by any design of human reason, intent, or *tour de force* of imagination.

Quite correctly, Erasmus was accused of having encouraged the Lutheran reform (he was said to have laid the egg that Luther hatched),[69] but when forced to take sides, he could not follow Luther all the way. The two men exchanged treatises defining their central differences, and the subject they chose was, significantly, free will.[70] In affirming it, Erasmus held to his allegiance with traditional Humanism, but the break with Luther distressed him profoundly, for the movements of reform and counter-reform now turned violent, and the war-mongering, bigotry and hatred which Erasmus all his life opposed, seemed somehow to have sprung up from the centre of his own best efforts to defend against them. Christendom had indeed fragmented from within, and the Humanist ship of fools, so gaily decked with wit, ingenuity, and imagination, was forced to weigh anchor, to cast off from the old cognitive anchorage of commonly-received ideas, to venture into strange seas, driven before the winds of mere unregenerate will, among the treacherous currents of a profane world.

It is highly likely that Shakespeare knew something both of Erasmus and Vives, if only because their writings were used as school text books. Certainly, the example of an Erasmian wise foolishness seems clear in *King Lear*, and traces of Vives' *Satellitum animae* have been located in *Hamlet* and elsewhere.[71] We might recall too that Erasmus' *Praise of Folly* was written for Thomas More, whose *History of King Richard the Third* is the source of Shakespeare's play on the same subject. Also, More wrote a defence of the *Praise of Folly*, and in a letter commends Vives' *Against the Pseudodialecticians* for having constructed an argument exactly in the spirit of his own defence of Erasmus.[72] It is of interest too that an early work of More's is entitled *The Life of Picus, Earl of Mirandula*, and in the web of such connections between texts, we can observe something of the transmission of Humanism into Shakespeare's England.

I will not speculate further about details of Shakespeare's Humanist affiliations, but rather talk briefly about *Hamlet* in the context of my remarks about Erasmian Humanism and Lutheran reform, and how these pertain to the dialectic of images and ideas. For if *Hamlet* is a Humanist document at all, it has the disturbed, saturnine caste of a late Humanism tainted by disappointment and unsure of its bearings, not least because of an unsettling sense of the dizzying gap between imagination and ideas, or the metaphoric and literal senses, precipitated by late developments within the movement itself, and which we see also reflected in the Reformation. Pre-eminently, Hamlet's imagination cannot find anchorage in commonly-received ideas at all, and its freedom is vertiginous, sickening and tragic, underming his own sense of identity as well as his personal relations with others.

It is as if Shakespeare created Hamlet in part to celebrate the free play of figurative language as Vives described it. Certainly, Hamlet's main advantage is his ability to see more in words, and do more with them than his interlocutors, who are slow and shallow compared to him. They take refuge in the general and conventional, while he has a thrilling, lively sense of language as metaphor, in all its wild peculiarity and bizarre impingements upon experience, so that imagination becomes a way of disarming and of dismaying his adversaries.

Typically, Hamlet sees the abstract as an evasion, so that his own penetrating irony and surprising metaphors become tokens for him of authenticity. Here, for instance, is Claudius early in the play giving the young Prince advice on mourning the death of his father, Hamlet senior:[73]

> Though yet of Hamlet our dear brother's death
> The memory be green, and that it us befitted
> To bear our hearts in grief, and our whole kingdom
> To be contracted in one brow of woe,
> Yet so far hath discretion fought with nature
> That we with wisest sorrow think on him
> Together with remembrance of ourselves.

> Therefore our sometime sister, now our queen,
> Th' imperial jointress to this warlike state,
> Have we, are 'twere, with a defeated joy,
> With an auspicious and a dropping eye,
> With mirth in funeral, and with dirge in marriage,
> In equal scale weighing delight and dole,
> Taken to wife.
>
>   (I,ii,1–14)

And a little later:

> Tis sweet and commendable in your nature, Hamlet,
> To give these mourning duties to your father,
> But you must know your father lost a father,
> That father lost, lost his
>
>   (I,ii,87–90)

Consequently, Claudius argues, too much grief is unnatural:

> Fie, 'tis a fault to heaven,
> A fault against the dead, a fault to nature,
> To reason most absurd, whose common theme
> Is death of fathers.
>
>   (I,ii,101–4)

Claudius' speech is full of balance and reserve. It is formal, well-turned, and largely conventional. It also gives the impression of cool deduction, and the particles binding it together suggest logical sequence: 'Though yet', 'yet', 'That we', 'Therefore'. Moreover, the advice against excessive mourning makes good sense: everybody has a father, and to survive your father is in the normal course of events. Ironically, Claudius is quite right, even though as a murderer and usurper he is wrong. And yet his ideas are glib, and the more so because so confidently formal, wearing the garb of received authority and proceeding through a series of public consolations and easy deductions.

Hamlet of course sees through Claudius in a flash, and detests him for assuming the veneer of such trite sententiousness. Consequently, when Gertrude comes in on Claudius' side and asks her son reprovingly, 'Why seems it so particular with thee', Hamlet turns on her:

Seems, madam? Nay, it is. I know not 'seems'.
Tis not alone my inky cloak, good mother,
Nor customary suits of solemn black,
Nor windy suspiration of forced breath,
No, nor the fruitful river in the eye,
Nor the dejected havior of the visage,
Together with all forms, moods, shapes of grief,
That can denote me truly. These indeed seem,
For they are actions that a man might play,
But I have that within which passes show;
These but the trappings and the suits of woe.
(I,ii,76–86)

Hamlet picks almost manically on the word 'seems', for 'seeming' and reality are incommensurate, and he is especially intolerant of the kind of hypocrisy that settles for a 'seemly' show of rehearsed ideas, such as we have just been given by Claudius. Hamlet is even consistent enough to know that for authenticity's sake he must turn his argument against himself: his 'inky cloak', tears, sighs, and so on are superficial, mere conventional hints, imperfect signs of grief, and he does not want Gertrude to be mistaken: these things too only 'seem'; they are 'actions that a man might play'. He draws here on the language of the stage: human behaviour, he implies, is a kind of drama, a mask of words and deeds, of ingenuity, metaphor and imagination by which we endlessly defer and conceal the truth. But it is essential also to notice that Hamlet is not so stand-offish as to refuse to play the game: after all, he stages a play to catch the conscience of the king, and he plays at madness, though it may well be that he becomes mad in doing so, and he plays at swordplay at the end, and at elaborate verbal games throughout. Far from refusing society's game, Hamlet plays it much *more* ferociously, elaborately, ingeniously, than all the others, so that he ends up turning the game itself inside out. The critical cliché depicting him as a malcontent brooding on the edges of society is therefore too simple: he is much more threatening as the enemy within, a fact clearly enough realised by Claudius when he packs Hamlet off in a hurry to England with Rosencrantz and Guildenstern.

Hamlet's speech to his mother is thus turned against himself as a token of uncompromising truthfulness. But Hamlet's truth has here broken loose from the consensus, for it is intolerant of the merely conventional. It is as if the logic of Folly's perpetual parade

of masks is pushed to the limit, for if language is a performance, a
false front, a metaphoric illusion, it can never come to rest securely
on any general statement, any idea which another might share.

Shakespeare's play, we can now surmise, resembles Erasmus'
Praise of Folly insofar as hidebound authoritarian formalities are
subjected to scrutiny in both works by a witty deployment of irony,
paradox, and a play of masks. And yet the fact that *Hamlet* was
written after the Reformation reflects everywhere in a certain weight
upon the wit and brilliance, imposed by the kind of question Luther
asked, and which Erasmus fudged: on what public consensus can
we rely if the relationship between language and reality, images and
ideas is, indeed, perpetually elusive? Hamlet, as we see, is plagued
by this problem, and his departure from the mood of such Humanists as Pico, Vives and Erasmus on the self-transforming potential
of the human being and his godlike, imaginative power to scale the
heavens, is caught in the speech to Rosencrantz and Guildenstern
where Hamlet gives his version of the cosmic scheme:

> I will tell you why; so shall my anticipation prevent your dis-
> covery, and your secrecy to the king and queen molt no feather.
> I have of late, but wherefore I know not, lost all my mirth,
> forgone all custom of exercises; and indeed, it goes so heavily
> with my disposition that this goodly frame, the earth, seems
> to me a sterile promontory; this most excellent canopy, the air,
> look you, this brave o'erhanging firmament, this majestical roof
> fretted with golden fire: why, it appeareth nothing to me but a
> foul and pestilent congregation of vapors. What a piece of work
> is a man, how noble in reason, how infinite in faculties, in form
> and moving how express and admirable, in action how like an
> angel, in apprehension how like a god: the beauty of the world,
> the paragon of animals; and yet to me, what is this quintessence of
> dust? Man delights not me; nor woman neither, though by your
> smiling you seem to say so. (II,ii,301–18)

At face value, Hamlet lets them know that he has become malcontent and cynical, out of step with the world. He can no longer take
pleasure in the 'goodly frame', and the spiritual potential of man
('how like an angel') means nothing to him. The idea of God's
great design is all very admirable, but if man is free within it,
he is free to be a misfit, to turn his back on it all, and Hamlet
claims to have done just that. The angel is diseased, and likes it.

And yet we cannot take his speech at face value, for Hamlet here is playing with Rosencrantz and Guildenstern, as he does throughout. His words have a tone of mock bonhomie ('Listen, and I'll tell you what they are really thinking of me') and are touched with contemptuous raillery. The conventional cosmic picture itself is too ornate, too frivolously overdrawn ('excellent canopy', 'the air, look you', 'fretted with golden fire', 'What a piece of work is a man', and so on). Just so, his own disaffection is touched with an exaggerated posturing which mocks at those who would depict him thus ('Why, it appeareth nothing to me . . . '). Hamlet in all this makes it hard for Rosencrantz and Guildenstern to know how to take him, and the pose of complicity among old friends is really the vehicle for ironic wariness opening upon an endless series of refractions. Indeed, a good deal of what he tells them about his malcontent disposition is true, but he is so conscious of conventional description that he undercuts it continually, holding it at ironic distance. Hamlet is not merely disenchanted with man the great wonder set free to transform himself within the scale of nature: the whole concept of a scale of nature itself is treated as just another metaphor, another mask for the hypocrites to hide behind, another false image posing as a true idea. And Hamlet isn't falling for any of it.

We recall that Pico thought man free to shape his destiny and to aspire to know God, whose providence has ordained man's unique status among creatures. Vives' *Fable* also declares man almost a providence unto himself, and extols man's ability to participate in the divine nature. Likewise, Erasmus recommends a kind of divine foolishness which leads to mystical union. In each case, a soaring declaration about human freedom is held on the rails, as it were, of an objective order, providentially designed and revealed as reasonable and acceptable to common sense (the scale of nature, the literal meaning of the creeds, the consensus of Christendom). Alone among these examples, Hamlet takes to its end term the suggestion that man might indeed act as his own providence, and if that is so, he of course does not really need an objectively created, guiding design.

The standard philosophical model of a tragic fall inherited by the Renaissance from the Middle Ages, was Boethius' *Consolation of Philosophy*. The rise and fall of a king was held to follow the course, described by Boethius, of a rise and fall on Fortune's wheel, which represents time and which turns continually. By contrast, at the centre of the wheel is the still point of eternity, which cannot be described in terms of time, and is the seat of providence. The usurping king who takes his chance and rides to glory on the wheel therefore places himself in Fortune's hands, and is always deceived, always let down.

As Maynard Mack[74] points out, *Hamlet* is based on this model, but with the crucial difference that, by a characteristic stroke of genius, Shakespeare applies the Boethian scheme in reverse. Hamlet does not ride on Fortune's wheel; Claudius does that, and, by contrast, Hamlet vilifies Fortune at every opportunity. Hamlet, however, makes the opposite error of usurping providence; of wanting, as it were, to play God, to stand outside history, untouched by its contradictions. Thus he decides not to stab Claudius at prayer, for it would be better to kill him in some more compromising situation, so that his soul would burn in hell. Thus Hamlet toys with suicide and tells Ophelia it would be better if she did not have children, and despite the ghost's warning him to leave Gertrude's soul to heaven, he does not. Thus he tends to diagnose the entire world's sickness, and to feel it, somehow, his own responsibility. Not surprisingly, he is overwhelmed by the burden of all this, and only at the end of the play, with death almost upon him, does he realise, 'There's a divinity that shapes our ends, / Rough-hew them how we will' (V,ii,10–11); 'There is a special providence in the fall of a sparrow' (V,ii,221).

I have now come close to saying that Hamlet's usurpation of providence and evasion of his own historicity is one consequence of his attitude to language, and to the relationship (or disrelationship) between metaphor and commonly accepted literal sense – that is, between images and ideas. Hamlet regards language as a set of satiric and ironic devices, of masks for expressing the force of a desire imaginatively, and within which the individual is free to move, transforming whatever resists him into a vehicle for his own will. But if this is so, there are no public certainties, no reliable ideas, but only the shaping force of individual aspiration, and a wilderness of coruscating, undependable meanings. Yet Shakespeare's special distinction is to record not only the sense of brilliant liberation in Hamlet's use of imaginative language, but also the personal derangement that follows upon the ensuing usurpation of the idea of nature's objective order. Shakespeare does not recommend going back to the simpler confidence of Pico, for he displays his hero's sceptical energy altogether too vigorously and sympathetically. But he also shows how self-defeating is a free-ranging imagination that refuses the contamination of publicly-accepted ideas. A world constituted merely of masks within masks, of play and counterplay, of seeming and appearance, ultimately stultifies purposeful action, and public meaning itself.[75] Within such a world, the human person disintegrates. Shakespeare's own imagination thus differs from Hamlet's in that Shakespeare grasps and expresses this truth, while Hamlet suffers it.

It is important, then, not to deny to imagination some relationship to the world that we investigate also by the kind of thinking that seeks for exactness, clarity and shared understanding. Criticism especially adjudicates this continuing interaction and dialectic between images and ideas and their relation to the world, not by reducing either pole to the other, but by maintaining the dialectic itself, the better to make it understood. Like literature, criticism is historically situated and shares in its fashion the struggle of imagination to awaken thinking to the simultaneous adherence to the world and distance from it, characteristic of our condition as persons. As I suggested in the first section of this chapter, imagination implies a degree of autonomy for the person as agent; yet, as I argued in the second section, imagination is marked also by hesitation and ambivalence. Through this shadow-drama of presence and absence, the truth of how things are can be glimpsed or recognised as convincing or plausible, but not as an absolute knowledge where concept and metaphor, word and body, are reconciled. Finally, I would like to suggest in this section that our alienations from one another and from the world are reproduced perennially by the gap between images and ideas. With this in mind, a modern approach to imagination needs to go on attempting to balance the uncertain identity and contingency of persons with their capacity for purposeful rationality, and surprising innovation.

5

Religious Promises

APOCALYPSE NOW

The Enlightenment offered a critique of religion that by and large affords to modern Western people the freedom of religious unbelief. This great good counteracts a general proclivity of religion to superstition and tyranny, and yet religious questions are of perennial concern to human beings and are a natural consequence of how human language enables us to frame questions about ultimate meaning and value: What is the purpose of life? What is our best hope? What is the meaning of suffering? Religion might even be thought of as the pre-eminent means whereby people describe their aspiration to ultimate meaning and purpose. Religious language is therefore especially a language of promises, and the possibility of a religious view of the world and of human destiny is an ineradicable consequence of our condition as persons in history.

Promises, however, carry a liability, and by failing to respect the relationship between promise and history, the world's religions have contributed greatly to suffering: tyrannical deities all too readily sanction tyrannical devotees worshipping their own desire for power projected onto a heavenly Father whose imagined will becomes their own. How sublime a submission. Voltaire's '*écrasez l'infame*' rang across Europe to protest against just such manipulations of fear and ignorance by the vested interests of the religious, and a century later Nietzsche lamented caustically that there was not even enough religion left in the world to destroy the world's religions. This secular critique promoting modern scepticism and secularism must either at last help to bring religion home to itself in the task of redeeming humanity and humanising nature, or help us to dispense with religion altogether.

My main comments in this chapter are directed from such a perspective especially to Judæo-Christian tradition, not only because it

144

expresses the main religious aspirations of Western literature and culture, and in so doing contributes to the idea of the person developed by that culture, but also because it received the full attention of the Enlightenment critique which, in a way, it produced from within itself.[1] Christianity is therefore especially pertinent to a discussion of how religious and secular languages might act co-operatively in negotiating the opacities of symbol and reflection towards a renewed humanity in a transformed world, the omega-point of eschatological promise. In Christianity, this final hope is addressed especially by means of the visionary genre of apocalypse.

Jürgen Moltmann tells us that the idea of history in apocalyptic writing was invented by the Hebrew prophets.[2] This is so, he says, because of the emphasis throughout the Hebrew scriptures on God's promise: God will show the way, bringing the exodus community home. Originally, for a nomadic people, being called out of a settled place was normal. Even when Israel settled in Canaan, its rituals maintained a powerful sense of the faith and hope required to follow a God who promised to lead his people through present crises towards a better future. The main sense here is not of a cyclically-ordered cosmos within which human culture has a place, but of a unique course of events, the story of a people's dislocation and wandering cast upon a unique trajectory through time.

After the division of the kingdom and the Babylonian captivity, Israel's prophetic message was developed in a more specifically religious and less nationalistic manner. The captive exodus community now especially must continue in faith and obedience to the covenant until Yahweh shows them a better future, and the message at this point opens up to the nations. Even the dead now might find their place in God's final disclosure.[3] As Moltmann tells us, prophetic eschatology gave voice to this message, and is linked in intricate, vexing ways to the kindred genre of apocalypse.

One way of explaining the differences between these genres is suggested by Adela Yarbro Collins,[4] who points to the prevalence in apocalypses of an ancient Near Eastern combat myth describing how monsters of the watery chaos are overcome by a divine warrior, and how the world is thereby formed. This cosmic myth becomes a way of interpreting recent history to show how God's final judgement is in the making through struggle and conflict. Apocalypses thus provide a cosmic interpretation of eschatological promises, and part of the strange, cryptic quality of apocalyptic writing comes from the interpenetration of these themes. Thus, apocalypses typically deal with expectations of cosmic catastrophe and renewal, while evoking a sense of imminence and tending strongly to a dualism whereby the forces of good and evil are pitted against one another. By contrast, the prophetic and eschatological tradition is less dualistic and communicates a fuller sense of Israel's immersion in history through which God's judgements are mediated in response to Israel's obedience. The Book of Daniel is the key biblical example of how prophetic eschatology opens up towards apocalyptic vision.[5]

Jesus can be seen in such a context as an eschatological prophet with strong apocalyptic leanings, and it is likely that Christianity arose as an apocalyptic sect within Judaism.[6] At the beginning of this century, Albert Schweitzer's famous *Quest of the Historical Jesus*[7] isolated eschatology as the key to Christianity, though Schweitzer concluded that Jesus was wrong about the imminent second coming, and that Christian hope is therefore unfounded. Yet, as modern commentators point out, the very contradiction between hope and present reality can itself be interpreted as a *via crucis* to be followed by the church through history. Jesus promises the kingdom not only in his parables but also in his insistence that the future is somehow present in his historical person: 'I and the Father are one' (John 10:30), he says, breathtakingly. In short, the kingdom is already present in those who recognise Jesus' significance, but is not yet come in its fullness as a cosmic event gathering in the nations. This fruitful tension between 'realised eschatology' and 'consistent eschatology' is sustained only if neither pole is surrendered and the paradox is accepted as it stands: the kingdom is really present, but is also to come. The interplay here between presence and absence, uttered by Jesus the human individual, reminds us how a religious evaluation of the world remains personal. And because religion is bound up with our historicity, its proclamations about belonging must encounter the challenge of the Flaw, the problem of suffering. Just so, the apocalyptic Son of Man will be crucified, confounded and humiliated by the world, and suffering is inevitably a condition of Christian hope, if only because hope always reveals present impediments to its realisation, the 'negative contrast' (as Schillebeeckx says) marking every historical present.[8] Religious language or religious promises that do not in some material fashion engage the negative contrast linking them to culture at large are at best escapist or decorative.

At this point it might be useful to notice how elusive are the gospels on exactly what happened at the resurrection, the event chiefly signifying the inaugurated, present Kingdom embodied in the person of Jesus. Whereas in all four gospels the passion narratives are quite definite and consistent, the resurrection stories are varied and perplexing. Significantly, none of them describes Jesus actually coming out of the tomb, thus discouraging us from identifying the resurrected Jesus simply with a revivified corpse.[9] And yet we are required to believe that whatever elusive mystery occurred at the resurrection did indeed happen to the historical Jesus. The perplexing accounts of his appearances thus confound our imagination, but in so doing they contrive to prevent us from relinquishing hope in the future or commitment to the present: we are claimed, that is, at once by the reality of suffering and by the vision of suffering overcome.

These concerns are central to the New Testament's eschatological emphasis, and are reflected in all its main elements: in the parables and the Sermon on the Mount, the Lord's prayer and the collection of sayings designated as Q, the discourses on the kingdom, the passion and resurrection stories, the so-called 'little apocalypse' of Mark 13 and its parallels (Matt. 24, Lk. 21), as well as in the Book of Revelation and Paul's letters.[10] Here and elsewhere Jesus tells us that the kingdom is revealed in his own person. Yet this revelation is itself a promise: he will come again and he is the future we desire as we carry the cross of the present. Indeed, the vitality of this hope and the faith underpinning it we might say are already Christ's presence, a real earnest of that to which history tends – the resurrection of the dead, a humanising of the person and of nature together. Thus, at the heart of Christianity the dialectic 'is and not-yet' assumes, once more, a central position. It is deeply ingrained in the way the New Testament is written, as it is in the culture that flowers under its influence.

With this in mind, I would like to look briefly at Revelation, the New Testament's example of a full-blown apocalypse. It is a strange, anomalous book, and makes an uncomfortable contrast to the Gospels: the impersonal avenging lamb, rampaging monsters and images of impenetrable hardness (stones, glass, jewels) are difficult to reconcile with the vulnerable and merciful Jesus.[11] And yet, Revelation confirms what the New Testament is all about, for, as Moltmann says, 'From first to last, and not merely in the epilogue, Christianity is eschatology',[12] and, as Schillebeeckx points out, Jesus' death remains the central fact that gives Revelation its historical foundation. The sacrifice of the lamb is mentioned repeatedly, and we are assured that martyrdom is not defeat, despite appearances to the contrary, for if the layers of manifestation were peeled back to reveal the true dynamism of history, martyrdom would appear in its true light as a victory blow for Christ.[13] In some such sense, Revelation encourages Christian martyrs in times of duress, and also (as is now increasingly suggested) counteracts complacency.[14] At any rate, as in the gospels, so also throughout Revelation we are recalled to the cross at the very moment of anticipating a promised future free from suffering.

Revelation and the resurrection stories thus have in common an intuition that the future is implicit in what is already present, and full disclosure of the promise will combine surprise and recognition. All of this duplicates in the mode of religious discourse our condition as persons immersed in language and seeking reconciliation with one another and with the world. Indeed, Revelation is highly conscious of the perplexities of people seeking through language for absolute certainty. Thus we are assured that Christ's real name is not known now, but will be disclosed at the *parousia* (3:12; 19:12), and the church in Philadelphia is told, 'I will write upon him my new name' (3:12), even though this name, as we learn later, 'no man knew, but he himself' (19:12). A good deal about names and naming throughout Revelation is connected in turn to this underlying idea that names fall short of the truth even though they give an earnest of it. In short, the reality we imperfectly call Christ is at once the crucified one and the resurrected messiah of our promised future.

The confusion and certainty produced by this combination of presence and absence mirror exactly our condition as persons called to the risks of evaluation and commitment. Such a condition is duplicated further in the various suggestions of design and structure throughout Revelation that, in the end, fail to come clear. As Austin Ferrar says, 'we are left unable to reconcile ourselves either to the hypothesis of formal order or to the hypothesis of its absence'.[15] For instance, it is easy to notice a fourfold pattern of seven: there are seven letters, seven seals, seven trumpets, and seven vials. Taken together, these describe a progress towards the lamb's triumph and the millennial rule of the saints. A conspicuous numerology and counterpointing of the powers of Babylon and Jerusalem, combined with further patterns of four (beasts, horsemen, elements), also indicate deliberate design. Yet the book as a whole is so densely-textured and wildly imagined that extending these indications to contain the avalanche of kaleidoscopic effects soon produces a theory so attenuated by complex adaptation that it ceases – almost – to be a theory at all. Improvised monsters, bewildering visions, fierce impersonality, cataracts of blood and pestilence, the daunting concept of a wrathful lamb, spectacles of monstrous armies, plague-afflicted nature and aerobic orchestrations of angels make for an originality as fascinating as it is strange and alien. The very abundance of such pictorial detail so overwhelms attempts at discovering a containing structure that our frustration even becomes part of the point.[16]

For instance, the number seven indicates completeness (as in seven days of the week), and the letters to the seven churches suggest that the Holy Spirit has a plan. Yet in the letters-section the anomalous figure with the 'sharp two-edged sword' coming out of his mouth issues repeated, dire warnings of unexpected intervention ('I will come on thee as a thief' [3:3]), so that the suggestions about design are undermined even as they are uttered.[17] If the spirit has a plan, we are assured that it will take us by surprise.

Again, in the section on the seven seals there is a pause after the sixth, during which destruction is held back and the children of Israel are sealed on their foreheads. At first, this reads like a respite preceding and therefore emphasising the climactic seventh, but when the seventh seal is at last opened, the effect is conspicuously anti-climactic (there is silence in heaven as an angel offers incense upon the altar) and serves merely as an introduction to the new sevenfold series of trumpets.

Again in the trumpet section, six are sounded to introduce the plagues and scourges, but in place of the seventh comes a series of 'seven thunders' (10:3) and John is mysteriously told not to describe them. There follows a further delay (the prophecy of the two witnesses) and at last when the seventh trumpet is sounded it announces a heavenly liturgy, followed by the section on the woman clothed with the sun. Once more, intimations of closure are disrupted and taken up into a further, unexpected set of events.

The last group of seven plagues seems an exception because they do make a complete list. Yet the sixth angel warns us against complacency ('Behold, I come as a thief. Blessed is he that watcheth' [16:15]), and at the end of this brief section an angel returns to deliver judgement against Babylon which, we come uncomfortably to realise, is the earthly city in which we dwell. Our own abominations are thus the target of the plagues about which we read objectively, as if they are part of a plan that does not involve us directly.

There are endless such puzzles and asymmetries throughout the book, and much commentary is taken up with pursuing intimations of design (the analogue of God's plan) into the labyrinth of episodes and panoplies of strange, dazzling imagery. But the design-seekers inevitably end up re-absorbed by the complexities, and I would like to connect this effect to Revelation's preoccupation with naming – that is, with the ambivalence of language.

As we have seen, Christ is not the messiah's real name, and his various titles are stumbling attempts to grasp a meaning that eludes our present powers of description. When the thrilling figure on a white horse, with flaming eyes and clothes dipped in blood at last comes to judge, we learn that he is the 'Word of God' (19:13), and on his garments is written 'King of Kings, and Lord of Lords' (19:16). And yet, the figure 'had a name written, that no man knew, but he himself' (19:12). In short, the names by which we identify the Word do not reveal his true being, which can be named only in the fulfilment of history. And in this secrecy or occlusion lie both reassurance and menace. Thus, another name for our horseman is 'Faithful and True' (19:11), which is reassuring; but a sharp sword comes out of his mouth (19:15) and he treads the winepress of God's wrath (19:15), which is menacing. A powerful ambivalence ensues, fraught with risk and danger, as is the divine promise itself.

The act of naming throughout Revelation re-enforces the rich perplexity of the book's structure in relation to its imagery. For instance, he 'that overcometh' (3:12) will receive God's name, 'and I will write upon him the name of my God . . . I will write upon him my new name' (3:12). This calls to mind the mysterious 'new name' of the previous chapter, written on a white stone again for 'him that overcometh' (2:17), but which nobody knows 'saving he that receiveth it'. In short, we do not yet know what names are written in the book of life, nor do we sufficiently penetrate the cryptogram of history to see clearly the dynamics of good and evil, or the identity and 'true name' of the triumphant Christ.

Yet Revelation insists on its own prophetic integrity, its own truth-telling. It records God's word (1:2), and the church in Pergamos is praised for holding 'fast my name' (2:13), as is the church in Philadelphia ('thou . . . hast kept my word, and hast not denied my name' [3:8]). The 144,000 blessed on Mount Zion have the name of the lamb on their foreheads (14:1), as do the blessed who shall see his face (22:4). Those shall enter the Holy City whose names are written in the book of life (21:27), and by the lamb's blood and 'the word of their testimony' (12:11) the powers of evil are overcome. Thus, the true word at last will coincide with the blessed community, which embodies it as it is embodied by it. Life, word, communion, and God's presence are then mutually inherent. Such is the end term of religious promise, imperfectly imaginable from the compromised and contradictory standpoint of our historical circumstances, where language is so insecurely related to its referents that we are likely indeed to fall for the blandishments and lies of the thwarters of a common good. For what is promised here is pre-eminently a personal fulfilment: a realisation of ourselves in one another and in the world, and not any imagined substitute that would deflect us from what we might be in our unalienated selves.

Not surprisingly, those whose names are not in the book of life (17:8) are condemned as liars (false namers) who will be cast into the lake of fire (21:8). 'Whatsoever . . . maketh a lie' (21:27) is condemned, and there is a good deal about blasphemy throughout: the beast of the sea has the 'name of blasphemy' (13:1) on his seven heads; those afflicted by the fourth vial angel 'blasphemed the name of God' (16:9); false apostles are found to be liars (2:2) and lies are blasphemy (2:9). In short, false words of unmaking parody the creative word, and so the beast also has a mysterious name: 'the name of the beast, or the number of his name' (13:17), the notorious 666.[18] Likewise, in parody of the blessed, the beast's followers have his name on their foreheads, just as the Whore of Babylon has a name written on hers (17:5).

This war of names is also a war between good and evil, the principles themselves underlying every name and informing the process of evaluation implicit in all naming. The opposition here is encapsulated in a remarkable further, encompassing opposition between 'him which is, and which was, and which is to come' (1:4), and the beast that 'was, and is not' (17:8). The redemptive principle is most fully present, that is, when its own past is seen as the means of realising its highest promise, and this also is the process of the true word, of authentic language. By contrast, the beast has no future, and therefore has a merely illusory present determined by necessary, mechanical repetitions of past practice, a kind of de-creative negation. Thus the Lord describes himself as 'Alpha and Omega' (21:6, 22:13), comprising the full potential range of language. But the beast and his minions are to be struck out of the book of life, losing their names altogether.

This remarkable vision of the ontological implications of naming throws us back upon the ambiguities of history where the very splendor of our hope for reconciliation and community reveals contradictions and opacities in our present circumstances. As we have seen, all this lies at the heart of what it means to be a person, and religious language needs to acknowledge these facts of our condition, so to resist the anodyne of mere escapism. Informed by some such intuition, Revelation declares itself fundamentally a witness to the crucified one (11:8), the slain lamb (5:9–12), the human Jesus who was pierced for love of us (1:7). So, shockingly, we are to go on watching the innocent suffer, believing through protest in the name of the resurrected God who died that the suffering innocent are to be vindicated. But even so we cannot be entirely sure where we stand, just as we cannot be sure of how the design is to unfold, either in history or in the perplexing book before us, mirroring our very condition.

It is always discomfiting to come to Revelation after the gospels, but Revelation states in striking terms some basic conditions of belief in the religious promises informing the entire New Testament. Throughout the New Testament, the cross signifies a perennial contradiction of hope for the liberation of humanity. Thus the cross and resurrection together embody in their fashion the central dynamic of presence and absence, necessity and freedom, by which each person is constituted, and on which all cultures draw. To examine further how this is the case, let us turn briefly to the Gospel according to Mark.

THE SUFFERING SAVIOUR

As we have seen, the divine impersonal power in Revelation is a counterpoise to the loving Jesus of the gospels. Yet this contrast can easily be overstated: Matthew also promises a last judgement, and John fairly bristles with difficult sayings. Gentle Jesus, it turns out, is not always so gentle: 'For judgment I am come into this world, that they which see not might see; and that they which see might be made blind' (John 9:39); 'Ye are of your father the devil, and the lusts of your father ye will do' (John 8:44); 'I have yet many things to say unto you, but ye cannot bear them now' (John

16:12). Also, as we have seen, Revelation is everywhere mindful of the lamb's sacrifice, and throughout the New Testament the suffering righteous one is identified with the eschatological Son of Man.[19] In short, a hoped-for fulfilment is known in the present also by what impedes it, rendering it absent. Yet this depiction of Jesus can readily be misunderstood, as the documents themselves keep warning us, partly by drawing our attention to the fragile uncertainties of religious language, mirroring our personal fragility and contingency.

For instance, Mark is the only New Testament writer to describe his book as a 'gospel',[20] and the good or joyful news implied by this title focuses on the apocalyptic promise. But Mark is also full of crisis and urgency, and the sense of how difficult it is to recognise and understand Jesus as the inaugurator of the Kingdom. After all, the scandal of the cross had dispersed and all but defeated Jesus' closest followers, and among other things Mark struggles to explain and interpret their amazement and incomprehension. There is thus a close connection in Mark between cross and apocalypse, and we can see this by turning first to the so-called 'little apocalypse' of Mark 13, where Jesus responds to the request of Peter, James, John and Andrew for a 'sign' (13:4).[21]

Jesus replies to this request in a pointedly indirect way. He tells the disciples first to watch for deceptions (13:5), because many will use Christ's name falsely. Also, there will be rumours of wars and various famines and troubles, but these are only the 'beginnings of sorrows' (13:8). The disciples will be persecuted and the times will be full of confusion and even family members will betray one another to death (13:12). There will be unexpected afflictions, false Christs and false prophets will arise, and signs and wonders will be everywhere (13:22). The closest Jesus comes to being specific is in verse 14: 'But when ye shall see the abomination of desolation, spoken of by Daniel the prophet, standing where it ought not, (let him that readeth understand,) then let them that be in Judaea flee to the mountains.' But this verse is notoriously problematic. It refers to a desecration of the Temple by Antiochus Epiphanes, as recorded in Daniel, except that Jesus does not mention the Temple directly, and the parenthesis seems to indicate that we should not take him literally. Also, this sign is itself only an indication that it is time to flee, but not that the real end has come. The message is perplexing, and oddly warped. Jesus makes quite clear that the Son of Man will come, and promises that despite false names and false signs 'my words shall not pass away' (13:31). Then, disconcertingly, he tells us that not even the Son knows the exact time, 'but the Father' (13:32).

Exegetes have struggled with the avowal that not even the Son knows the time and clearly it is an embarrassing statement if one holds, from a high Christological perspective, that Jesus as Christ must have foreknowledge. Yet it is pointless to soften the plain sense of Mark's report, and it seems that not even the Son can read the signs accurately. Here, as everywhere, Mark emphasises our anxious uncertainty before the God whom we are also to trust. And here again as in Revelation the battle is between different kinds of naming. On the one hand are false rumours (13:7) and false prophecies (13:22), and Christ's name will be used to cover deceit and treachery (13:5). On the other hand, those who endure in Christ's name shall be saved (13:13), the elect will speak truth in the Spirit (13:11), and 'my words shall not pass away' (13:31). Although there is a plan, we do not know exactly how we fit in with it, and the promises are simultaneously reassuring and disorienting. As in Revelation, eschatology and the process of naming, like the reading of signs, are absorbed in the deep ambiguities of our desire for a transcendental signified that always eludes us. Mark thus warns against naive apocalypticism and too eager a search for signs that would enable us to escape the ambiguity of signs. The chief corrective to such idolatry is, ironically but not surprisingly, itself another sign – that of the cross before which all the consolations of religion and of the world are alike broken.

Clearly, then, the 'little apocalypse' is anxious to tell us that looking for proof signs is wrongheaded and leads to misunderstandings. Although Jesus is already a sign present among us, and his miracles are signs, Mark is anxious to establish how easily all this is misinterpreted, as the cross pre-eminently attests. Mark's concern helps also to explain why the disciples should stumble so often and so uncomprehendingly, and why there is such stress on secrecy and the betrayal of secrets. This last theme is the subject of William Wrede's famous book, *The Messianic Secret*,[22] positing that Jesus during his lifetime was not recognised as the Messiah. The early church offered to explain this potential embarrassment by claiming that Jesus wanted to keep his messianic status a secret. Certainly, injunctions to secrecy are everywhere: the cured leper is told to say nothing (1:44); nobody is to know about the cure of Jairus' daughter (5:43); the deaf-mute is not to tell what has happened (7:36), nor is the blind man at Bethsaida (8:26); Peter is not to tell others about recognising Jesus as the Christ (8:30); nobody is to know about the cure of the child with the evil spirit (9:30).

Despite Wrede's original debunking intent, his central argument has stayed very much alive in Markan criticism,[23] and one way to accommodate it to the present discussion of the 'war of names' in the 'little apocalypse' is by seeing it as another reminder of how readily people misunderstand religious language, and how Jesus' messianic status inevitably is misunderstood if the cross is ignored. Because the miracles and other manifestations of divinity occur before the crucifixion, observers are especially liable to misread them. Consequently, Mark's Jesus offers warnings and injunctions to secrecy to prevent premature enthusiasm and to discourage a sense of false security among his followers.

At this point, it is worth reconsidering some of the secrecy passages in more detail. For instance, the cured leper promptly disobeys ('he went out, and began to publish it much, and to blaze abroad the matter' [1:45]), and so do those who witness the cure of the deaf mute ('but the more he charged them, so much the more a great deal they published it' [7:36]). Also in the case of Jairus' daughter and of the blind man, it is clearly impossible to keep the cure secret, as Jesus would have known. All this suggests that Jesus' divine power *cannot* be kept secret because it is so obviously present among us. And yet the miracles must not be interpreted just as proof signs to legitimise a messianic claim.[24] Rather the miracle secret, like the messianic secret,[25] is to be grasped in light of the cross and resurrection or not at all.

Significantly, Jesus does not perform miracles unless he is asked, and his cures come as a surprise. They are amazing restorations, as it were, of things to their natural condition. Likewise, we are to learn that the kingdom of God is the restoration of what we already are, but we will find it by following the way of the cross and not by seeking any other kind of security, including the solace of special magical interventions. Thus in the miracles and injunctions to secrecy, Mark's Jesus insists as in the 'little apocalypse' that God's power is present and yet to come. Mark's way of showing this is both coarse and subtle. Notoriously, his writing is jagged and unpolished, full of discontinuities and awkward transitions. Yet the compelling, central intuition linking apocalyptic prophecy to the way of the cross drives him back upon various nuanced interpretations of signs and names, and his meaning is conveyed partly by a careful distinction between the reader's point of view and the participants'. Thus he forces us constantly to interpret and re-interpret, and so to feel a perilous insufficiency in the signs and images even as they assure us.

Mark's transfiguration scene is especially significant in this context. Here Jesus reveals the messianic secret to a select few, but Mark's account is carefully prefaced by the strange story of curing the blind man at Bethsaida, and by the equally disconcerting episode of Peter being rebuked after recognising Jesus as Christ. The transfiguration occurs directly after, when Jesus takes Peter, James and John 'into an high mountain apart by themselves' (9:2), and appears in glory with Moses and Elias. A voice from a cloud declares 'This is my beloved Son: hear him' (9:7), and the disciples are suitably terrified. Then the vision passes, and as they come down from the mountain, Jesus tells the disciples to 'tell no man what things they had seen, till the Son of man were risen from the dead' (9:9). The disciples are puzzled, and question one another 'what the rising from the dead should mean' (9:10).

The disciples in all this are insufficiently aware of the implications of Mark's titles, for Jesus is pronounced Son of God and then refers to himself as Son of Man. Although the exact meaning of these titles is disputed, there is a firm core of opinion linking 'Son of Man' to the eschatological prophet in the book of Daniel; Son of God by contrast, indicates Jesus' special relationship to the Father, and in the present context calls up an echo of Isaiah 42:1, where God announces his servant, his 'elect, in whom my soul delighteth' Thus, the suffering servant of Isaiah ('Son of God') is brought together with the apocalyptic prophet ('Son of Man'), and this potent conjunction shapes Jesus' identity.[26] But again, the titles (another form of naming) are not quite commensurate with the new meaning that they indicate but do not encompass, and the disciples do not clearly see the connection between them.[27] Neither apparently, do they see the significance of coming down again from the mountain into the ordinary world of 'the multitude' (9:14, 17) The transfigured Jesus has offered them a clear sign, but even so the disciples do not quite understand what he is about, or that the kingdom is not to be found just in a blaze of light on a mountain top, but down among the afflicted, and by way also of suffering that affliction.

Let us now backtrack, first to Peter's recognition of Christ before the transfiguration, and then to the cure of the blind man a

Bethsaida. Jesus first asks the disciples 'Whom do men say that I am?' (8:27), and they give various answers. Then he asks, 'But whom say ye that I am?' and Peter replies, 'Thou art the Christ' (8:29), upon which Jesus (yet again) 'charged them that they should tell no man of him' (8:30). On the face of it, the messianic secret here should be easy enough to keep, but Jesus' reasons for charging the disciples with secrecy are not plain. They are, however, implicit in the teaching that follows. 'The Son of man,' Jesus says, 'must suffer many things, and be rejected of the elders, and of the chief priests and scribes, and be killed, and after three days rise again' (8:31). At this point Peter interrupts and objects: surely that is not what the Son of Man is all about. In reply, Jesus offers a rebuke of alarming vehemence: 'Get thee behind me, Satan' (8:33). Jesus then calls the people to him, and addresses them and the disciples together: 'Whosoever will come after me, let him deny himself, and take up his cross, and follow me' (8:34).

Peter has read things correctly by identifying Jesus as Christ, but he has also misread because he cannot understand the cross. Jesus' vehemence alerts us to the danger of such partial understanding, and in the battle of names the sign of the cross again contradicts our easy securities and confident identifications. Christ is among us, but his way calls for the renunciation of our desire for a privileged perspective, clear understanding, and complete presence. Faith, rather, mirroring our condition as persons, is poised on the perilous way between what is (the facts of suffering) and what is not yet (the promised kingdom).

The story of the blind man at Bethsaida also impinges on this theme, and indeed prefaces the episode where Peter is rebuked. Jesus first attempts to cure the blind man by applying spit to his eyes, but has only partial success: 'I see men as trees, walking' (8:24), says the man, unforgettably. And so Jesus tries again, this time with complete success. The point is that the blind man has to be cured by repeated applications, and in this he resembles Peter, who sees at first imperfectly and has to be treated again, until he comes to recognise more fully the Messiah who is both Son of God and Son of Man, the eschatological prophet whose triumph is issued in by his becoming the suffering servant.

We are forced, then, to read and re-read, to construct meaning retrospectively and grasp the implications of shifting viewpoints, relationships between episodes, and so on. In short, Mark's 'literary' method of awakening his readers duplicates Jesus' own method (as the gospel records it) of instructing the disciples.[28] Thus, throughout Mark's account, the passion is hinted at or anticipated, and becomes an index of how well the reader, as well as Mark's characters, understands what is happening. For instance, early in the gospel the Pharisees are already seeking to kill Jesus (3:6) who in turn observes how a prophet is 'not without honour, but in his own country, and among his own kin' (6:4), alluding to the lament – beginning with Nehemiah – that Israel kills its prophets. Later, Jesus declares that even the Son of Man comes 'to give his life a ransom for many' (10:45), a point already made clear to the uncomprehending Peter (8:31). These indicators of the passion at once signal to readers how implicit is the cross to Jesus' preaching the kingdom throughout his mission, and how we might understand his titles and the signs he offers.

We have seen how this is the case with the cluster of stories about the blind man of Bethsaida, Peter's confession, and the transfiguration. It is also the theme of the story directly following the transfiguration, where the child possessed by a malign spirit is cured. The disciples are unable to cast out the spirit, and Jesus reflects, with some exasperation, 'O faithless generation, how long shall I be with you?' (9:19). He then tells the child's father, 'If thou canst believe, all things are possible to him that believeth' (9:23), to which the grief-stricken man replies with piercing humility, 'Lord, I believe: Help thou mine unbelief' (9:24). Jesus then drives out the 'dumb and deaf spirit' (9:25), but it tears at the child, leaving him for dead (Gk. 'a corpse'), until Jesus at last raises him up.

The poignancy of this episode gains immensely from its position following the transfiguration. Here we are down from the mountain and among the afflicted, the bearers of crosses. The disciples have been less than perceptive about what Jesus' messianic status really means, and have missed the point about the cross and, consequently, about the meaning of faith. This is why they cannot cast out the devil. The exorcism then is itself another sign to them of the very point they are missing, as a reader might detect. Jesus wrestles here with a demon, and it leaves the child as a corpse, which is then raised up. This is a little allegory of his own death and resurrection, and, significantly – even with a degree of provocation – the devil is described as 'deaf and dumb', the very spirit of recalcitrance, of inability to hear the meaning of words and to speak of their significance correctly that Jesus encounters in the 'faithless generation', including his own disciples. If the blind man at Bethsaida represents the disciples' condition before the transfiguration, the deaf and dumb spirit suggests the unregeneracy among them that Jesus must still confront after the transfiguration. Mark everywhere is hard on the disciples, and is consistently so because they fail to read the signs. The battle of names in Revelation thus remains close also to the heart of the gospel, and in both books the language of religious promises remains transparent to the perplexities of our condition as persons, immersed in language that both contains and liberates us.[29]

The same principle obtains in the story of the anointing at Bethany, where an unnamed woman pours precious ointment on Jesus' head. She is rebuked by the disciples, whom Jesus in turn rebukes, saying that she anoints his body for burial and that her act 'shall be spoken of for a memorial of her' (14:9). The episode takes place directly after the 'little apocalypse', which as we see is concerned with the ambiguity of signs.[30] The anointing at Bethany is also an example of ambiguous sign-making, and again the pressing issue is the cross.

Clearly, the disciples who accuse the woman of squandering money do not grasp the significance of her actions: Jesus, Son of Man, is to die and she is anointing him for burial, not adorning him. It might well be that Mark is anxious here to avoid the scandal of Jesus being buried without proper rites, and the story provides an assurance that these were performed in advance.[31] But it is more pertinent to Mark's gospel as a whole to see how the disciples again miss a sign of the cross. Pointedly, the woman 'brake the box' (14:3), an act recalling the practice of snapping the necks off ointment jars to be interred with the body.[32] Also, the fact that she anoints Jesus on the head might suggest the anointing of a King of Israel (2 Kings 9:1–13; 1 Sam. 10:1), thereby indicating that she recognises Jesus as Messiah. And yet it is impossible to say what exactly she perceives. The disciples and Jesus both interpret her action, but she herself gives no explanation. Does she grasp the significance of the broken container, and does she think Jesus is a political messiah? The matter remains shrouded in ambiguity, as Mark's narrative and the several points of view of the participants open upon possibilities that are left perplexingly unresolved.

And so at last we come to the crucifixion, devastator of comforting signs, breaker of worldly securities, revealer of radical contingency. All this is driven home by the mockers who challenge Jesus to come down from the cross and thereby prove his power (15:30). Instead, he utters his terrible cry: 'My God, my God, why hast thou forsaken me?' (15:34). It is the exact opposite of a sign that might console, and again it is a rebuke cast in the teeth of those who misunderstand Christ's mission. But now at last the rebuke is thrown up simply as a comfortless cry: it is as if the titles and visions, names and signs, distract us from the suffering, abandonment and loneliness that in fact separate the world from God. The cross thus becomes a sign drawing us in protest against everything that impedes the 'not yet' of hope. Jesus, who consistently in the gospels proclaims his special closeness to the Father, just as unyieldingly proclaims that the way of the apocalyptic prophet is also that of the suffering servant.

It is generally agreed that Mark's gospel ends at 16:8, after the two Marys find the tomb empty and are told by the mysterious young man to seek the crucified and risen Jesus. The women go off, amazed and frightened, and Mark's gospel ends abruptly. Again, the empty tomb is a sign, but it is also negative, indicating an absence. Mark does not have any resurrection appearances, and we are left destabilised, still in the grip of the apocalyptic mood of chapter 13, looking for signs, discomposed amidst startling illuminations, strange secrets, and the terrible invitation to suffering. The *parousia* in Mark is therefore not distinct from resurrection, and he leaves us with the sense of anxious waiting for an imminent event, in the proximity of promises to be fulfilled.

The other synoptic gospels modify this view without surrendering Mark's central vision, but by converting it into a myth of the time of Jesus, as Perrin points out,[33] and separating the resurrection from the *parousia* which is to come at the end of history. Thus, Matthew and Luke add the birth narratives and resurrection appearances, giving the story of Jesus a beginning, middle and end, and thereby establishing the church as commemorator of the special historical period of the birth, death and resurrection of Jesus. Consequently, the apocalyptic 'not yet' of the heavenly Jerusalem is delayed, but Jesus remains nonetheless present among the faithful ('lo, I am with you alway, even unto the end of the world' [Matt. 28:20]).

The further implications of these shared gospel teachings on signs and naming, hope and the relinquishment of power, faith and the fragility of the human state, suffering and protest against suffering, are recorded throughout the literature, history and culture of Western Europe that has called itself, in broad terms, Christian. As Moltmann says, Christianity is nothing if not eschatological, but eschatology in the New Testament is the way of the suffering servant, and this, as we also see, has far-reaching consequences for how we read the signs and names of Christ. The root paradox is that Jesus crucified and Christ risen are one and the same, and this drives us back to the intolerable difficulty of accepting that God's way is at once to restore all things to health, beauty and perfection, and on the other to permit the death by torture of his own Son.

The moral unbeliever at this point refuses assent, and with good reason. Yet believers and unbelievers alike might protest equally against the outrage of suffering from which no religious observance protects us. The difference is, that believers go on hoping for the 'not yet' of the promise to be revealed as the future of the crucified. As Edward Schillebeeckx says, the cross is to be understood less as an event between God and God than as an 'index of what is to be opposed as the anti-divine in our human history'.[34] The cross therefore is a sign of the radical contingency of human existence, and of the anxieties occasioned by realisation of this fact and the overwhelming questions that accompany it, concerning the purpose of life, its possibilities, and direction, which every human person can be expected to encounter.

From such a perspective, which I take also to be generally post-Enlightenment or post-critical, it is possible to see what believers might call the Christ-principle present in whatever power opposes suffering and injustice by energising hope. A believer's faith, of a kind compatible with the right to unbelief and with the several other positions outlined in this book, is founded basically on the notion that the religious promise of a redeemed humanity will come to pass in a form yet to be discovered but already in the making: already rooted, that is, in our selves as persons. However, we are warned repeatedly by the New Testament that God's energy in Christ is invariably misrecognised if it does not serve the poor directly, and that there is no recognition of Christ in the world that does not have a material form, a real embodiment. Whatever else the resurrection stories mean, they tell us that recognising the resurrected Jesus is a concrete encounter in the midst of things.

To summarise: we do not name Christ accurately until at last his true name is disclosed, as Revelation tells us, at which time word and body will be as one. Meanwhile, the signs are ambiguous, and the contradiction is upon us, to recognise and endure through protest and hope, as we can. Religious promises, like religious language, thus take their place within a diverse, pluralist culture labouring for the liberation of human beings on a variety of fronts. In this context, the distinguishing function of religion is to address the problem of liberation in absolute terms, to state absolute aspirations and hopes and then to describe its beliefs accordingly, but without distorting the rights and claims of persons, and their historical embededness. And although I deal here with Christianity because it is the principal religion of the literature and culture that concern me most directly, I expect that the terms of the analysis are appropriate for assessing the relevance of other religions in a post-critical society. But to repeat: none of this is to deny that the disciples and advocates, crusaders and witch-hunters, clerks and scribes, have managed throughout history to go on crucifying in Christ's name, perpetrating the one truly anti-Christian and radically de-personalising act. In counterstatement, a partial solace only, we might point to the traditions of spiritual literature which have struggled through the centuries to keep alive imaginatively the essential apocalyptic drama of ourselves in the making. To these I now turn briefly.

PERENNIAL PHILOSOPHY

In this section I do not take the term 'perennial philosophy' in its usual sense to indicate the common core of all religions, but rather some common principles in the spiritual traditions of Christianity in the Latin West. My main claim is, simply, that these traditions by and large remain faithful to the insights about language and signs, presence and absence represented by Mark's transfiguration narrative, maintaining that the way of the cross is also the way of the triumphant eschatological prophet. In turn, this spiritual tradition confirms and has helped to produce the idea of the person as I have described it.

The term 'perennial philosophy' straight away raises the old problem of describing spiritual experiences that are held to be ineffable. But here we might remind ourselves that no experience is ever fully described, and always contains more than words can say: language never fully captures the moment. Nonetheless, it is useful to distinguish between experience and interpretation: the cat we saw in the bushes can, on inspection, turn out to be rustling leaves and shadows and not a cat at all. 'I thought I saw, I found it was' is a common occurrence, and shows how experience and interpretation differ, however complexly interinvolved. In some such manner, every special epiphany or visionary moment forces on us a renewed awareness of how the impediments of ordinary language, apparent ego and social structure prevent that special moment's consciousness from being adequately interpreted or understood, even though, paradoxically, we need ordinary language to realise this fact and to examine whether or not we have suffered under an illusion. The mystics themselves emphatically reassure us that visions always need testing, for they might be the devices of charlatans or a madman's fantasy. So it is indeed with all the visions, whether sacred or secular, that would reform and liberate.

But what is mysticism and who are the mystics? A degree of solace might derive from the fact that the church has nowhere attempted to define mysticism,[35] and the wisdom of this evasion lies in a certain tacit acknowledgement that Spirit transcends and outreaches human prescription. But I should now suggest also that it seems futile to attempt discussing mysticism outside some framework of belief, if only because mysticism attests and then asks us to explain our relationship to an ultimate reality that is always an object of belief rather than understanding. We must begin somewhere, but, as we have seen in earlier chapters, we cannot step far enough outside what we already believe (and disbelieve) to assume some kind of neutral or impersonal stance, even though we admit the provisional status and imperfection of our current beliefs and symbols.[36]

Two examples will help to clarify the problem. Evelyn Underhill tells us that mysticism is 'the science of union with the Absolute', involving, she says, a 'movement of the whole self towards the Real'.[37] This is a general, philosophical description, and it does not tell us much about specific representations or determinations of the 'Real' in the literature with which her book mostly deals. By contrast, Heribert Fischer in *Sacramentum Mundi* tells us that mysticism is 'consciousness of the experience of uncreated grace as revelation and self-communication of the triune God'.[38] This is mainly theological, and describes a much more specific kind of experience. Underhill's Absolute now becomes the triune God who offers to meet the human soul by an act of self-disclosure. Defining the Christian God as triune is itself a reflection on the central claim in the New Testament that Jesus is divine. For, as J. P. Mackey points out, the doctrine of the trinity is first of all a Christology: that is, an attempt to grasp the theological implications of the fact of incarnation.[39] According to Christianity, God comes down to us by choice, making himself a human person who is able to suffer.

Just as for Mark and Revelation, so also for Christian spirituality in general, experiencing or thinking about God without the way of the cross is futile and dangerous. Fischer's definition encompasses this Christian understanding and is grounded in a prior acceptance of incarnation. It does not contradict Underhill, but describes more closely the terms of a specifically Christian mysticism.

Although mystics by and large remain uncomfortable with definitions, in a broad sense descriptions of their own experiences are poised between the tendencies suggested by Underhill and Fischer. On the one hand, the special adventure that the mystic attests is felt to break through the limitations of conventional theological and linguistic categories, and to be in contact with a Reality that words (at best) intimate in a veiled, imperfect manner. On the other hand, this special adventure can be overwhelming and the mystic needs to find exact language to understand and assess it, thereby communicating it for the benefit of others, bringing it down into the culture it should irradiate and renew.[40] Such language usually will derive from theologians and other spiritual writers whose opinions and directives have been tested by communal experience and by careful sifting and analysis in conformity with what is taken to be orthodox opinion. Mystics, it seems, break through the limitations of culture and convention to encounter a transcendent reality, but they come to know their experience as fully human and personal by testing it in the common life.

One result is a tension between the institutional church and its visionaries, and this we might see as a special case of the relationship between images and ideas we examined in Chapter 4. Each needs but resists the other: the institution needs to be challenged and revitalised, and the mystics need to understand and communicate their experience. Understandably, the church tends to hold its mystics, at least initially, under suspicion, for part of its task is to separate out the cranks from the saints. Likewise, the mystics remain acutely aware of the arbitrariness and shortcomings of institutional concepts and dogmas for describing the supremely real thing they have encountered. It is fair to say that the greatest achievements of Christian mysticism have occurred when the tension between institution and individual mystic is especially heightened, though avoiding schism. In such a context, unconventional voices might register a claim based on capacities and experience that orthodoxy might find uncomfortable or would prefer to deny. For instance, although women during the Middle Ages were excluded from official positions of power, they were influential in moulding a spiritual literature, as we see in the writings of Hildegard of Bingen (1098–1178), Mechthild of Magdeburg (1217–1282), Gertrude the Great (1256–1301), Angela of Foligno (c. 1248–1309), Bridget of Sweden (1303–73), Catherine of Siena (1347–1380), Julian of Norwich (c. 1342–1420), and many others.

At this point it is worth noticing that Christian tradition is carefully elusive on the subject of what actually is experienced in the varieties of mystical experience, even when these are held to be genuine. Although there is general agreement that in some sense God is present, there is reluctance to conclude that God's essence is known directly.[41] Thomas Aquinas and Augustine argue that it is not theoretically impossible to experience God's essence: such a thing might occasionally happen (as with Moses and St. Paul), but outside the Scriptures this would be impossible to verify, and by and large mystical theologians avoid making the claim. Thus St. Teresa of Avila tells us that there always remains more to discover and to know about God.[42] The point is conceded by authorities such as Jacques Maritain and Cuthbert Butler, the first of whom describes mysticism as an 'experimental knowledge of the deep things of God', and the second as an 'experimental perception of the Being and presence of God in the soul'.[43] The words 'deep things' and 'Being and presence' indicate revelation, but not a claim that God in his essence is present. This principle is important to grasp if the varieties of spiritual experience are to be accorded their due: as David Knowles says, in dealing with mysticism we are not trying to define a truth of revealed religion, but to assess God's dealings with individual souls whom he always leads in a particular way.[44] Careful investigation of particular cases might indeed suggest the outlines of a perennial philosophy, but describing such a thing calls also for imaginative discrimination and critical judgement whereby generic and particular elements are carefully balanced. In effecting this balance, the literature of mysticism resembles other kinds of literature, entailing personal evaluation and critical reflection.

As is often noticed, mystics tend to experience the God in whom they believe. As we now see, this is because mystics – like all of us – are pre-formed to a degree by the language and culture within which consciousness arises. Yet mystics claim also a vision of things beyond the limitations of culture and language, and are not truly mystics until they attempt to communicate this vision for the benefit of others, which entails engaging and transforming their own immediate culture and society. Calling the realm beyond culture and language either God, Reality, or the Creative Unconscious is, in one respect, less important than the impulse deriving from an experimental knowledge of such a realm and expressed as a hope that others can share, for a humanised nature and the overcoming of separation, oppression and suffering. Indeed, one insistent demand both from mystics and theologians concerned with 'discernment of spirits'[45] is that the main criterion of a genuine experience of the 'deep things of God' is its expression in good works and the recognition by others of a morally-strengthened character. As the mystics keep insisting, such a change of character does not occur only in the apparent ego. As Erich Neumann says, although genuine mysticism does indeed extend consciousness and strengthen the ego,[46] it also shifts the human centre away from the ego's narrowness through experience of what he calls a 'creative unconscious', experienced also as a creative nothingness that returns us, re-invigorated, to an imperfect and contradictory world. Here Neumann the Jungian psychologist helps to confirm the observation of the Freudian Norman O. Brown, that psychoanalysts are the inheritors of mystical theology, a point to which I will return by and by.[47]

Meanwhile, I want to suggest that Western mysticism remains in the spirit of Mark's teaching on coming down from the mountain and accepting the contradictions of the cross, and this teaching is reflected especially in how mystics describe their experiences as a personal encounter, engaging a complex dialectic of presence and absence. In short, visions pass and epiphanies fade in the hollowing of the present moment into the ceaseless drift of time, and vision then takes its place, re-admitted to the present in the form of hope and promise. It remains as the not-yet that will stand up to criticism and contradiction, alienation and false consciousness, as we awaken to ourselves in one another. This again is a dynamic of the personal, and, as with other forms of literature we have discussed, the perennial philosophy confirms the centrality of this dynamic to our human concern.

The development of spiritual writing in the Latin West becomes, then, at once an intricate history of the care of souls (a history of psychology) and of the institutional church (an ecclesiastical history) as well as the history of a theology keeping alive and interpreting the symbols of Christ's original revelation. Certain passages, especially in St. Paul ('I live; yet not I, but Christ liveth in me' [Gal. 2:20]) and St. John ('as thou, Father, art in me, and I in thee, that they also may be one in us' [Jn. 17:21]), imply a mystical experience of the soul's union with God. Yet Christian spirituality from the inception rejected any mystical path through knowledge and special techniques for illuminating the understanding.[48] Here again the way of the cross humiliates the aspirations of the elite visionary or intellectual. Even so, gnosticism and neo-platonism did not relinquish their hold on Christian thinking, as is clear in the Alexandrian Fathers, Clement and Origen, who strive to show how faith and gnosis are complementary. St. Paul had already suggested that children should be given milk and adults meat (I Cor. 3:2), and had distinguished between body, soul and spirit.[49] In so doing, he laid the ground for a theory of spiritual progress as a series of stages, increasingly perfect but never dissociated from Christ crucified. In some such spirit, Clement of Alexandria suggests that true Christian gnostics proceed by way of mortification until able to cast themselves into Christ, searching blindly until knowing (*gnosis*) descends. There is progress here through the world, the soul's desire, and into spiritual knowledge, and this scheme anticipates the familiar way of purgation, illumination and union widely deployed throughout the Middle Ages. Origen likewise teaches that asceticism is the way to gnosis, and he introduced a distinction between active and contemplative lives (represented by Martha and Mary). He also developed a doctrine of spiritual senses, and in his commentary on the *Song of Songs*, he brought to Western tradition a sophisticated version of bridal mysticism.[50]

Through Athanasius' *Life of Anthony* (c. 357) and the *Lausiac History of Palladius* (d. before 431), the practices of the Desert Fathers also contributed to the ascetic Western spirituality. In one sense, the flight to the desert was a protest against the worldliness of a decaying empire, and a scouring of paganism by a fierce imitation of the crucified and risen one. Thus for Methodius the celibate are truly called martyrs.

For Origen's disciple Gregory of Nyssa, spiritual life remains an ascent through prayer which leads into a dark cloud in which the soul remains passive until illuminated from above by God's free self-communication.[51] Gregory here draws from Clement and from Philo of Alexandria who had described Moses' encounter with God as an encounter with darkness. And although Gregory of Nyssa drops from view in Western tradition, his teaching remained in the writings of Dionysius the Areopagite, whose influence on Western mysticism was extraordinary, as we shall see.

As with many theological issues, all roads meet in St. Augustine, and in him are combined the influence of St. Paul and Neo-Platonism, desert asceticism and the quest for gnosis, a conviction of sin requiring God's grace, a threefold way of corporeal, spiritual and intellectual vision, a distinction between active and contemplative, and a version of bridal mysticism. And yet Augustine is not mainly a mystic and does not thematise mystical experience by treating it as a special state. Rather, he sets out a broad programme for cultivating a Christian understanding of history and psychology, learning and prayer, and allows that in the higher stages understanding merges with increasingly intense illuminations of God's love.

By and large, the Augustinian spirit prevails during what Cuthbert Butler calls the 'Benedictine centuries'[52] (extending roughly from 550–1150), and contemplation by and large is regarded as the fruition of ordinary prayer in which everyone participates. As Ernesto Buonaiuti says, the liturgy is dedicated to safeguarding the spiritual life of Christians as a whole, and without individualism.[53] As Butler claims, this kind of approach is the backbone of Western spiritual tradition, represented by such figures as Augustine, Gregory the Great, Bernard, and Bonaventure. It is roughly equivalent to what has become known as the 'affirmative way', an approach to prayer stressing the positive contribution of language and signs in our journey towards contemplation. Thus we are to see in things a trace or symbol of the divine creator, and allow this particular illumination to guide our spirit upwards through imagination ('spiritual vision' Augustine calls it), leading to the one, unimaginable source of all manifest order and energy. In contrast, the 'negative way' operates by our cancelling out of experience and imagination everything that is less than God, until at last there remains only a darkness in which God's presence then might be revealed, dark yet paradoxically brilliant.

Neither of these 'ways' can in fact exist in isolation. On the one hand, the way of affirmation needs a certain order and discipline, and must stop short of idolising the creation. It needs to acknowledge that God, who is different from the things he has made, is not present to us in his essence, and must at last approach us freely. On the other hand, proponents of the 'negative way' also participate in the world and require some basic comfort and securities. They must not encourage us to reject the creation, for God blesses what he has made and leaves in it a trace of his presence. Still, there are two distinct tendencies here, and by and large contemplatives during the Benedictine centuries lean to the first, expressed in a corporate or communal spirituality, whereas the second comes to the fore during the second half of the twelfth century, together with a renewed interest in Dionysius the Areopagite.

Dionysius appears to have been a sixth-century Christian monk with strong Platonist leanings, influenced by the imagery of divine darkness explored by Gregory of Nyssa. He was long mistaken for St. Paul's convert at the Areopagus, described in the Acts of the Apostles, and today the title Pseudo-Dionysius reflects a consensus about his true date. Partly because of Dionysius' supposedly illustrious origins, his writings were held in high esteem during the Middle Ages. They were translated from Greek into Latin in the ninth century by John Scotus Eriugena, and commentaries were provided by Hugh of St. Victor and Thomas Aquinas. But Dionysius' influence on European mysticism was most extensive during the fourteenth century, and was accompanied by a strong new emphasis on the negative way. Words and ideas break down, says the Dionysian mystic, because the real thing is quite other.

It is easy to see how the negative way would be favoured by – and indeed would encourage – the anti-institutional tendencies of a mysticism of individual experience. As rumblings at the foundations of Catholic Christendom were caused by schism, black death, and institutional corruption during the fourteenth century, so mysticism increasingly embraced the way of discontinuity, the way of God's absence, thereby also coming increasingly to explore mystical experience as a special state, the preserve of special individuals admitted to a presence at the other side of the absence experienced by most of us. Thus, the negative way becomes aligned with a theory of mysticism as a special kind of prayer, in contrast to the affirmative way of corporate worship during the Benedictine centuries. Yet by and large a necessary, fructifying tension still holds between institution and individual, church and saint. Only with the rise of secularism, as we shall see, does the mystical dynamism seek other means of expression as Christendom dwindles and theology relinquishes its position as queen of the sciences.

Bonaventure's (1221–74) little treatise *The Mind's Road to God*[54] is an example of spiritual writing in the 'affirmative' Augustinian tradition, adapted to Franciscan spirituality of the High Middle Ages. Bonaventure describes the stages of an ascent towards God who is reflected 'in his traces in the universe' (I,1). The world, that is, clamours with significance: it is a book that the mind reads, or can

learn to read. Just as the divine, creative light pours down into the material world, giving form and shape to things (for Bonaventure, matter itself is a kind of light), so the mind, attending to nature and finding significance there is already on the path back towards the 'Father of Light' (Prologue), the supreme originator. Consequently, the human sciences are 'like rays of light descending from the eternal law into our minds. And thus our minds, illumined and suffused by such great radiance, unless they be blind, can be led through themselves alone to the contemplation of that eternal light' (III,7).

The creation, in short, is an inexhaustible multiplicity of formal relationships that human intelligence infused with desire can detect and appreciate as traces of divinity. In turn, these signs and traces are more or less intensely brilliant and coherently organised according to their closeness or remoteness from the Father of Light, and a good deal of Bonaventure's effort goes into describing progress towards the vision of God as an ascent by means of a ladder. Because 'the world is itself a ladder for ascending to God, we find here certain traces [of His hand], certain images, some corporeal, some spiritual . . . consequently some outside us, some inside' (I,2). There are, for instance, stages of ascension, 'to wit, sense, imagination, reason, intellect, intelligence, and the apex of the mind, the illumination of conscience (*Synteresis*)' (I,6). These six stages are analogous to the six days of creation, as well as various other patterns of six, and are in turn an extension of an even more basic threefold structure whereby the human is constituted by body, spirit and mind (I,4), mirroring in turn the single threefoldness of the Trinity, and duplicated also in the threefold way of purgation, illumination and perfection. Because the human being has an inner and an outer aspect, the mind's threefold structure becomes six, corresponding to the six days of creation. The six stages of ascent thus lead to a mystical seventh (or sabbath): just so, Bonaventure's book, as he tells us, has seven chapters (Prologue).

Bonaventure places before us all kinds of such patterns, analogies, and correspondences, in order to suggest how the variety of human crafts and sciences and are rungs on a ladder. It is all very intricate, but based also on a conviction that we can trust the world and language to provide insights into God's design. Nature responds co-operatively to our intelligent gaze, and as we ascend the ladder of spiritual knowledge, illumination becomes increasingly intense.

Yet the affirmative way is never quite altogether affirmative, and

Bonaventure well knows that in the end every image fades before the vision of God, and this also is part of what is meant by the cross: images are imperfect and indicate our imperfect knowledge by faith, our suffering incomprehension. Bonaventure points out that the symbolic six-winged seraph 'signifies the six states of illumination' leading to God, but then adds, 'to Whom no one can enter properly save through the Crucified' (Prologue).

In this context, Bonaventure several times cites Dionysius, at one point quoting the *Mystical Theology* to the effect that the senses and intellectual operations must be abandoned if one is to pass over into union (VII,5). Such abandonment is painful, like the cross: 'let us pass over with the crucified Christ from this world to the Father' (VII,6). This is the experience of not, finally, being able to achieve the highest contemplation by our own efforts, but only by a *via crucis* wherein all our securities are abandoned and our visionary schemes in the end made desolate. Yet, by contrast, Bonaventure's own treatise is a conspicuously public and objective document. It is not at all an account of a special experience or of the unique suffering or abandonment of a particular soul. Rather, Bonaventure implies that contemplative experience is continuous with general experience and ordinary prayer. Although our individual trials and crosses are to be borne uniquely by ourselves, the shared world of prayer and ritual guides us reliably along the way.

Perhaps the finest example of mystical spirituality written originally in English is the anonymous fourteenth-century treatise, *The Cloud of Unknowing*.[55] In contrast to Bonaventure and in tune with its times, the *Cloud* follows the negative way, and is plainly influenced by Dionysius: 'Indeed,' we are told, 'anyone who will read Dionysius's works will find that he clearly endorses all that I have said, or will yet say, from beginning to end' (145). Yet the *Cloud* is also enriched by a warm and friendly appreciation of the foibles of ordinary people seeking God in a common world and through the many-sided institutional life of the church. The result is a sophisticated account not only of mystical prayer and its special rigours, but of its place in the church and in a largely unmystical world.

The first thing we encounter in the *Cloud* is a concern about who is reading the book. The prologue asks the present owner not to let it into the hands of those unprepared to read it properly, for 'If a man saw the matter only partially, he might easily go wrong' (51). This misgiving is repeated towards the end:

> Not all those who read this book, or hear it read or spoken of,
> and as a result think it is a good and pleasant thing, are therefore
> called by God to engage in this work because of the pleasant
> sensation they get when they read it. (150)

The author here mistrusts his own words, suggesting how they
might be dangerous. His book is not for everybody, just as mystical
experience is not for everybody because it is a special state – a
'special life', as our author says, where the chosen one becomes
'a servant among his [God's] own special servants' (59). This idea
recurs throughout the *Cloud*, and we are assured that not everybody will have such special experiences; certainly these cannot be
expected to come from reading a book. The author even shows
some embarrassment at the idea of writing about what he knows,
for words too often leave us with a mere illusion of substance.

I will return to the idea of special states, but I would like first
briefly to consider one significant consequence of the author's
distrust of language and espousal of the negative way. This is
his repeated urging that imagination be put aside, for although
it helps in the earlier stages of prayer, in the end it provides only
distractions. Consequently, the 'pride and inventiveness of the
imagination' must be 'stamped out' (65), and we must 'try to forget
all created things' (61). The 'vigorous working of your imagination'
must be 'suppressed' (73), even though it is an exceptionally fertile
faculty and persistently disobeys our desire to suppress it. (139)

There is much of this kind of thing in the *Cloud*, and the author's
main idea is that when we cease thinking in images, we enter into a
kind of darkness, 'a cloud of unknowing' (61). We must wait there
in pure longing for God until the divine mercy breaks through,
illuminating us. Will and love are central in this process, but it is
important to notice how waiting suggests that we are approached by
another. Because the author of the *Cloud* prefers the way of negation,
he has little sense of approaching the heights gradually through
the process of reading God's design, as does Bonventure. Instead,
God's self-revelation comes as a sudden, piercing experience, and
the *Cloud* repeatedly uses language suggesting violent surprise.
Such experience comes 'without warning' (104); it is 'a shaft of
spiritual light, which pierces this cloud of unknowing between you
[and God], and shows you some of his secrets' (95). It occurs in the
twinkling of an eye (64), and is like a spark or a flash, or a 'sharp
dart of longing love' (68).

This piercing shaft of light is mentioned frequently, but the author assures us that words cannot say anything more about it (95), and it is risky even to think of doing so. Although mystics have always made claims like this about ineffability, the *Cloud* leaves us with an especially strong impression of how startling, extraordinary, and private is mystical prayer. And at this point we might even begin to suspect the author of a kind of elitism, except that such a tendency is counteracted by two further, strongly defined characteristics of his writing. First is his teaching on humility; second, his insistence on balanced judgement, confirmed by a particular sense of humour. Here, ironically, the author's imaginative range rescues his book from excesses consequent upon his own repudiation of imagination.

Humility, we learn in a famous sentence, 'is nothing else but a true knowledge and awareness of oneself as one really is' (78). If we see ourselves clearly – which requires a complex imaginative act – we will know our wretchedness and weakness, and how none of us has any right to dominate anyone else. This sense of shared fallenness is labelled 'imperfect humility', and is contrasted to a 'perfect' kind that comes from understanding the 'superabundant love and worth of God in himself' (78). Faced with this, 'all nature trembles, all scholars are fools, all saints and angels blind' (78). Given God's power and glory, that is, nobody has any right to feel anything other than humble. Our hearts must therefore be all the more up lifted with love (61).

These teachings promote a balanced attitude towards one's non-contemplative fellows, and throughout the *Cloud* runs a strong current of commonsense. For instance, we are to take care of our physical health and not overstrain our bodies (109, 111). We are not to judge the inner lives of others (97), and we should know that true contemplatives are recognisable by the effects of their vision on ordinary behaviour (125). We are to submit to the uses of Holy Church, accepting its guidance and counsel. At one point the author admires Jesus' 'courtesy and propriety' (86), which we should try to emulate. And despite his attack on images, he admits 'paradoxically' (69) that they are the foundation of progress towards contemplation.

Part of the reassuring warmth to which many readers respond affectionately in the *Cloud* comes also from a distinctive tone, which can be felt even in modern translations. Thus the author explains in a conspiratorial way a spiritual 'dodge' for avoiding distractions by looking over their shoulders (98). He describes false contemplatives with amused gusto, as fidgeting, looking like sheep that have been hit on the head, or bowed in attitudes of conspicuous piety as if they had a worm in their ear (123). 'Ah, Lord God! where there are so many humble bleats without, there must be pride within' (126).

There emerges from this side of the *Cloud* the sense of a person we might trust; one much like ourselves, engaged in the business of common living, well-balanced and good humoured. These qualities, the expression of which is itself an imaginative achievement (the affirmative way, as it were, re-admitted) provide the reassurance we need that, however special we think mysticism to be, the mystic is not above us, but all the more emphatically among us precisely because of the special experience. As the *Cloud* keeps telling us, there is no true mysticism without a foundation of world-transforming charity. In short, the *Cloud* everywhere imparts the sense of a person whose belonging among other human beings is enhanced by the higher vision that might at first seem to set him apart. That is also what the New Testament tells us is Jesus' way in the world, and the mystics, among other things, describe how we might imitate and follow such a way, affirming God in a world where imagination always falls short, though we must continually engage and deploy it.

In the late Middle Ages and early Renaissance, literature of spiritual experience flowered with special luxuriance and variety. But with the Age of Enlightenment and the emergence of secularism and widespread scepticism, 'discernment of spirits' became increasingly a matter of particular religious preference rather than of general social concern. Spiritual classics continued to be written, but they often reflect the changed conditions of their broader social context, as we can see in Jean Pierre de Caussade's (1675–1751) *Abandonment to Divine Providence*.[56]

Caussade's main idea, repeated insistently, is that we should abandon ourselves to the present moment, for God's will is always hidden there. This is 'the sacrament of the moment' (24), and 'Our only satisfaction must be to live in the present moment as if there were nothing to expect beyond it' (51). Yet we must also get on with our duties, our 'external' life, where we will appear entirely ordinary and unexceptional, even though remarkable things are occurring secretly within (77, 65). Like everything else, our duties are vehicles of the divine will (23), and 'If we carefully fulfill the duties imposed on us by our state of life, if we quietly follow any impulse coming from God, if we peacefully submit to the influence of grace, we are making an act of total abandonment' (66). Such duties consist in obeying superiors (86), resisting evil and practicing virtue (81), and we can even become so busy with such things that 'we forget ourselves and all our needs' (82). This leads Caussade to a simple, if startling, conclusion: 'leave to God what is his business and carry on peacefully with your work' (82). It seems that interior abandonment to God's will at the present moment enables us to get on with our everyday tasks as if God did not exist at all.

The notion of 'hiddenness' is crucial here, and Caussade insists on it: God's will is 'hidden beneath every little detail of our lives' (41); his power is like a 'hidden scent' (60); his 'hidden activity' (93) takes place in darkness and through those whose influence on others goes unrecognised (60), even though it leaves a seed, ready to 'work in other souls' (98). Thus we must be reconciled to the fact that in the eyes of the world God's purposes are not evident and so, in turn, we must be 'detached' from worldly concerns: 'a certain detachment of soul . . . enables us to handle any situation and every kind of person' (64). Therefore, 'We must keep ourselves detached from all we feel or do if we are to travel along his path and live only for God and the duties of the present moment' (80).

Only by acquiring such 'detachment' (a version of François de Sales' 'indifference') can we allay the fears and anxieties besetting everyday life. Thus 'detached' souls feel 'no anxiety' (69), and Caussade returns frequently to the idea of abandonment to the present moment as a principal means of allaying mental distress. This abandonment partly involves also relinquishing a concern for past and future: 'We must stop all imaginings about the future, keep our attention on what is happening now and not bother about anything that has gone before or what may follow' (80). After all, we cannot know where we have come from, or where we are going (98).

Late medieval interpretations of mysticism as a special state are here pushed to an extreme, and Caussade has to be careful to avoid being thought a quietist (80). Certainly, his emphasis on inner experience markedly divides the world of private religious experience from that of everyday events. The comparable interiorising tendency in the *Cloud* is now developed by Caussade to the point where even the directives of the Christian community and of traditional literature are all but jettisoned. The *Cloud*'s nervousness about the efficacy of words and imagination becomes a wholesale

attack. Thus we are assured that because we cannot see the path
we are on, 'nothing we have read is any help to us' (83); 'Neither
books nor laborious delving into history will instruct us about the
wisdom of God' (49) and we are to avoid seeking after systems for
guidance (92). Rather, each is on a unique, interior journey: no path
is marked and we are reassured with a kind of deadpan audacity
that 'We cannot get lost when there is no road to be found' (99).
It seems, there is very little to say about the interior life, for 'we
understand nothing' (45), and even God's name is veiled among so
many names that we cannot decipher it (51).

Clearly, with Caussade the negative way teeters at the very edge
of self-contradiction, for if there were nothing at all to say, there
would be no book. Yet even here Caussade presents us with a
unique brinkmanship, because in fact he did not know he had
written a book: the letters that make up *Abandonment to Divine
Providence* were collected and published after his death. Still, of
course there were letters, and there is (after all) a book, and so,
at least, some degree of commitment to the efficacy of words,
however laden with constraints. Yet by telling us so emphatically
to avoid dwelling on the past and future, Caussade runs the risk
of utterly de-historicising the human person. And by coupling this
advice with the idea of obedience to our superiors and attendance
to duty, he removes from religious life any function critical of the
status quo, or of the dynamisms of secular affairs. Moreover, the
attack on books, systems of guidance, imagination, names, and
even on the sense that we can know ourselves as being on any path
at all, effectively cancels any means of mediating between Spirit
and the world. Guidance becomes otiose, and symbols impotent
to communicate a creative unconscious to the human community.
One price of Caussade's theory of 'the present moment' is that it
empties spiritual experience of any direct world-engaging energy
or significance. In so doing, it highlights one pressing problem of
religion in the secular society.

Still, there is also a counter-tendency throughout the book, modifying these extreme positions. This is evident first, as I have said,
in the very fact of Caussade's having written, and then also in an
ambivalence about books in general. For instance, Caussade admits
that in some circumstances we might indeed be helped by them (80)
because they can take on meanings not dreamed of by their authors
(106), which shows how God might use them for his purposes.
Likewise, Caussade admits that his recommended freedom from

anxiety is not easy to attain, and indeed that specially blessed people often suffer acutely because 'They must live on this bitter bread of anguish and exist under unrelenting pressure, for they have a conception of sanctity which never ceases to torment them' (90). In short, we are to accept sorrows (102), and faith comes alive when it experiences contradiction, which is a kind of crucifixion (39). It is as if the sacrament of the present moment, freed from anxiety and pain, is itself always to some degree a hope contradicted by experience reminding us of how unfulfilled the present moment really is.

After pushing the negative way to a limit that might easily tip over into the total privatising of spiritual experience, Caussade thus at last returns from the brink, via the cross, to a world we all share. Interestingly, in this context, he links the *via crucis* both with the Book of Revelation and with Mount Tabor (65). Faith, we learn, is 'a gulf of shadows' (42) and historical events are dark and mysterious, for the just are persecuted and this will remain so until the end of time. Here we are to recall the plagues of Revelation (42) and realise that our way through history is a way of darkness and suffering (42). Jerusalem will be built at last from the fragments of Babylon destroyed, and history remains a story of conflict between the powers of these two cities (119).

Thus Caussade also comes down from his own interior mountain into the shadows and uncertainties of a world that needs to be made whole.[57] And as with other mystics, he finds his own personality strengthened to endure and transform the world through a vision of God's deep things. Yet this personality, as St. Paul insists, is not any more that of the 'old man', but one in which Christ moves. It is not, that is, the apparent subject of everyday consciousness re-engaging the world, but an ego pervaded by an experiential, felt participation in a creative unconscious that pre-possesses it, and is antithetical to its narrow grasping and dominative selfishness. In some such context we might return to the idea that psychoanalysis inherits the traditions of mysticism. In one sense, this is a hidden or concealed inheritance, mediated by the Romantic movement wherein, by and large, Caussade's kind of privatised religious experience re-emerged into public discourse as a mysticism without systematic theology. The story of such a development would be intricate, but in Jung's teachings on self and ego, as in Lacan's on the apparent subject, or in Erich Neumann's discussion of mysticism as an encounter between ego and the archetypes of a creative unconscious, the old science of discerning genuine vision against the subterfuges and techniques of selfishness and domination remains with us. As ever, the symbols by which we represent such discernments of power are part of the culture we make.

Finally, it might be worth noticing how these suggestions of the transmission of a perennial philosophy are complemented today by a powerful, renewed interest in explicit rapprochements between secular politics and mystical theology, especially among Liberation theologians. Thus, Schillebeeckx calls for a form of 'political love' wherein 'love of God – ultimately mysticism – can enter the concrete social and political commitment of Christians'.[58] In the making of a modern, global and international culture, the old and new, spiritual and secular, might still take strength from one another. But as we have seen, the dialectic of 'is and not yet', the dramatic consolidation of the apocalyptic Son of Man and the suffering Son of God continues to underlie a perennial experience of broken visions, an epiphany on the mountain obscured and persecuted in the byways of the world. As historical persons, we do not yet know how to name what we hope for; the word indeed is made flesh, but flesh and word are not yet one. In the shadows, we go on interrogating our symbols that remind us of the absence we do not name, the self we do not know, the condition of our contradiction. In negotiating such labyrinths towards the homecoming of humanity to itself, and the liberation of each person through the realization of a common good, religious language might join again with the other languages of culture that would assist us on the way.

6

Social Communities

MARX AND PRESENCE OF OTHERS

T. S. Eliot once observed that a Christian ought to have good reasons for not being a Marxist. Eliot himself did not dwell much on the reasons, but he recognised the basic challenge Marxism offers to Christian praxis. As history shows, the exercise of charity as the main rule of life has hardly measured up to the theory of charity as selfless giving to others. A Marxist would claim that history shows instead how modern Christianity has been widely appropriated by the competitive and self-serving ideology of liberal bourgeois individualism, just as it was previously by feudalism. Consequently, to a large degree Christianity has served as the instrument of oppressive forces against which, in theory, it raises its voice.

By contrast, Marx approaches history by looking first to the material conditions of production.[1] He tells us that labour is the chief instrument of human self-creation, and control over the means of production confers control over the human beings whose labour produces what is necessary for the satisfaction of human needs. The result is a perennial condition wherein the wealth of a dominant few is founded upon the enforced labour of many. Thus, in the ancient world, slavery was the basis of an economic life sustaining sophisticated civilizations. In the Middle Ages, feudalism developed under Germanic military organisation, compelling the labour power of an enserfed small peasantry, and as feudal hegemony spread to encompass the towns, it shaped the development of trade guilds and the emergence of a burgher class. Eventually, the rise of manufacture and development of industrial capital in the eighteenth and nineteenth centuries produced conditions for the economic and political dominance of the modern bourgeoisie and the liberal ideology that still supports capitalism. Under the capitalist system, money no longer symbolises labour, but has acquired autonomous power.

Marx identifies the beginning of capitalism as the moment when the owner of capital encounters the labourer whose only property is his or her labour power, thereby creating the circumstance in which human labour is treated merely as another commodity, and natural relationships are resolved into money relationships. Marx tells us that communism will abolish this state of things, liberating people from exploitation and anxiety caused by the rule of money. Yet Marx also holds that communism can come about only after full industrial development.[2] Only when the productive forces of labour are maximised by efficient industrial technology can human beings be relieved of alienating work, and human need satisfaction be achieved by all. Increasingly serious collisions between relations of production and forces of production will herald an eventual stultification and breakdown of capitalist economy, and whether or not this is happening in the twentieth century is the most fervently-debated aspect of Marxism. The unconvinced point out that Marx's predictions have not taken account of the diversity and flexibility of modern markets, and that many of his economic theories are discredited. Besides, the so-called communist states at the present time are in evident disarray.

Nonetheless, Marx's attacks on the alienations and oppressions perpetrated by industrial capitalism and its enshrining ideology are often devastating. The description in *Capital I* of how the factory system enslaves families, the horrors of vagabondage, child labour, addiction to opium, dehumanising work and working conditions, is an indictment simultaneously blood-chilling and imperative. And in this context, Marx's criticism of religion occupies a special position. Basically, this criticism draws on Feuerbach, whose book, *The Essence of Christianity*, proposed that God is the human species in alienated form, and that veneration accorded to God ought to be directed back to its true object, humankind. For Feuerbach, the Christian claim that the human Jesus is divine is at least a step in the right direction.

In the *Economic and Philosophical Manuscripts*, Marx develops the Feuerbachian idea that humans are alienated from their own species being, and he describes communism then as the 're-integration and return of man into himself'.[3] In the *Theses on Feuerbach*,[4] Marx affirms this general position, and praises Feuerbach for resolving religion 'into its secular basis' (IV). Yet, for Marx, Feuerbach's critique remains limited because it stops short of a thoroughgoing revolutionary 'practical-critical' engagement (I): Marx points out

that religious sentiment 'is itself a social product' (VII), and altera-
tions effected in consciousness by means of a mere philosophical
critique are insufficient. Rather, the structures that produce religious
consciousness must themselves be changed. 'Man', says Marx, 'has
found only his own reflection in the fantastic reality of heaven'[5]
and we must understand that 'man makes religion; religion does
not make man' (131). This point underlies every effective critique
of religion, and, in turn, 'the critique of religion is the prerequisite
of every critique' (131).

The language of religious promises is thus the fundamental
example for Marx of how ideologies offer illusory prospects of
happiness that turn attention away from attaining real happiness
'of this world' (132). Here is the famous paragraph:

> The wretchedness of religion is at once an expression of and a
> protest against real wretchedness. Religion is the sigh of the
> oppressed creature, the heart of a heartless world, and the soul
> of soulless conditions. It is the opium of the people. (131)

Although religion here is allowed to protest against an oppressive
world, it is also condemned for providing an artificial escape. Yet,
in general, Marx's distaste for how the ruling classes manipulate
religion to subject the poor outweighs his appreciation of authentic
religious protest. 'The abolition of religion as the illusory happiness
of the people,' he holds first and last, 'is a demand for their true
happiness' (131).

But if we take the critique of religion as the premise of all
criticism, and grant that humans indeed are caught up in illusions
and self-alienation, the problem of how to describe our true 'species
being' becomes urgent. Marx takes us to the heart of the difficulty
when he points out that human nature itself changes in the process
by which nature is changed through human labour: man 'acts upon
external nature and changes it, and in this way he simultaneously
changes his own nature'.[6] Marx never relinquished this idea that
consciousness is not so much 'natural' as a product of social conditions. Thus, he tells us in the *German Ideology* that 'men, developing
their material production and their material intercourse, alter, along
with this their real existence, their thinking and the products of their
thinking. Life is not determined by consciousness, but consciousness
by life'.[7] And in a well-known sentence from the preface to the
Contribution to the Critique of Political Economy, we are assured that

people's consciousness does not determine being, 'but their social existence . . . determines their consciousness'.[8] It follows that part of the revolutionary and 'practical critical' activity missing from Feuerbach is an engagement in the class struggle whereby oppressive structures are changed, and false-consciousness discovered for what it is.

However, if consciousness is produced by social structures and if these are oppressive, how are the revolutionaries to escape the ideological net entrapping all the others? And what then can it mean to define communism as the 'return of man to himself'? Lenin's pragmatic solution was to call for a vanguard party to effect changes that would enable the less perspicacious proletariat to see the light of day. Thus, although the masses are blinded by false-consciousness and kept in thrall to the economic *status quo*, a critical minority is apparently able to detect the mechanisms of oppression and resist them. Yet if this is the case, the social determinants must be less than determining after all, and Marxist intellectuals by and large concede the point to some degree. One favourite way of doing so is by insisting on how complex and subtle are relationships between base and superstructure, cultural formations and class struggle, as Marx himself helps to show us in his own complex analyses of actual social change. Thus the Italian Marxist Antonio Gramsci deploys but adapts the notion of a vanguard party to his call for 'organic intellectuals', by which he means an intelligentsia capable of using the resources of a culture to bring to light the real experiences of the masses. Gramsci laments the historical breach between intellectuals and the people and claims that 'cultural hegemony', or the control of intellectual life by cultural means is essential to revolution. But Gramsci is also a strong proponent of the view that 'human nature' is not fixed, and that education can reveal tendencies or trends whereby people can recognise their condition and react against oppressive elements. Clearly, for Gramsci the human subject is produced by a many-layered history it cannot observe directly, but which it is able to influence.

Gramsci's line of thinking overlaps with the more stringent and styptic analysis of subjectivity by Louis Althusser, maintaining that social relations shape consciousness to the degree that the very experience of subjectivity is itself ideologically produced 'empiricism of the subject', we are assured, 'always correspond' to an idealism of the essence'.[9] Althusser explains that ideology is so inherent in language as to constitute even our most intuitive or 'obvious' sense of ourselves. To develop this claim, he draws on his one-time psychoanalyst Jacques Lacan, whose theory of the 'mirror stage' (as we have seen) proposes that our earliest sense of personal identity depends on a misrecognition of ourselves in others. For Althusser, ideology is likewise an imaginary mis-recognition, and is necessary for the ruling classes to maintain control. Yet such misrecognitions are so much a part of what we take to be 'natural' that we remain unconscious of their arbitrariness: 'those who are in ideology believe themselves by definition outside ideology.'[10]

The problem of how Althusser gets outside ideology sufficiently to make such pronouncements is, again, the 'false consciousness' question pushed to its limit, and his answer, in the end, resembles Gramsci's. Some of us can come to recognise how ideology is 'a structure essential to the historical life of societies', and 'only the existence and the recognition of its necessity enable us to act on ideology and transform ideology into an instrument of deliberate action on history'.[11] One function of literature, for example, is to effect the kind of distantiation from our apparent selves that enables us to break the mirror of ideological mystification in which 'an age can recognise itself (but not know itself)'.[12] With this in mind, Althusser analyses Bertolazzi's play *El Nost Milan*.

Althusser begins by pointing out that the play has two time schemes, one operating as 'chronicle', the other as 'tragedy'. The first is empty: it is the time of the cheap fun-fair and run-down eating house of the Milan sub-proletariat, a time with no future and no hope, marked by chronic unemployment and powerlessness. This empty time is sustained by illusions, suggested by the fun-fair and by Nina's father who encourages her romantic dreams, and then, out of a deluded sense of honour, kills his daughter's would-be seducer. But this empty time co-exists with a full, properly dialectical time, marked by lightning-moments when 'some history must take place' 137). This is a time when illusions and false-consciousness are ruptured by encounter with otherness. This is pre-eminently the time of Nina's decision to take her destiny into her own hands and to leave her father's world in order to sell herself in the other world, the world of pleasure and money, containing she knows not what.

Nina does not realise the distinction between the two kinds of time: 'the structure is nowhere exposed, nowhere does it constitute the object of a speech or dialogue' (141–2). Rather, it exists tacitly as a set of balances and imbalances. Althusser proposes that this co-existence of 'dialectical temporality and a non-dialectical temporality, is the basis for a true critique of the illusions of consciousness' (142). Such a critique is basically an encounter between 'false dialectic' and the 'disconcerting reality which is its basis and which is waiting for recognition' (143). Consciousness, that is, needs 'the radical discovery of what is *other than itself*' (143), such as occurs when Nina makes a new beginning, even though she does not know exactly what she is doing. In turning away from the familiar myths in which a society 'can recognise itself (but not know itself)' (144), she breaks with a confining ideology, taking a step towards the real.

This process constitutes the characters' 'deep meaning' (145), which is hidden from them because not centered in their ideologically imprinted subjectivities. For this reason, Bertolazzi, like Brecht, is careful to offset the play's centre, placing (or displacing) it 'always to one side' (145) in a way that shows how the spectator's experience is analogous to that of the play's characters. The spectator has no better claim than they to 'absolute consciousness of self', or even to a reliable sense of personal identity, but experiences the play 'in the mode of a questioned false consciousness' (148). Thus the audience in a sense is already in the play, sharing history and false-consciousness in the same ways as the characters, but now better able to recognise this fact. 'The only question, then, is what is the fate of this tacit identity, this immediate self-recognition . . . ?' (150)

Again, recognition is the lynch-pin and, as I have argued especially in Chapter 3, a capacity to recognise degrees of significance is basic to what I have been describing as the idea of the person. Not surprisingly, then, even despite his resistance to the notion of personal identity, Althusser insists that the promised 'disconcerting reality' indeed awaits our 'recognition' (143) and choice to engage it despite our enclosure in 'spontaneous ideology' (144). The open-endedness of our encounters with reality is explainable partly by the fact that culture (or ideology) does not bear a simple relationship to the economic base, and Althusser especially argues for a complex, non-synchronous set of relationships between them. In doing so, he intends to attack theories of 'expressive totality' among such Marxists as Lukács, but he wants also to establish a place for the Marxist intellectual as one who could discover and explicate the 'deep structures' of Marx's own texts. Althusser tells us that the work of intellectuals is important, because 'Marxist philosophy . . . has still largely to be constituted',[13] and the intellectual is especially an agent of those key recognitions necessary to dispel the worst effects of ideology. Yet in so arguing, Althusser makes himself vulnerable to the charge of privileging the cultural superstructure, a deviation to which he eventually confessed.[14] Ironically, this urgent deconstructor of subjectivity ended up being accused of egoism.

Marx's own broad view is that people do indeed make their own history, but in circumstances not of their own choosing. Clearly, a good deal here depends on how much scope there is for choice in any given set of circumstances, and how much autonomy is granted to persons unconsciously held in thrall to ideology. Althusser pushes the argument so far in one direction that the autonomous subject becomes entirely illusory, and it is therefore impossible to erect criteria upon which debate about the relative adequacy of ideas to politics or history could be conducted at all. Indeed, one main reason for the eventual shelving of the Althusserian project by many French Marxists is precisely Althusser's inability to deal effectively or coherently with actual political events.[15]

My main suggestion in relation to this difficulty is that the idea of 'false consciousness' needs to be interpreted in light of my arguments in earlier chapters about our capacity as persons to recognise and describe aspects of a common world. It is therefore heartening to discover that some Marxist commentators also confirm this way of thinking. For instance, Alan Wood and David-Hillel Ruben stress that Marx held a commonsense view of the world as independent of ourselves, and Charles W. Mills builds upon this position to argue against attributing to Marx the view that all thought is determined by a ruling ideology.[16] Human beings can indeed assess some empirical facts independently of ideological illusions, and, for instance, Marx himself relied on facts about wage-rates, factory conditions, and so on, recorded by government officials. Mills suggests that a multi-causal model, responsive to a variety of tendencies and interactive patterns, best reflects Marx's intent. Consequently, the term 'contradictory consciousness' is often more fruitful than 'false consciousness' for describing our immersion in, and capacity to criticise, a dominant ideology. Some such perspective, grounded in a commonsense epistemology such as I have been proposing, helps to check the Althusserian position from spilling over into an endlessly self-involved play of the kind invited by extreme deconstruction.

This caveat is worth noticing because Althusser's influence on literary intellectuals remains extensive, and his thinking on decentered subjects, conflicting meanings, and the perpetration of ideologies has been disseminated by such as Pierre Machery, Fredric Jameson and Terry Eagleton, as well as through a variety of scholars and critics associated with 'New Historicism' and 'Cultural Materialism'. After surveying some of this recent criticism-in-the-making, Raymond Williams recommends that a literary analysis should be directed at the 'historically-based conventions of language and representation',[17] so that texts can be read as history. Thus, we are to discover ways in which texts mediate contradictions within the society that produced them, presenting us at once with the ideological determinants of the sense we have of ourselves as persons, while simultaneously transgressing against those determinants. This kind of reading shows how subjects are not what they take themselves to be, and also how persons dwell perennially in the welcoming shadows of ideological self-misrecognition.

Literature, then, can discover to us something of our personal contradictions and their social embededness, the dark places of our motivations, the fragility and uncertainty of consciousness, and literature is thereby a means of recognition that we are not just what we think we are. And so we return once more to the centrality of recognition and to the question of who does the recognising, and what is recognised. As we see, Althusser points to a 'disconcerting reality'[18] that awaits us, and claims that only by 'recognising' ideology as necessary to the historical life of societies can we set about making a liberating instrument of that same ideology. Likewise, for Fredric Jameson the 'shock, or the failure, of recognition'[19] is central to dialectical criticism, the way in which latent content works its way to the surface and we are released or sprung from our hardening ideas. Gramsci tells us that people need to criticise their own conceptions in order to organise against oppression, and one function of the 'organic intellectual' is to enable such self-recognition: 'In this sense, recognition is power.'[20] For Ernst Bloch, the sheer astonishment accompanying our recognition of the latent potentialities of objects and situations is a key to the revolutionary *novum*,[21] as he tells us repeatedly.

For all these thinkers, the dispelling of contradictory consciousness entails a degree of recognition that what we take to be a stable self is shot through with misapprehensions, and tacit assumptions shaped by language and culture. For Gramsci, the main distinction of Marxism is to have expressed this truth for its own times better than any other theory, but he insists that the field of struggle is 'absolutely mysterious, characterised absolutely by the unforseeable and by the unexpected'.[22] In other words, Marxism is itself a transitional value and itself an ideology, as Althusser also says. The point is made again by Lukács, who sees Marxism as a 'method' that will take new forms:[23] it is itself 'a form moving in time'[24] as Jameson tells us. And for Ernst Bloch, no one knows what a developed human nature would be like: 'the human capacity for such an absolute concept of goal is the tremendous aspect in an existence where the best still remains patchwork, where every end again and again becomes a means to serve the still utterly opaque, indeed in and for itself still unavailable fundamental goal, final goal.'[25]

Indeed, if recognition is an awakening from the contradictory to the more adequate, we must beware of hypostasising any set of doctrines that are themselves historically produced, including Marx's own. But we must be careful, likewise, not to surrender entirely our criteria of objectivity, or our willingness to propose grounds for preferring one theory to another in accounting for the phenomena.

In short, we ought not to dispense with the idea of the person altogether just because persons are deeply entangled in contradiction and do not see themselves clearly: such entanglement, indeed, is part of what it means to be a historical person. Admittedly, mechanical, Zhdanovite models of the base-superstructure problem have been by and large discarded today by Marxist intellectuals, and one consequence has been the surrender of dogmatic attempts at over-simple kinds of uniformity. Liberation from contradictory consciousness in the variety of the world's cultures is clearly a task so multivalent, complex and ungraspable from any single viewpoint, and the prospect itself so haunted by – among other things – the spectre of Stalinism (and its varieties in other so-called communist states), that one countenances today a variety of Marxisms, a range of applications of the founder's thinking, more and less progressive. Yet in a simple way, the premise that we live alienated lives, not yet truly ourselves, remains basic as the engenderer of critical protest and hope alike, all of which is compatible with the notion of the person I have been describing. And these concerns in turn might reduce to the disarmingly simple issue of whether or not we regard the human person as selfish and egotistical 'by nature': that is, to how we interpret the fundamental problem of the Flaw, and the prospect of human self-improvement.

Repeatedly and to a surprising degree, David Conway's confident

book *A Farewell to Marx*,[26] turns on just this issue. Conway outlines
Marx's main positions, and then tells us what is wrong with them.
Thus, Marx took over from Feuerbach the idea that egoism and
selfishness prevent other-directed concern for species-being (21).
Marx's critique of Hegel's *Philosophy of Right*, like his essay *On
the Jewish Question*, is based on a realisation that the only rights
protected by the state are those of egocentric individuals in civil
society, bent on acquisitiveness and personal gain. Likewise, his
attacks on capitalism in the *Economic and Philosophical Manuscripts*
and *The German Ideology* centre on the fact that capitalism fosters
egoism, and that communism stresses altruism, co-operation and
disinterestedness (44).

Conway's rejoinder is that people are acquisitive, and, on the
whole, self-seeking, a fact that communist societies discover when
they succumb to the dictatorship of power elites, as they invariably
have done (51). Rather, Conway favours the argument proposed
by the classical economists, that self-interest is the most powerful human motive, and that persons are selfish by nature (184).
He points out that 'human beings, as a rule, are disposed to
be self-centered in their concerns and to have only strictly limited sympathy' (198), and, consequently, that private property is
necessary to avoid inter-personal conflicts. In short, we are to
acknowledge the limitations of human nature – its self-centeredness
and acquisitiveness – and conclude that capitalism makes the best,
most productive use of our imperfect human resources: capitalism,
in short, best reflects our nature as persons. By contrast, Marxism
promotes merely an illusory, utopian concept of human nature,
and this illusion is dangerous because it passes all too easily into
intolerance and self-righteousness. Thus communists have shown
a disastrous willingness to sacrifice people to the Party, and to
raise consciousness by liquidating and otherwise repressing those
who are held to be insufficiently altruistic. Michael Polanyi[27] adds
a dimension to Conway's analysis by noticing how the doctrine of
original sin traditionally reminded believers of an inherited Flaw in
the form of unregeneracy and selfishness, thus placing a check on
unlimited moral aspirations to bring about the kingdom here and
now. In dispensing with original sin and with religion in general,
Marxism is vulnerable to a messianic fervor in a secularised, supposedly scientific form, a pure moral impulse unwilling (or unable)
to compromise, and thus too easily set on a path of destructiveness
in the name of liberation.

Insofar as the Marxist concept of individualism means selfishness, exploitation, and egoistic prejudice, indeed individualism is properly denounced. But it is less clearly evident that the words 'individual' and 'person' should be confused. The distinction between them is longstanding in theology and philosophy, and the idea of the person acknowledges (among other things) that the human being is endowed with a degree of freedom, finding an identity in relation to others, and comprising conscious and unconscious dimensions. A person's ego sustains a sense of identity and continuity, but the ego is not identical with the person. Indeed, equating one's personality with the ego, which by definition is appropriative and grasping, is what the mystics mean by sin, and Marxists by 'individualism'. From a broadly Marxist viewpoint, then, literature enables us to recognise the limitations of ego-consciousness and individualism, and to see ourselves as decentred, alienated, both more and less than we think we are. But as I have argued in earlier chapters, literature is also mimetic, and what we recognise is partly a common world we know and share empirically in a manner that is personal, and not just individual. To show something of how this is so, I would like to turn again to Shakespeare, whose *The Merchant of Venice* is deeply concerned with matters pertaining to religious ideology and the economic base – in this case, venture capital in relation to church teachings about usury.

THE ALIEN INSIDE: READING *THE MERCHANT OF VENICE*

Despite its modern diversity, one main thrust of Marxist literary criticism is to show how texts mediate or disclose what I have described in the previous section as contradictory consciousness. The text then becomes a site for understanding history, and criticism helps us to recognise our present condition and act to change it. That is, by showing the historical embeddedness of a text we are better able to see it as the product of a certain shaping situation, part of a continuing 'dynamic, unstable, and reciprocal relationship between the discursive and material domains', as Louis Montrose says.[28]

In recent years, literature of the English Renaissance has offered especially fruitful ground for such analyses, and a body of work is at present forming in England under the rubric 'Cultural Materialism', and in the United States, 'New Historicism'. Not all Cultural

Materialists and New Historicists are Marxists, but I would like to begin by considering a strongly materialist interpretation of *The Merchant of Venice* by Walter Cohen,[29] who argues that the play shows Shakespeare combining two contrasting theories of socio-economic relations. The first derives from English history and reflects a widespread anxiety in Shakespeare's day about the rise of mercantilism and the shifting of financial power away from the landed aristocracy. The second derives from Italy, where capitalism was more advanced and confident. Cohen argues that fear of usury among the ruling English nobility faded once they adapted to capitalism. But the transitional phase – which was in process during Shakespeare's lifetime – was fraught with uncertainty. In this context, Cohen notices that Shylock does not always act like a conventional usurer: for instance, his demand for the pound of flesh even when he is offered great sums of money does not make financial sense. This goes to show that Shylock does not really belong in the world of sixteenth-century Venice, but rather in the Venice of two or three centuries before: he is a medieval figure of folklore, and is archaic, diabolical and obsolete. By reworking history in this way, Shakespeare expresses an English fear of bad old times, while presenting modern Italian bourgeois mercantilism as a way of allaying it. Consequently, Antonio is not permitted to be too progressive or too conservative, and through him the aristocratic landed wealth of Belmont and the mercantile capital of Venice are reconciled. Cohen also suggests that Shakespeare's theatre itself exemplifies petty commodity production in process of making the transition to capitalism, and (like the monarchy) it survived by catering simultaneously to anarchic instincts and traditional aristocratic authority.

In this context, Cohen provides a brief analysis of the play's religious themes. Shakespeare, he tells us, 'combines a formally dominant, Christian, aristocratic ideology' with a set of demystifying qualifications, thereby producing the characteristic 'central creative tension of Shakespearean drama' (781). Cohen especially associates the play's orthodox religious elements with allegory (a technique for affirming unity), and points out that the malapropisms and jumbled theological language of Launcelot Gobbo ('devil incarnation', 'my young master doth expect your reproach', and so on) effectively complicate 'and thus demystify the serious religious issues of the plot' (780). At this point, Cohen's argument merges with a variety of other critical analyses showing how Christians in *The Merchant of Venice* espouse values in contradiction to their actions (they preach mercy and charity, but show none). Yet the connections between allegory and religious ideology in the play seem deeply entangled also with a pervasive allusiveness to the Bible, engaging in turn a set of concerns deriving from contemporary debate about usury laws. All of this raises again in a strong form the relationship between charity and economic practice that so concerned Marx, and which in turn brings into question the status of personal choice in relation to the powerful and unconscious effects of ideology. I would like now to examine further, and thereby attempt to develop, some of Cohen's thoughtful arguments.

In an obvious sense, *The Merchant of Venice* keeps bringing us back to a distinction between two kinds of riches: those associated with money, and those associated with the worth of personal relationships. This broad contrast between material and spiritual treasure is broadly Biblical, and is part of the debate throughout the play on mercy and justice, which in turn involves the theme of love and forgiveness of one's enemies, and the entire relationship between Shylock, who is frequently referred to simply as 'the Jew', and the Christians who berate him from what they take to be their superior position. The word 'gentle' occurs frequently as a pun on 'gentile', and Shylock swears by Jacob's staff, by father Abraham, and cites the story of Laban, thus confirming his allegiance with what Christians call the Old Testament. When his daughter runs off with Lorenzo and becomes a Christian, and when conversion is forced upon Shylock after the trial, the general issue of the relationship between Christian revelation and the Jewish scriptures, and between gentiles and Jews, is urgently upon us. 'I stand for Justice' (IV,i,103) says Shylock at the trial, a remark echoing Portia's earlier declaration, 'I stand for sacrifice' (III,ii,57). This opposition conforms broadly to the Christian conception of how Jesus' sacrifice redeems us from the rigours of the law, and Shakespeare keeps probing these ideas, which, as we see, are closely associated with the two central attitudes to money.

The binary structure of these various thematic elements is fairly obvious: justice-mercy; revenge-love; money-value; Jew-gentile. Indeed, as if to confirm such a design, the play throughout is built up in sets of linked yet opposed pairs. On the one hand is the enchanted, golden world of Belmont, with its touches of sweet harmony, brimming silence and haunting moonlight, where the heavens are inlaid with patens of gold, and mysterious longings brought provocatively to the rim of consciousness through the fairy-tale motif of the caskets are fulfilled at last in surprise and delight: 'you are all amazed' (V,i,266), says Portia. On the other hand is Venice, a centre of nascent capitalism, opulent and hard. 'I know not why I am so sad', says Antonio in the play's first line, but the choric duo, Antonio's so-called friends Salerio and Solanio, help to remind him why. Antonio's mind is 'tossing on the ocean', where his 'argosies with portly sail' are 'Like signiors and rich burghers on the flood' (I,i,8–9), and yet at risk, for his merchant venture involves committing his capital to the vagaries of foreign trade and the dangers of sea-voyaging. In their elaborate concern about Antonio's anxiety, Salerio and Solanio express also something heartless and menacing, ready to shrug with ambiguously gratified commiseration at the shipwreck of their friend's fortunes. This is opulent, venture-capital Venice, where entrepreneurs are equal, where dog eats dog, and where the general spirit is a good deal short of charitable. Venice is an anxious world, and Antonio the merchant is tainted by it, even though he does not exact usury.

Basically, the contrast between Belmont and Venice could not be stronger, and is duplicated in a whole series of further oppositions. Thus, there are two trials, one in Venice, the other (involving the rings) in Belmont. There are two daughters, the first, Portia, under the rule of a magically benign father; the second, Jessica, under the rule of the father as ogre. There are two 'venturing' lovers, Bassanio and Gratiano, who make two pairs with Portia and Nerissa. And there are even two merchants, Antonio and Shylock. When we put all this along with the thematic twofoldness I have outlined (mercy against justice, and so on), it seems easy to conclude that Shakespeare's play asks to be read through a series of oppositions that control the action.

In this context we are especially invited to assess the Biblical themes. Various critics touch on the subject, and I would like for a moment to have Barbara Lewalski stand as their representative.[30] Briefly, Lewalski argues that *The Merchant of Venice* is about Christian love and its antitheses. Antonio is a Christ figure, ready to give his life to redeem his friend's debt, while Shylock sinks further into vengefulness and evil, the opposite of redemptive love. The casket plot represents Everyman's choice of spiritual life and death, and at the courtroom scene, Antonio's plight resembles the crucifixion, with Portia representing Mercy. This is the allegorical side of Lewalski's argument; the other side deals with Biblical allusions.

For instance, the venture theme is associated with Christian love through Matthew 6:19–20: 'Lay not up for yourselves treasures upon earth . . . / But lay up for yourselves treasures in heaven.' Gratiano's speech on loss and gain ('You have too much respect upon the world; / They lose it that do buy it with much care' [I,i,74–5]), recalls Matthew 16:25–6 ('For whosoever will save his life, shall lose it . . . / For what is a man profited, if he shall gain the whole world, if he lose his own soul?'). The Sermon on the Mount, calling for forgiveness and love of one's enemies, is exemplified by Antonio's eventual patient submission to Shylock, and Matthew's exhortation, 'do good to them that hate you' (5:44) is what Antonio attempts to enact. In laying down his life for his friend, Antonio exemplifies the injunction in John 15:13 ('Greater love hath no man than this, that a man lay down his life for his friends'). Matthew's version of the Lord's prayer in the Bishops and Geneva versions has the words 'Forgive us our dettes, as we forgive our detters' (6:12), and is alluded to twice in the trial scene, as Portia pleads with Shylock to 'render / The deeds of mercy' (IV,i,200–1) rather than demand exact justice. Her famous speech on the quality of mercy that 'droppeth as the gentle rain from heaven' closely follows Ecclesiasticus 25:19 ('O how faire a thyng is mercy in the tyme of anguish and trouble: it is like a cloud of rayne that commeth in the tyme of drought'). There are clear allusions also to Genesis and the Book of Daniel, where Daniel is called Baltasar, paralleled by Portia's taking the name Balthasar when she goes in disguise, and by the fact that the ecstatically-vindictive Gratiano welcomes her as 'A Daniel come to judgment' (IV,i,222). Shylock's cry, 'The curse never fell upon our nation till now; I never felt it till now' (III,i,80–1) alludes to the curse pronounced on Jerusalem in Matthew 23:38, 'Behold your house is left unto you desolate.' And when Shylock says, 'I have a daughter; / Would any of the stock of Barabbas / Had been her husband' (IV,i,294–5), he alludes to the choice of Barabbas over Christ described in Matthew 27:16–21 (though no doubt mediated by way of Marlowe). There is a good deal else of the same sort, on the strength of which Lewalski concludes that in *The Merchant of Venice* 'patterns of Biblical allusion and imagery' are 'so precise and pervasive as to be patently deliberate' (328).

Many of these passages are cited also by other critics and editors, and it is hard to deny their relevance. But as far as I can tell, no critic has focused on the simple fact that the preponderance of such allusions derives from the gospel according to Matthew. This is the case with practically all of the examples I have cited from the New Testament. Matthew gives us the Sermon on the Mount and the Lord's prayer, and Matthew's is more concerned than any other gospel with the relationship between Jewish law and the new Christian church. Moreover, Matthew's gospel is more explicitly concerned with money than any of the others. Matthew's special material, by which he is distinguished from the synoptics, shows a marked emphasis on people dealing with money: the story of the treasure in the field (13:44), the pearl of great price (13:45), the labourers in the vineyard (20:1–16), and the wise and foolish maidens (25:1–13) occur only in Matthew.

For a long time, the church regarded Matthew's gospel as first-composed, and it is still printed that way in most bibles. One reason for this opinion is Matthew's special relevance to a newly-institutional Christianity: his is the only gospel to use the word *ekklesia* ('church'), and he is everywhere concerned with the new ecclesiastical identity and mission of the Christian movement.[31] To a degree unmatched by the other gospels, Matthew insists on symmetry and balance, and he is fond of rhetorical structures exploring relationships between opposites. Thus the Sermon on the Mount is developed within the antithetical framework, 'You have heard that it was said . . . But I say unto you' (5:27ff). Two senses of fire are counterpointed in John the Baptist's promise that the Holy Spirit will baptise with fire, but also that 'unquenchable fire' will burn up the chaff when the wheat is separated out (3:11–12). A man cannot have two masters (6:24), and houses built on rock and sand are compared (7:24–7), as are the fruits of good and corrupt trees (12:33). Whoever saves his life will lose it, and whoever loses it will save it (16:25), and so on.

Matthew's fascination with antitheses is confirmed also by his concern with doubles and pairs, and a peculiar habit of giving us two where Mark gives us one, even when it does not make much sense to do so. Thus in the country of the Gadarenes, Jesus meets two men possessed by devils (8:28); after he cures Jairus' daughter, two blind men follow him (9:27); and again, later, he cures two blind men (9:30). He sends two disciples for an ass and a colt, and is strangely said to ride into Jerusalem on both animals (21:2). Other examples come readily to mind: if a man takes your coat, give him your cloak also (5:40); if you are forced to walk a mile, go two (5:41); there are parables about two brothers (20:24) and about two sons (21:28).

Indeed, other gospels have their share of antitheses and dualities, but the fact remains that no other gospel shows such a concentrated and unremitting interest in binary structures. This emphasis is partly pedagogical, for repetition facilitates teaching. Yet it is also connected to the fact that Matthew alone among the evangelists gives an account of the Last Judgement in which the Lord's pronouncement divides the opposites: on the one hand, 'Come, ye blessed of my Father, inherit the kingdom prepared for you from the foundation of the world' (25:34); on the other, 'Depart from me ye cursed, into everlasting fire, prepared for the devil and his angels' (25:41). Matthew is fierce on this matter, and keeps reminding us how the fate of the iniquitous is 'a furnace of fire' (13:2). In the final accounting, that is, the difference between the opposites is absolute and terrible. And yet there is also the parable of the wheat and tares, which, again, is unique to Matthew (13:24–30). In it, the weeds (or tares) are allowed to grow along with the wheat, for fear that uprooting the young weeds would also uproot the young wheat. Only at the harvest will two piles be made, and the weeds burned. The idea is, then, that fierce and final as the last judgement will be, we are not really in a position to make it yet, while we are alive and kicking along the furrows of human existence. But if this is the case, how does the parable fit with Matthew's unremitting insistence on antitheses?

To help to answer this, I would like to re-consider briefly an argument I have proposed elsewhere[32] about Matthew's special fondness for the Greek word *seismos* (in the verb form, *seio*), which means a commotion or shaking, and is translated as 'tempest' or 'earthquake', or 'to shake' or 'move'. There are only two occurrences of this word in the other three gospels together: Matthew uses it seven times, for instance to describe the commotion in Jerusalem when Jesus enters (21:10), the earthquake that occurs when he dies (27:51) causing the centurion's terror (27:54). Translations obscure the fact that Matthew uses the same word to indicate Christ's renovating power breaking in upon the world, and also the radical upheavals upsetting normal order and expectation. Symmetry, law, and organization, that is, are of our own making, but by themselves they are inert. The Christian *energia* does not dispense with such foundations, but is brilliantly unsettling, and makes of them the mediator of something new and strange. Thus, Matthew's Jesus is especially upset about the over-reliance on formal order among certain Pharisees, and continually points to hypocrisy as

a dangerous triumph of precept over practice. The hypocritical
Pharisees for Matthew are whited sepulchers 'which indeed appear
beautiful outward, but are within full of dead men's bones' (23:27).
It seems clear also that Matthew realises he is to apply the lessons
of his seismic Christ and the story of the wheat and tares to
his own, heavily catechetical, highly-organised discourse. In short,
God's ways remain disconcerting, surprising to our expectation,
and the measure of such disturbance is precisely that there is a
foundation of expectation, a pattern to fulfil. Matthew seems quite
aware of presenting us simultaneously with order, with clearly
defined pairs, antitheses and doubles, and then with the disturbing
tertium quid, the unsettler of our best-laid rhetoric, our best-dressed
self-righteousness.

This effect is especially prominent in Matthew's money stories.
His parables about investments and riches and treasures are in
fact unnerving bits of subversive narration when we look at them
closely. For instance, the parable of the labourers in the vineyard
(20:1–16) tells of workers hired early in the morning, and who work
all day. Then, at the eleventh hour, some new workers are hired, and
at the end of the day everyone is paid the same wage – one denarius.
On the face of it, if the householder is God, he acts unfairly. Exegetes
of course do their best to evade the problem by claiming for instance
that the parable describes how the gentiles came late into Israel's
history through Jesus, but are no less worthy. Or, since one denarius
is a subsistence wage, the employer really wanted to be sure nobody
starved.

In the parable of the ten maidens (25:1–13) which is carefully
paired with the parable of the talents directly following, the five
who garner oil for their lamps are allowed to accompany the
bridegroom, but the other five, less prudent ones, are not. When
these five ask to borrow oil from the five who have it, they are
refused, and told to go and buy some. Yet this refusal, we might
reflect, sits ill with Jesus' earlier instructions in the Sermon on
the Mount: 'Give to him that asketh thee, and from him that
would borrow of thee turn not thou away' (5:42). Indeed, by the
standard of the Sermon on the Mount, the wise maidens ought
to have given *all* their oil away, on the principle that if you are
asked for your cloak, you should give your coat too (5:40). Again,
exegetes argue that the parable is really about persevering in virtue, and how at the day of accounting we cannot borrow virtue
from another if we have been lazy ourselves. But again, I am

not sure we should approve of those selfish girls who refuse to share.

Perhaps I am over-particular, but even Matthew's brief pericope about the pearl of great price is puzzling. We are told (13:45) that the kingdom of heaven is like a merchant man who discovers a costly pearl and sells all he has in order to buy it. But this is buying more of the same; it is like selling your house to buy gold shares, or to invest in diamonds. Pearls are another kind of worldly treasure, even though the commentators invariably want to say the pearl means something spiritual, and is different from other worldly goods.

Uncomfortable money stories are Matthew's specialty, and they belong with the strong tendency in his gospel to deflect us from plain pairs of opposites which nonetheless we need to know about. And now I am about to bring this back to *The Merchant of Venice* by claiming that Shakespeare's play also is an uncomfortable money story in which the binary symmetries of his moralising structure and themes are upset. But is it likely that Shakespeare would have read Matthew in this way? There is no commentary, for instance, on the rhetorical use of *'seismos'*, and I am not sure how interested Shakespeare would have been in studying Matthew's doublets. But the money stories are another thing, and, as I have shown, they link with everything else, including the parable of the wheat and tares. Moreover, Shakespeare knew the moralising glosses on the parables in the Geneva bible and Tomson's New Testament, the Bishops' bible, and (perhaps) the Reims New Testament, and he was well aware of the kind of spirituality that informs these, deriving from Calvin and Beza, in contention with various shades of Catholic and other opinion.[33] It is highly instructive to watch how frequently these commentators paper over the cracks between the gospel narrative and their own special, often politically-interested interpretations.

In his commentary on the parable of the labourers, Calvin dodges and weaves from the start.[34] 'If any man should resolve to sift out with exactness every portion of this parable, his curiosity would be useless' (II,409), he tells us. And yet, he goes on to say that 'there will be no harm in examining the words, that the doctrine may be more clearly evinced' (II,409). This self-conscious bit of throat-clearing suggests that Calvin feels some pressure, and well he might. The parable for him means simply that the Lord 'owes no man anything', and Calvin draws this tough conclusion without flinching, even though it does threaten to leave God the unabashed exploiter of human labour. But Calvin prefers to avoid 'all subtleties' (II,410), as he says, pertaining to issues like that. Not surprisingly, he was advanced for his times in arguing that the taking of interest on loans was not un-Christian:[35] if redemptive love transcends economic calculation, then, presumably, economic practice must be allowed to work by its own laws. By contrast, the kinds of subtlety Calvin avoids are highlighted in the gloss to the Reims New Testament of 1582,[36] which claims that the denarius (or 'penny') is 'life everlasting', and that different kinds and degrees of labour contribute to earning it. Calvin at least sticks to the story and allows his penny to be a penny. Reims tries to rescue a hard case by making it a different case: the penny is not a penny, but something else.

The pearl of great price fares no better. The 'natural meaning' (II,132) of the words, Calvin says, is that the pearl is the gospel and we are to prefer it before all worldly things. But Calvin does not like the idea of *buying* the pearl, for the gospel is God's gift. Therefore 'buy' does not really mean 'buy', but means that we 'cheerfully relinquish the desires of the flesh' (II,132). To confirm the kinds of strain to which exegetes often submit the text on these matters, I cannot resist citing a gloss by Cornelius à Lapide, the Catholic commentator contemporary with Shakespeare, though Shakespeare would not have read him. Lapide says that Matthew's pearl is similar to Wisdom in Proverbs (8:11, 19): 'For wisdom is better than rubies; and all the things that may be desired are not to be compared to it.'[37] This comparison opens up a difficulty Lapide does not seem to notice, for Proverbs says quite plainly that Wisdom is 'better than' rubies: it is something different, and as such it is not a true parallel to Matthew's pearl at all.

Finally, a word on the ten maidens. Once more, Calvin begins defensively: 'Some people,' he says, 'give themselves a good deal of uneasiness about the lamps, the vessels, and the oil,' but we must not enter into 'minute investigations' (III,170). The plain sense is that we should persevere until the end, though once again Calvin balks at the idea of *buying* the oil: this cannot mean a literal purchase, because we cannot attain worthiness by our own efforts. Again, this commentary (reproduced fairly directly in the Geneva gloss), intimates misgivings almost in the same breath as it proclaims self-evidence, and in the midst of the various tensions we can again feel something of Calvin's concern, however uneasy, to tease apart economics and religion. And so, once more, as in all these commentaries, we are forced uncomfortably upon the difference between worldly calculus and spiritual economy, and upon the simultaneous awareness that the two seem more distinct than they are. Evidently, Shakespeare was exposed to a variety of such fitful attempts to make plain distinctions come clear, and to separate sheep from goats, good from bad, wheat from tares, in a manner that often only shows how problematic such an enterprise is.

The difficulties of all this are compounded when we turn to the contemporary anti-usury tracts.[38] Henry VIII had allowed the taking of interest up to 10 per cent, but under Edward VI interest was banned altogether. However, the Edwardian statute rapidly proved un-enforceable, and Elizabeth I passed the act of 1571, making invalid all loans exceeding 10 per cent. The Elizabethan statute resoundingly condemned interest-taking in general, but in effect permitted what it was unable to prevent, up to the limit of 10 per cent. A wide variety of tracts then offered advice on the whole perplexed subject, and reflect everywhere the subterfuges of those who practiced what they preached against, and then found ways either to justify their actions, or to prevent themselves seeing what they were doing. Thomas Wilson, John Jewel, Philip Caesar, Miles Mosse, Nicolas Sanders, Henry Smith, Thomas Lodge, and many others allow us into the intricacies of this debate, and I want here only to highlight some of the most prominent, repeated concerns among these writers, over-riding even their disagreements.

Typically, the tracts offer a central core of denunciation. Thus Nicolas Sanders says that 'usurie is utterly against God and Nature, even as mankilling is';[39] Miles Mosse assures us that usury is utterly forbidden in the New Testament, and 'usurers are a meanes of God's curse upon men';[40] Philip Caesar proclaims there is no question but that usury is unlawful.[41] One main reason offered for these blanket condemnations is that usury offends against charity, and is therefore a prime example of not treating your neighbour as yourself. The tracts never tire of telling us how usury overthrows Christ's rule of love by attacking the chief bond of society which is, as Philip Caesar says, treating one's neighbour as one's self. It is an easy step then to see usury as against the law of nature – 'against all lawe, against nature', as Thomas Wilson[42] says – and there are frequent allusions to Aristotle's condemnation of money unnaturally breeding money. God told the beasts to 'increase and multiply', says Henry Smith, but when this applies to money it 'begetteth a monstrous birth'.[43]

Such a prospect of monstrosity and unnaturalness leads easily to the further notion that usury is the devil's work. And because Jews were supposedly allowed by their own law to exact usury from strangers or enemies,[44] it was easy enough to include Jews with devils, serpents and biting dogs – all popular epithets for usurers.

Even a cursory reading of the tracts reveals the marked concern about landed wealth to which Walter Cohen draws attention, and in light of which objections based on charity, natural law, and the devisings of Satan can be linked to a ruling ideology. As the tracts keep telling us, usury threatens the commonwealth because it overthrows noble families. The problem is that the younger generation – 'prodigals', as Thomas Lodge[45] calls them – flock to the cities and pawn the ancestral lands to support their spendthrift habits. Alarm is often sounded about the decay of the landed nobility under the impact of financial entrepreneurship among unscrupulous city slickers without breeding or morals. Thus Thomas Lodge goes on at length about the 'divellish usurer', a 'limme of Sathan himselfe' (3r) who with 'more then Iudaicall cousonage' (3v) robs families of their ancestral lands. They will eat our English gentry out of house and home; they are 'Caterpillers of a Common weale' (6v), and 'painted Sepulcres' (6r). Certainly, they will ruin the noble families in whose wellbred expertise the safety of the commonwealth rests, and Thomas Wilson laments the high incidence of bankruptcies and 'decayed gentlemen' (227). All usurers are 'cormorants of a commonweale', says the anonymous author of *The Death of Usury*,[46] and Miles Mosse assures us that 'Usurie consumeth private families' (Fourth Sermon, 95). As Cohen says, a degree of relief would come when the nobles learned to do business, but by and large the indications of this were insufficiently encouraging for those who worried about moneylending practices in Shakespeare's time.

Still, I have given thus far only one half of the picture these tracts present. For, despite the high-mindedness about charity, natural law, loving one's neighbour and maintaining the commonwealth, most writers about usury admit that merchant capital is necessary, and whether one approves of it or not, usury keeps on being taken by a great variety of means. One way of reconciling this apparently unavoidable fact with the moral imperative to condemn usury as anti-Christian, is to redefine the term 'usury' itself.

As Norman Jones[47] shows, the main point of contention in the usury debate lay between conservatives who condemned all usury as unlawful (the term traditionally meant contracting intentionally for more than the principal of a loan without risk to the lender), and those who wanted a more liberal acknowledgement of the good frequently effected by lending money at a price. However, the liberalisers also condemned usury, but redefined the term by enquiring about when usury *really* occurs, and how charity is *really* exercised. In the liberal interpretation, usury was mainly a matter of conscience, and should not therefore be adjudicated so much by civil law as by an individual's assessment of intent.

As Mosse confides, this whole subject turns inevitably into a maze or labyrinth, and the cloaks and cunning devices by which usury is concealed are infinite: trying to control it is, he says, like trying to contain rising water. In the same spirit, Sanders describes various tricks for falsifying documents; *The Death of Usury* notices how usurers will lend for short periods of three months to create a dependency; Smith describes the various operations of legal thieves, as does Wilson; and Lodge notices how much more ingenious the concealments become when usury is threatened by law. Though much of this is predictable, it can leave a reader with a poignant sense of quandary and confusion. Mosse neatly, though hopelessly, concludes that the sin of usury is one thing, and usury itself is another, and Smith concludes with the perplexing exhortation, 'let every man hereafter be a usurer to God'.

Even from these brief observations, it is evident how, in theology and politics alike, precept and practice were wildly confused and confusing. Taking interest on loans was contrived by innumerable pretenses, despite the fact that, theoretically, charity is everywhere praised and usury condemned. The official ideological position pitched the opposites – charity and usury – clearly against one another, thereby simultaneously producing and concealing a wilderness of hypocritical behaviours and sharp practices. Everywhere the tract writers keep struggling for a solution, but mainly they reproduce instead enmeshments that parodically invert Matthew's seismic re-constitution of the whole question of God and Mammon, fracturing the tombstone that seals up the Christ, and also, I will want to say, exploding the allegory in Shakespeare.

But first – to recapitulate briefly – it is useful to notice how embedded Shakespeare's play is in this contemporary debate, and how many of his key situations and motifs are part of a widespread concern about current economic practice. Agrarian Belmont and merchant capital Venice exemplify the conflict between the landed nobility and new monied classes that the tracts describe. We can identify Antonio as a merchant rather than a usurer because his money is at risk abroad.[48] Shylock lends for three months, the common sharp practice, and he carefully avoids taking interest, but settles for a forfeit, which is legal, though he is clearly also a mental usurer. Bassanio is described as a prodigal, and exemplifies the spendthrift sons who are on the way to ruining the country. Along with Gratiano, Lorenzo and Antonio, he does not admit the hypocrisy of his own condemnation of Shylock, the Jewish money-lender who is called a devil and a dog, the popular language of opprobrium for those who want an easy mark, a target against which to release their own frustration and alienation while concealing from themselves how much they resemble what they condemn. But what, then, is the equivalent of Matthew's seismic effect in Shakespeare's play?

For a start, the series of pairs in *The Merchant of Venice* that I outlined earlier, sits uncertainly in relationship to a relatively undeveloped, yet insistently subtending interest in threes.[49] Shylock's 3,000 ducats are loaned for three months, and there are three caskets, and three suitors make choices. At the end, three pairs of lovers are united, with Lorenzo and Jessica turning up in Belmont on their own recognizance to support the principal two pairs. And although the ring trial at the end parallels the courtroom trial, it is possible to see the casket scenes also as a trial, thus making three. Also, it has recently been argued that the really effective merchant in the play is neither Antonio nor Shylock, but Portia, who, because she is a woman, is even more subversive in re-writing all the male bonds, financial and otherwise.[50] Consistently, the play has a way of making us aware of a *tertium quid*, even in the midst of its foregrounded display of paired opposites.

Earlier, I suggested how the most obvious of these pairs is the setting at Belmont and Venice. The first is a golden, enchanted world, the second, where Antonio finds himself unaccountably sad, is the real world of financial anxiety and venture capital. Yet, when we move from Act I, sc.i (that is, Venice), to Act I, sc.ii (Belmont), we move from a scene written entirely in poetry to one entirely in prose. It is not exactly what we might expect: the poetry, surely, should belong to Belmont. Moreover, Portia's first words are 'By my troth, Nerissa, my little body is aweary of this great world.' The tone is at once brisk and deflated, and the line echoes Antonio's lament about being sad, so that Shakespeare obscures the contrast between Venice and Belmont even as he draws it. Indeed, the more we think about it, the more the inter-dependency between these two worlds becomes increasingly, and uncomfortably, evident.

For instance, despite her golden fleece and caskets, mysterious music and generally enchanted ambience, Portia is well-monied, resilient, capable of vindictiveness, cosily vigorous in the conduct of character assassination from within her protected estate, and an accomplished manipulator. Certainly, she can knock the stuffing out of the Venetians at their own hard games. Moreover, her glamorous, eloquent and true lover, Bassanio, explains to Antonio that he is off to Belmont because a lady there is 'richly left', is 'fair', and has 'wondrous virtues' (I,i,161–3). That is, she has an inheritance, is good looking, and also virtuous: Bassanio's order of priorities is markedly disenchanted[51] and again we see that values in Belmont and in Venice are not as distinct as we might want them to be: the very Venetian worldliness of Portia's attractions is, apparently, necessary for her to find the romantic love that ought, apparently, to be above such venality.

The unsettling effect of all this is aggravated in several further ways. Bassanio is not really at risk in the casket trial, if only because Morocco and Aragon have already made the wrong choices of gold and silver. By the fairy-tale law of threes, it is quite clear that Bassanio will choose correctly. Indeed, the main action at Belmont is so perfectly and poetically just (each of the suitors chooses in character, and true love is vindicated), that we suspect our own self-indulgence in such a fantasy, as W. H. Auden points out.[52] On the other hand, Shylock's bond for the pound of flesh is itself an age-old fairy-tale motif, so that the supposedly real and threatening prospect of Shylock using the knife he so menacingly whets before us, is effectively absorbed. But again we feel this is evasive, for so powerful is Shylock's resolve, and so ferocious the animus he expresses, that we hesitate somehow to commute it by a structural subterfuge (it is only another fairy-tale motif). The opposition between Belmont and Venice that would, on the surface, provoke our moral judgements on the issue of money and human community, is thus repeatedly unsettled and destabilised.

Something of the same effect accompanies the play's best-known speeches. Portia's famous words on mercy in the courtroom scene of Act IV, sc.i introduce an amazing, momentary stillness into the tense, half-demented atmosphere of the trial:

> The quality of mercy is not strained;

It droppeth as the gentle rain from heaven
Upon the place beneath . . .

(IV,i,183 ff.)

The feeling of release and refreshment is unmistakable, and
unmistakably welcome, as soft rain, and as a gift. Such mercy is
'mightiest in the mighty', and is more powerful even than the power
of monarchs. It is greater even than that, and yet 'It is entroned in
the hearts of kings': it is concealed at the centre, in the secret heart of
things where overarching transcendence and vulnerable interiority
are presented as mysteriously at one. We pray for that quality of
mercy, says Portia, 'And that same prayer doth teach us all to render
/ The deeds of mercy.' There is a kind of confidence that in its very
defenselessness is free from anxiety, and Portia recommends it. But
then, even in mid-line, she snaps out of it. 'I have spoke thus much
/ To mitigate the justice of thy plea / Which if thou follow, this strict
court of Venice / Must needs give sentence 'gainst the merchant
there.' It is back to business: she knows that he will want the bond,
and she knows already how she will trip him up on a technicality.
The mercy speech is beautiful, but is oddly dislocated from what
precedes and follows, abruptly relinquished, almost a kind of move,
we might suspect (though, again, uncomfortably), designed to drive
another nail into Shylock's coffin, for he will soon learn that he has
not listened. But she *knows* he will not listen, and the speech rounds
out the design of her entrapment. She goes on to enclose him entirely,
exacting a financial revenge justified by her persuasion that she is
really, at heart, merciful.

Or take Shylock's famous plea in Act III, sc.i, in reply to Salerio,
who asks what good is the pound of flesh:

Hath not a Jew eyes? Hath not a Jew hands, organs, dimensions,
senses, affections, passions? – fed with the same food, hurt with
the same weapons, subject to the same diseases, healed by
the same means, warmed and cooled by the same winter and
summer as a Christian is? If you prick us, do we not bleed? If
you tickle us, do we not laugh? If you poison us, do we not die?
And if you wrong us, shall we not revenge? (III,i,55–63)

Indeed, these words enliven us to our common condition – we all
have senses, blood, are vulnerable to disease, and so on. Shylock is
one of us, and in the name of the body's vitality, basis of all human

community as Terry Eagleton[53] points out, he makes his demand. And yet, the very meagreness of Shylock's scope, here, is menacing: he sees the reflex actions of the autonomic nervous system as our only common inheritance. And the aggressive questioning expresses an antagonism which comes to light at last, again in the riveting conclusion: 'And if you wrong us, shall we not revenge?' There is no sense of difference between the account of hands, organs, bleeding, and disease, and the moral issue of revenge. For Shylock they appear the same (or he makes them appear so): revenge is as instinctive as eating. We might have thought revenge to be another kind of thing, and yet the vindictiveness of the play's Christian gentlemen and husbands is also very much as Shylock describes it. As with Portia's speech, we are stopped at the very moment when we might extend a degree of unguarded sympathy, and thrown back on something altogether less self-indulgent, less secure.

Much else in the play resembles these examples, but I would like to move towards a conclusion by citing one brief point that highlights again the theme of material and spiritual wealth. The annoying and verbose Gratiano has just told Bassanio and Portia that their success with the casket test has enabled his betrothal to Nerissa. He then turns enthusiastically to his bride to be, his heart full (presumably), and, then, dumbfoundingly, he says to her, 'We'll play with them the first boy for a thousand ducats.' That is, let's make a bet of 1,000 ducats on which of us couples produces the first baby boy. It is another bargain, another bond, this time dealing with a few extra pounds of flesh, but no matter. It seems obvious that we are meant to see this *louche* insensibility in relation to the pound of flesh story in Venice, but this Belmont version, though in one way a merrier bond than Shylock's, is a tainted enough thing, and it seems that love and money, charity and revenge, accountability and accountancy, are not after all distinct, but rather more like Mosse's labyrinth. Only by acting as though the alien were the outsider – the Jewish usurer – and as if the precepts of Christian self-giving were embodied in those who preach them, do the play's Christians disguise from themselves the alien within.

I agree with Barbara Lewalski that scriptural references in *The Merchant of Venice* are 'so precise as to be patently deliberate', and they gain special urgency from the fact that Shakespeare in this play so explicitly argues a Christian case. But the way the Bible is used is another thing. I have argued that the gospel according to Matthew seems especially important here, and that Shakespeare responds to it, not just as a commentator or allegoriser. Matthew's money stories themselves are uncomfortable, and relationships between Jew and Gentile, law and mercy, worldly treasure and spiritual worth, are antithetical in theory, but in experience terribly complex. The temptation to divide the wheat from the tares easily yields dangerous self-righteousness, as we see in the pervasive contradictory-consciousness among the blithe Venetians, unwittingly in collusion with what they condemn. Indeed, fragments of a happy and blessed condition do occur, and the comedy rejoices. But their provenance is surprising, a shock to our easy assumptions about order, expectation, and our just desserts.

As Cohen says, the temptation to allegorise the play's religious dimension reflects a drive to assimilate alien experience and to restore unity, confirming a dominant, Christian and aristocratic ideology. But the play also resists, and Cohen cites Launcelot Gobbo and the various kinds of disguise as examples of how religious issues are demystified, presenting us with tensions inherent in the social conditions of the play's production during a period of transition to capitalism. I have suggested that the temptation to allegorise, such as Lewalski presents it, is itself resisted by the Gospel on which the allegory largely draws, and that the aristocratic, ruling ideology of Belmont is undermined also by Shakespeare's knowledge that separating sheep from goats, wheat from tares, is often an easy way to avoid loving your neighbour as yourself. The condition of persons in the grief of human history remains perennially alienated, and it is all too easy to deny the alien within by labeling another as the real alien, and then blaming that other for our own anxieties.[54] Matthew's hard money stories and the rhetoric of his gospel present this fact compellingly; but the commentaries on Matthew that Shakespeare knew, like the usury tracts, have a singularly difficult time avoiding the self-delusions that the gospel warns against in its own very refusal to be made into allegory. In this context, I have suggested how in *The Merchant of Venice* Shakespeare engages the contemporary usury debate by incorporating Matthew in a way that foregrounds the whole flawed *ensemble*, calling for something revolutionary in our apprehension of the very question of God and Mammon, and in our acceptance of the practices upon which the question is based. Such a thematising of contradictory consciousness is one hallmark of literature and of the way literature foregrounds the gaps between behaviour and explanation – knowing how and knowing what – characteristic of our predicament as persons called to evaluation and commitment, yet acting against what we hold to be our best interests. In this context I have tried also to suggest how, as with Christianity, Marxism might be regarded as a transitional value, more or less progressive in the hands of its interpreters.

COMMUNITY, AUTONOMY, AND PERSONS

As we see, contradictory consciousness and hypocrisy are closely linked, and the problem of formulating our best, 'seismic' hope might devolve at last upon such a plain enough matter as how ineradicably selfish and hypocritical we take ourselves to be. The familiar terms central to debates about what is ineradicable in 'human nature' – terms such as self, ego, person, identity, character – are notoriously imprecise, and remain as elusive as the problem they are deployed to explore. Thus, Maritain and Jung describe 'ego' as an energy bent on appropriation and material control, in contrast to 'self', the generous and creative spirit active in each of us.[55] But in ordinary usage, 'self' frequently indicates the possessive, and words with the prefix 'self' became current especially during the eighteenth century, a period when people increasingly were able to possess property and power by industry as distinct from inheritance.[56] In this context the 'self' is an owner, whether of self-consciousness or self-esteem or individual rights. Still today we name an excessive, grasping desire for exclusive possession 'selfishness'. By contrast, in Freud's estimate, the ego's appropriative side – its 'selfishness' – is exactly what needs strengthening, and culture should enable it to achieve consciousness and coherence, pitched against the irrational turmoil with which it merges and from which it struggles to develop.

In these several contexts, 'ego' and 'self' refer to no observable entity, and, as we have seen, the Cartesian assertion of the ego's clarity and distinctness has been efficiently and properly criticised. Nonetheless, philosophical debate on personal identity deriving from the tradition of Descartes, Locke, and Hume remains vigorous, and I began this study by noticing such modern contributions as Derek Parfit's. My own inclination all along has been to stress how the elision of discussions about ego and self into such closely-allied notions as mind, soul, character, and identity, involve us not so much in the definition of a term – or set of terms – as in a sense

of how the history of human consciousness remains sedimented
in the evolution of language and in the tacit evaluations language
entails. With this in mind, and following the arguments of Polanyi
and Taylor, I have taken the word 'person' as neither subjective
nor objective but as evaluative, indicating what we hold most
worthwhile about ourselves and others. As Marcel Mauss[57] has
shown, such an approach to the idea of the person has itself evolved.
The Greek word *prosopon* became in Latin *persona*, the mask through
which an actor spoke, and which in turn was associated with rights
to sacred functions or prescribed roles. In Roman law the concept
then emerged of a civil persona who enjoyed certain rights, so that
the legal and dramatic senses of 'acting' remained together even
as the idea of the person evolved. Especially among the Stoics, the
legal concept expanded to include free, responsible action, and the
interpretation of *persona* as an assumed mask or as the underlying,
true nature of the moral individual who assumes the mask, varied
with context. These legal and moral developments found further
application in the revolutionary Christian extension to all humans
of immortality and the opportunity of salvation. The eschatological
core of Christianity offers final judgement to everyone, whether
Jew or gentile, slave or citizen, woman or man. In a slave-owning
and patriarchal society, this extension of personhood was seen as
dangerous, and not surprisingly Jesus was executed as a political
insurrectionist.

Theological definitions of the Trinity in the early Christian centuries took the further bold step of describing God as a paradoxical
relationship among persons, and distinct theological and psychological senses of the person began to emerge, though remaining interrelated. Boethius' cornerstone definition of a person as
the 'individual substance of a rational nature'[58] remained at the
heart of subsequent scholastic enquiries, and although Thomas
Aquinas stressed that the person is a unity, he emphasised an
equally fundamental, relational aspect, as Richard of St. Victor
had insisted.[59] During the Renaissance and Reformation, much
effort was expended trying to describe the spiritual, 'individual
substance' animating our physical bodies, and Descartes is as much
the last scholastic as the first modern in describing the human
as a composite of spiritual and extended substances. Also, in a
revolutionary way Descartes assimilated soul to consciousness and
to a simple centre of autonomous, interior, and unified action
the ego. Although, as we have seen, his doctrine of substances

did not long withstand scrutiny, a tendency to treat the person as an individual, self-conscious agent remained strong, especially in Locke. But the inter-relational view also endured, mediated by the Cambridge Platonists and explored especially by Hegel, who describes the ego exteriorising itself in order to recover itself in the other. Persons, that is, discover themselves through others, and as Hegel correctly realised, the concept of the person is its history, fraught with interlocking and laminated emergences and inconsistencies.

The relevance of this brief recapitulation to the present, final phase of my argument in this chapter is that it helps to gather various strands of the previous discussion towards the idea that the person needs to be engaged in a community. As I have everywhere stressed, a capacity to assess significance is crucial to personal identity, and is especially connected to our use of language. Human concerns, that is, are focused in language, through which we develop plans of action and interpret ourselves to ourselves. This being the case, persons are self-creating to a limited degree,[60] capable of taking stock of an elusive self-presence that is also the presence of a burdensome yet informing past entailing an orientation to a future in which we hope to be more truly and actively ourselves. Yet is is clear also that we are not pure persons,[61] nor do we speak pure language. Although we gain ourselves by giving being to others, we do not identify totally with others, and to that degree remain still in potential, our language and bodies grievously at odds, our standards still beyond ourselves and perennially at risk, our presence to one another marked also by a sense of absence. The very notion of person is itself thus to be assessed in all the weighty confusions and contradictions of its historical emergence. But insofar as it entails some such understanding of language and literature as this book exemplifies, we might also suggest that the idea of the person points us towards the political, for we are persons only through others and in relation to a community.

It is easy to mis-estimate the interrelationship between individual and community by claiming too much for either pole. Glorification of a unique self, possessor of whatever it can appropriate by its own power, yields utilitarian individualism and encourages a blind acquisitiveness masquerading as freedom. For many, such freedom remains more apparent than real, sustained by an ideological fantasy that has done much to transform human selfishness into a public virtue, calling then on private benevolence to offset the inevitable damage. True charity, we are assured by the current President of the United States (current, that is, as I write this), will shine from a 'thousand points of light' to solve the plight of the homeless in the world's richest, freest nation.

Yet Leszek Kolakowski concludes in turn that Marxism 'has been the greatest fantasy of our century',[62] not least because its pretensions to scientific socialism ignore, among other things, the fact that the choice of ends is not itself scientific. One consequence is that Marxism 'presents its temporal eschatology as a scientific system' (526), and minimises the freedom of individuals to evaluate and interpret conflicts between that freedom and the common good. Again, Kolakowski centres on the question of selfishness: Marx, he argues, seems to have imagined that 'one had only to forbid private ownership of machines or land and, as if by magic, human beings would cease to be selfish and their interests would coincide in perfect harmony' (527). Indeed, living for others requires overcoming selfishness, but this is scarcely to be brought about by the *a priori* denial of personal autonomy and by the imposition from without of the necessary disciplines of self-denial and sacrifice. Transformations of significance are assessed and recognised by *someone*, who cannot be dismissed as merely fictional and who in this respect is not unlike those who presume themselves sufficiently advanced to correct the ideological determinisms binding all the others.

It is distortive, then, to conceive of the person as a unique, free claimant of rights from a society that at best ought to ensure only that such uniqueness and freedom are preserved. This is the fallacy of individualism, and it regards the person as an atomic consciousness looking out on a neutral world, choosing and creating a course of life. But it is also distortive to deny personal autonomy altogether, claiming that individual consciousness is constituted by and indistinct from the prevalent ideology. We need to remember that an entanglement of values in contradiction has developed through history, and cannot be understood outside the language by which we recognise and affirm (or deny) their several claims upon us. With this in mind, it is instructive to look at Samuel Johnson's *Rasselas*, which thematises this problem with unusual circumspection.

'The only end of writing,' Johnson says, 'is to enable the readers better to enjoy life, or better to endure it.'[63] The measured sobriety of this statement remains evident throughout Johnson's writing, and not least in *The Vanity of Human Wishes*, where he invites our

'extensive view' to 'Survey mankind, from China to Peru' and then
to notice in a variety of ways 'How rarely Reason guides the
stubborn choice'.[64] People, that is, perennially induce unhappiness
by ignoring the most general constraints upon human action, and
especially by failing to understand, as Imlac teaches Rasselas, that
life is a condition in which 'much is to be endured, and little to
be enjoyed'. Ezra Pound claims that in all this Johnson, like Pope,
makes 'mainly a negative statement' even though affirming 'the
value of intelligence, the right to be impatient with fools, the
value of being undazzled'.[65] Certainly, Johnson's sombre view of
humanity is far from either dazzling or bedazzlement, as he seeks
to impart a judicious understanding of general truths, locating the
best, most reliable self in that which is least individually differenti-
ated, least peculiar, and clearest in its grasp of principles confirmed
by common experience.

Johnson's surveillance of the human condition might call to
mind Foucault's adaptation of Bentham's 'panopticon'. According to Foucault, the development of liberal, critical ideas in the
eighteenth century was accompanied by a systematic classifying
and institutionalising of individuals decreed out of order by the
panoptic control tower: that is, the central, authoritative, omniscient
arbitration point for assessing reasonableness and 'normality'.[66] In
his fashion, Johnson also strives for a panoptic viewpoint, and in
so doing is at one with the broadly Cartesian and Lockean notion
of the self-contained ego as surveyor of a neutral material world,
transparent to the reasoning of other like-minded individuals. In
this context, imagination is mainly a breeder of illusions and an
inciter of dangerous eccentricities or abnormalities.

However, the tale of Rasselas,[67] Prince of Abyssinia, provides an
oddly mixed assessment of the relationship between reason and
imagination. The paradisal Happy Valley into which Rasselas is
born offers all the comforts, but he is unhappy there. We sympa-
thise, for life in the valley is after all tedious, and when he complains
that one day is much like the next, we understand how he needs a
change. But when he then says he hopes to see the miseries of the
world, we know also that he is set on a dangerously naive course.
We who live outside the Happy Valley understand these miseries
sufficiently so that we might hesitate to prescribe them as a relief
from boredom. And so the prince devises a plan of escape, taking
a small retinue on an educative voyage to the world outside. As
they enter Cairo, Imlac tells Rasselas that now 'you shall see all the

conditions of humanity, and enable yourself at leisure to make your *choice of life'* (XVI,16). Johnson's early title for the story was, simply, *The Choice of Life*, and Rasselas is presented as a privileged spectator, freed from financial worry by the treasure he has brought with him. Reasonably enough, he looks around to see what is available before choosing.

Rasselas is attracted especially to those who seem to have their own definitions of happiness worked out rationally and clearly. He admires a stoic sage who discourses elegantly on governing the passions, and who offers a variety of persuasive precepts and examples. Rasselas 'listened to him with the veneration due to the instructions of a superior being', but Imlac charily attempts to dampen this enthusiasm, saying that teachers of morality 'discourse like angels, but they live like men' (XVIII,18). But Rasselas is unconvinced, and must learn by experience,[68] as he does when the sage declares himself broken and inconsolable after the death of his daughter: 'I am now a lonely being, disunited from society' (XVIII,19).

The same kind of thing happens with the hermit, whose supposed sanctity is in fact an agony of loneliness and discontent. Likewise, 'the assembly of learned men' (XXII,21) who voice broadly Deist principles about their concurrence 'with the great and unchangeable scheme of universal felicity' (XXII,21), turn out to be self-deluding egocentrics, the more incomprehensible the more one hears from them.

Imlac then guides Rasselas once more to the steadying observation that in human experience there is never much happiness and always a lot of illusion. 'Of the blessings set before you,' he advises, 'make your choice, and be content' (XXIX,27). The problem is that imagination of absent pleasures keeps us striving to be happier than we are, but as the various episodes of the tale illustrate, the state of life we imagine as happy always turns out to be less than that when we examine it closely. The quixotry and sheer attractive power of fancy all too easily drive people to extremes preventing the very fulfilments they would bring about:

> By degrees, the reign of fancy is confirmed; she grows first imperious, and in time despotic. Then fictions begin to operate as realities, false opinions fasten upon the mind, and life passes in dreams of rapture or of anguish. (XLIV,38)

This passage might remind us that a principal achievement of the English Enlightenment was its resistance to absolute monarchy, and the appeal to publicly-shared judgements of clear-thinking individuals arriving at a consensus was a chief moving force in this resistance. Not surprisingly, as the antithesis to reason, imagination could seem a ready ally of political absolutism, as we see here in the way fancy's 'reign' is described as 'imperious' and 'despotic'. Soon after, Rasselas admits to 'an indulgence of fantastic delight more dangerous' than a daydream just confessed by his sister the Princess Nekayah. 'I have frequently endeavoured,' he tells her, 'to imagine the possibility of a perfect government.' He has dreamed up 'innumerable schemes of reformation', all imaginary, and Imlac hastens to advise him about the danger of such 'visionary schemes' (XLIV,39). The political implications of aberrant imagination disturbing the consensus of reason are again plain, and Imlac concludes that 'All power of fancy over reason is a degree of insanity.' And yet there is nobody over whose mind 'airy notions do not sometimes tyrannise, and force him to hope or fear beyond the limits of sober probability' (XLIV,38). As these passages make clear, when the threat implicit in imagination shows up, it is called insanity, and therefore needs surveillance and correction.

It is not hard to feel Johnson's personal concerns thinly veiled in the character of Imlac, the wise though less than perfect poet who keeps offering sensible advice even though Rasselas keeps ignoring it. At one point Imlac even sets out a theory of poetry containing the famous words about not numbering the streaks of the tulip but attending instead to 'general properties and large appearances', and examining the species rather than 'the individual' (X,11). This reflects Johnson's own theory, but there is a moment of distancing irony as Imlac's account concludes:

> Imlac now felt the enthusiastic fit, and was proceeding to aggrandise his own profession, when the prince cried out, 'Enough! thou hast convinced me that no human being can ever be a poet. Proceed with thy narration.' (XI,12)

Admittedly, we do not see the 'enthusiastic fit' affecting Imlac's language, but he is prone to it nonetheless, just as he later acknowledges that everybody is subject to disturbances caused by imagination. Poetry can indeed lead to excess, but we discover this in a passage praising poetry and confirming our perennial need for it.

Individualism, imagination and political absolutism are thus closely linked, and in Johnson's view this combination offers a fearful prospect: therefore general principles based on the consensus of autonomous, reasoning agents making public judgements, need to prevail. Yet nobody is proof against fancy, and Johnson (himself a compulsive neurotic) knew more than to let Imlac stand inviolate in any simple or uniform theory about the reasonableness of human affairs. And here we come upon some of the inconsistencies and tensions by which *Rasselas* is riven.

The tale itself is, after all, contrived throughout to indulge the fancy. There is an exotic Eastern setting with a paradisal valley, an adventurous escape, a kidnapping, strange castles with secret passages, a trip into the interior of the pyramids, and much more. The reader is therefore attracted and led by the same promise of adventure and discovery as Rasselas, and Johnson ensures that both are brought to the same remorselessly sobering disappointments. Moreover, and with splendid irony, it turns out that the apparently reasonable, unextravagant notion underlying Rasselas' pilgrimage – that he should make a survey of how people live and then choose what to do with his own life – turns out to be among the grandest illusions of all. Initially, Rasselas assumes he is free to stand outside and observe things neutrally. Yet, the advocates of this kind of detachment whom Rasselas meets are all unhappy because their imagined autonomy breaks down under pressure of the reality it seems to preclude. Once again, the 'hunger of imagination . . . preys incessantly upon life' (XXII,29), and in this context Johnson's allusions to rivers are especially suggestive.

When Rasselas first experiences discontent in the Happy Valley, he seeks seclusion and spends 'day after day on the banks of rivulets', telling himself 'I am not at rest' (II,4). The agitated water here resembles his uneasy state of mind, and Johnson quickly establishes a link between the river and the book's psychological themes. Later, Rasselas confesses to Imlac his desire to 'mingle' with the 'mighty confluence of nations' (XI,12) outside the valley. But as we see, 'mingle' is not quite what he intends, as he ventures forth to survey his options. This tension between participation and detachment recurs when Imlac lectures Rasselas on not endeavouring 'to do more than is allowed to humanity', and then confirms his advice by alluding to the river: 'no man can at the same time fill his cup from the source and from the mouth of the Nile' (XXIX,27). The river is life, and we must take our appropriate pleasures at the appropriate points: the freshness of the source and the fullness of the rivermouth are different, and we should not try to have them both at once. Filling our cup suggests that we are not only travellers, lookers-on during the course of a voyage, but also participants in the river's substance. Also, the waters suggest life's fluid and restless course, mirroring in turn imagination's fickleness and turbulence. In the concluding chapter, the Nile has overflowed, and the company cannot take excursions. Instead, they discuss 'the different forms of life which they had observed'. Each describes the most desirable existence, including Imlac's wish 'to be driven along the stream of life' without taking any particular course, but they all know at last that the ideal cannot be attained (XLIX,44), and so they return to Abyssinia.[69]

The river in all this is something to travel on and mingle with, simultaneously. It is within us, as the stream of our pleasures and discontents, the fluctuations of imagination and desire, and although its waters can overflow, they normally take their course between the containing banks. Indeed, only because there is a containing structure can there by a river at all, making its way from source to ocean. And in a sense Johnson depicts here imagination's relation to reason, the general, containing structure within which run the currents of a disturbing, necessary energy, at once potentially fertilising and destructive. This analogy extends even to Johnson's style, containing such variety within the famous, calculated and weighty grandeur. In short, *Rasselas* is full of a certain pre-Romantic self-involvement, and Johnson is aware of how human beings are driven by the flood tides of emotion and volatile feeling, and how these also need to find expression.

All this stands uneasily in tension with the surveyor from the panopticon, the cultivator of a public consensus of reasonable individuals. The necessary afflictions of our particular strangeness, the peculiar turbulences of our imagining, creative and self-destructive selves, make complex the account of personal identity and the choice of life that Rasselas seeks. Johnson's text confirms how we are always to a degree prepossessed by the inarticulate body and by the society that we partly observe even as it structures our observing gaze. The 'choice of life' is thus discovered as a synthesis worked out tentatively, and not just by agreement among atomised, clear-thinking Cartesian egos. Yet public consensus remains valuable, as Johnson keeps telling us, even though it does not provide a full enough account of human motivation and action. And here we can see *Rasselas* especially as the product of its historical occasion, offering to explore contending evaluations of the idea of the person that we can identify as at once late-Enlightenment and pre-Romantic. This historical occasion remains present also as part of the consciousness it has helped to produce, and today we are likely to feel the value both of a critical consensus resulting from rational investigation, and of the self as obscurely taken up and inspired by natural forces. Nor is this all we are likely to value about the idea of the person, but Johnson's *Rasselas* recovers at least something of how we have come to know and understand it as a site of such contradictions and complex emergences.

To summarise: the person as agent, self-aware in relation to others, as an interlocutor engaged in assessing significance, transforming values and making plans, is neither fully self-present nor fully detached; neither fully constituted by the communal, nor wholly autonomous. The notion of a 'communal autonomy' (to use a phrase of Jung's)[70] implies that language and culture are bound together in the task of making a society in which the good of all together is also the good of each. Insofar as literature is a means of exploring the labyrinthine emergence of such a sense of personal identity, it is a promoter at the very least of a political position consistent both with the claims both of autonomy and community.

7

Coda:
Dialogical Networks and
the Unfinished Humanum

I have been concerned in this book with how language operates through a play of presence and absence, and how in this context we can clarify the meaning of persons. Through language we meet as interlocutors within a community where we might share goals in common, make plans, and assess values. Yet the language that gives us things in common also makes us aware of our separations and of the problem of suffering. At the point of 'negative contrast', as Schillebeeckx says, between a perception of the good and whatever impedes it, protest and hope arise together, and thus the *humanum* remains in process through a dialectic between what is and what might be. Each living, invisible present carries within it a past, the body's history: as Heidegger says, our 'factuality' is the way we are prepossessed by the world, and our present concerns direct this state of affairs towards a future. Retrieving a past without distortion, repression and compulsive repetition is a way then to grasp and understand the most arresting contradictions in which we dwell as historical persons.

The problem of suffering and the experience of negative contrast are already thematised in the ancient myths of a primordial fall. These myths are later explained by theologians as recording the origins of sin, and then in secular terms as pertaining to our sense of contingency, anxiety and alienation. Experiences of a radical 'Flaw' are perennial in human culture, and are a concomitant of language disclosing a tragic absence at the heart of our self-discovery in history.

In this context, literature is characterised especially by its power of disclosure, showing us once more and anew the latent, value-impregnated union of ourselves with things and with others, the secret life of ourselves recovered from the habits of convention and distortion. We are thus invited to a complex act of assessment and evaluation, in which recognition is an irreducible component, for thus we affirm a work's mimetic force, its power to re-discover familiar things. Contesting evaluations of the same text can then render objective our different modes of subjectivity, and enable some reassessment of standards and beliefs, the 'prejudices', as Gadamer says, informing our personal point of view.

It follows that literature is indirectly testable against the world insofar as it effects a felt change of consciousness that we judge satisfactory, adequate, a probable account of how things are, and to which we give assent in the form of convictions more or less passionately held, as Polanyi says. We do not judge works of literature only against other works, for the great books tell us how to live, and if they not do this, they are at best escapist. Still, the process of assessing literature and of exploring thereby some social expressions of repressed needs and desires, is not ordered scientifically by general covering laws established in advance, but through a multiplicity of dialogical networks and committed positions. Assessments and theories need to be compared, just as texts do, so that judgements are established by a process resembling eliminative induction, by which I mean that the explanations we choose to affirm will be the ones that seem best when compared to others. This does not mean that different interpretations might not make equally valid claims on us: only that some accounts might seem more valid than others. Literary critics can learn at least here from the procedures of empirical scientists and from philosophers of science who stress the importance of theory-comparison and of shrewd choices made by practitioners within specialised communities. It follows that although critical discourse attempts to clarify and explain, it is never free from advocacy, however implicit, based on what is personally recognised by the critic as valuable.

Human language making present an absence helps also to explain imagination. Whether at the level of our recognising a familiar world through the configurating processes of a thought-imbued perception, or in the making of fictive worlds in the image of which we are invited to re-make our own, or in the displacement of ourselves into another's point of view, imagination is an agent of synthesis. It is the forger of new but imperfect meanings that disclose and yet distantiate simultaneously, re-narratising the past and seeking intimations of a future good, outflow from a fragile present. Thus imagination is instinct in the workings of language itself, but in its usual, strong sense imagination is the maker of fictive worlds. These in turn call for reflection and clarification, and it is part of the dialectic of culture that the languages of reflection engender fresh metaphors to enable and promote acceptance and understanding of the clarifications reflection provides. The process exemplified by Plato's critique of Homer that gives us the *Republic* replete with its own poetry, is duplicated in the development of all vital cultures, and critics remain also personal persuaders.

In some such context I have attempted to deal with religious language, confining the enquiry to Judaeo-Christian tradition. I have suggested that religion gives voice to an ultimate hope for community realising the potential of every person and encompassing also the material creation, the world's body. In so doing, religion throws into vivid contrast the scandal of present suffering and injustice, and insofar as it offers incentives for change, it stands opposed to selfishness, the exclusive possessiveness and *libido dominandi* of individual human egos, and whatever social institutions (including its own) promote such possessiveness.

Although religious claims rest on absolute, personal commitments, these are no less open to debate, comparison and evaluation than other texts and theories, and I draw no line between sacred and profane texts. Rather, I have suggested that eschatology in light of the cross reproduces the conflict implicit in all personal choice: our every means of promoting a desirable end return us inevitably to the facts of present suffering. It follows that a minimal requirement of acceptable religious commitment is that it should be aware of the transitional value of its own formulations and procedures, admitting the right to unbelief while remaining open to criticism of the means it adopts to express and promote its ends. I might add that one implication of Jesus' death outside the pale of every institutional protection is that 'religion' does not save, and there is a deep paradox in the fact that Christian religious institutions bear the responsibility of promoting this message, confirming their own institutional authority as imperfect and transitional. One function of what I have been calling the 'perennial philosophy' is to remind us of how this is so. In short, religious symbols and doctrines are open to criticism in the same way as literary symbols and critical theories.

Any progressive, modern religious culture depends on the vitality of this dialectic.

Marx considered the critique of religion the basis of every other critique. He held that dominant ideologies shape social consciousness to serve the interests of the ruling class, and then denounced religion for complicity in the history of oppression. Only by the overthrow of materially exploitative institutions and practices will the emancipation of persons in community be effected.

In this context, I have been concerned especially with how Marxist critics assess literature's presentation of historical contradictions to enable a discovery to ourselves of our ideological pre-formation. Because relationships between base and superstructure are complex and asynchronous, the literary intellectual has a place in society, working to 'constitute' Marx's ideas. As Althusser, Gramsci and Lukács point out in different ways, Marxism too is 'a form moving in time', a transitional value calling for assessment, itself as open to tragic and exploitative misapplications as the religious and other oppressive ideologies it criticises.

Through the various strands of this discussion, dealing with presence and absence, language and body, suffering and hope, mimesis and structure, images and ideas, self and other, I have attempted to assess the person not as some entity superadded, but rather as implicit in the several parts of the argument. Broadly, I cannot see that the problem of the Flaw (anxiety about contingency, death, suffering, selfishness, power) is likely to be absorbed by the designs of an extreme scientific socialism denying personal autonomy, nor by extreme liberal individualism unwilling to make sacrifices for the common good. Community remains necessary for personal identity, but that does not mean social structures constitute the identity of persons who can assess values, assume obligations, and undertake to bring about change. Moreover, the meaning of the word 'person' itself has evolved, its development caught up in the complex imprecisions and discontinuities of such closely-related terms as self, ego, character, soul, mind, and so on. Consequently, my emphasis has not been to define 'person' rigorously and then apply the results to a discussion of literature, but rather to deduce from the discussion a set of criteria for assessing the idea of a person.

As we see, a person is neither wholly autonomous nor wholly communal nor wholly self-identical, but in process, exigent, fragile, self-divided, and centrally engaged in culture through language. One value of literature and criticism is precisely to produce and enable clarification of the very claim that persons are emergent in this way, situated historically, prepossessed by the body, socially formed, with a degree of autonomy and responsibility. The good of persons thus understood is then the good of all which is returned as the good of each, so that a realisation of communal goals is also the self-creation of the people who bring them about.

How such an argument might affect the academic study of literature – the literature industry – remains problematical because today communal goals within the literary community are themselves so much in conflict, and so diverse. Yet this fact itself might help to explain why literature and the arts have acquired the authority they now hold in modern Western cultures. Competition among theories and theory proliferation have so obscured universally acceptable principles for assessing the common good that we find ourselves best persuaded in more local, particular ways by visions and ideas to which we subscribe because we recognise and affirm their validity, part of which resides in the personal signature they bear, the 'personal co-efficient' of which Polanyi talks, and the 'personal resonance' described by Taylor, substituting for the absence of shared intellectual frameworks. The hazards and responsibilities of choice, and of a limited self-creation are thus foregrounded by the complex elaborations of literary language, indicating at once our courageous circumspection and tentativeness, hallmarks of a richly considerate, if bewildered, way of knowing.

The passages of exegesis in the present study are meant as examples of such a way of knowing and of the idea of the person that informs it. As with every evaluative procedure, meaning inheres also in *how* evaluation is expressed, and critical exegesis remains a skill: we need to acquire the knack – to embody it, in Merleau-Ponty's sense. Culture then is, in part, a tradition of such tacit ways of knowing and evaluation and, as Polanyi shows, this is true also of the sciences. Yet I have resisted surrendering altogether the claim that language is referential and that it describes, however inadequately, aspects of the world over and against ourselves. Literature, I want to say, is also mimetic. This implies that *what* we claim to be the case can be regarded seriously as a more or less adequate description of the way things are, open to assessments taking account of evidence.

My position might therefore be described as an attempt to synthesise the claims of hermeneutics and realism, rather as Richard Miller has undertaken to do for the natural and social sciences. In such a quest for a 'hermeneutic realism' as a model for critical practice, one point of entry is, simply, the foregrounded interplay in literary texts between implicit evaluations and what the most explicit meanings and claims appear to be. Along such lines, I have suggested that literature and criticism provide unique means for understanding how persons also are constituted within such a dialectic of tacit participation and objective distance, duplicating the play of presence and absence within language itself, so distinctively foregrounded by literature. While the horizon of the not-yet remains obscurely pre-figured through all that impedes it in the present inherited from the past, it seems that the task of reading and interpretation will remain, however modestly, one aspect of the labour of culture to bring us home to the world in one another.

Notes

CHAPTER 1: INTRODUCTION

1. Derek Parfit, *Reasons and Persons* (Oxford: Clarendon Press, 1984).
2. *The Spectator*, May 19 (1984), pp. 24–5.
3. Charles Taylor, *Sources of the Self. The Making of the Modern Identity* (Cambridge, Mass.: Harvard University Press, 1989), pp. 49 ff.
4. Various scholars stress this general emphasis. Besides Taylor, *Sources of the Self*, pp. 51 ff., *et passim*, see R. S. Downie and Elizabeth Telfer, *Respect for Persons* (London: George Allen & Unwin, 1969), pp. 18 ff.; Jonathan Glover, *I. The Philosophy of Personal Identity* (London: Allen Lane, 1988): this study develops Parfit's arguments in a direction situating the person historically; Marcel Mauss, 'A Category of the Human Mind: The Notion of Person; the Notion of Self', trans. W. D. Halls, *The Category of the Person. Anthropology, Philosophy, History*, ed. Michael Carrithers, Steven Collins, Steven Lukes (Cambridge: Cambridge University Press, 1985), pp. 1 ff.; Michael Polanyi, *Personal Knowledge. Towards a Post-Critical Philosophy* (New York: Harper, 1964. First published, 1958); Richard Rorty, *Contingency, Irony, and Solidarity* (Cambridge: Cambridge University Press, 1989), especially Part I, 'Contingency', pp. 3–69. Interrelations between philosophy of mind in the Lockean tradition and an evaluative, broadly hermeneutical stance are intricate, but beyond the scope of this study. For alternative approaches, see for instance Geoffrey Madell, *The Identity of the Self* (Edinburgh: Edinburgh University Press, 1981); Sydney Shoemaker and Richard Swinburne, *Personal Identity* (Oxford: Basil Blackwell, 1984); Bernard Williams, *Problems of the Self. Philosophical Papers 1956–72* (Cambridge: Cambridge University Press, 1973).
5. *Personal Knowledge*, pp. 104, 174, 303, *et passim*.
6. See especially Paul Ricœur, *The Symbolism of Evil*, trans. Emerson Buchanan (New York: Harper & Row, 1967), pp. 161 ff.
7. Jonathan Glover, *I. The Philosophy of Personal Identity*, pp. 139 ff.
8. Don Cupitt, *Taking Leave of God* (London: SCM Press, 1980), p. 166.
9. George Steiner, *Real Presences* (London: Faber, 1989). p. 86.
10. See Bruno Snell, *The Discovery of the Mind: The Greek Origins of European Thought*, trans. T. G. Rosenmeyer (Oxford: Basil Blackwell, 1953), pp. 1 ff. For a cautionary reaction to Snell, see Hugh Lloyd-Jones, *The Justice of Zeus* (Berkeley: University of California Press, 1971), pp. 158 ff.
11. See Ernst Bloch, *The Principle of Hope*, trans. Neville Plaice, Stephen Plaice, and Paul Knight (Oxford: Basil Blackwell, 1986), 3 vols. The tension between the present and the allure of the 'not yet' is the leitmotif of Bloch's thinking.

12.   Jonathan Swift, *Gulliver's Travels*, ed. Herbert Davis (Oxford: Basil Blackwell, 1965). Page numbers to this edition are cited in the text.
13.   See Dolores J. Palomo, 'The Dutch Connection: The University of Leiden and Swift's Academy of Lagado', *Huntingdon Library Quarterly* 41 (1977–78), 27–35.
14.   See David Renaker, 'Swift's Laputans as a Caricature of the Cartesians', Publications of the *Modern Language Association*, 94 (1979), 936–44; Marjorie Hope Nicolson and Nora M. Mohler, 'The Scientific Background to Swift's *Voyage to Laputa*', and 'Swift's "Flying Island" in *The Voyage to Laputa*', Annals of Science II (1937), 299–34 and 405–30.
15.   Thomas Sprat, *History of the Royal Society*, ed. Jackson I. Cope and Harold Whitmore Jones (London: Routledge & Kegan Paul, 1959), p. 113.
16.   For an account of this attachment, the 'balance of power' and lack of autonomy, see Kathleen Williams, *Jonathan Swift and the Age of Compromise* (Lawrence: University of Kansas Press, 1958), pp. 161 ff.
17.   Dennis Todd, 'Laputa, the Whore of Babylon, and the Idols of Science', *Studies in Philology* 75 (1978), 114.
18.   These points are developed by Todd, 'Laputa, the Whore of Babylon, and the Idols of Science', pp. 116 ff.
19.   J. M. Synge, *The Playboy of the Western World*, ed. Ann Saddlemyer, *J. M. Synge. Collected Works*, vol. IV, Plays, Book II (London: Oxford University Press, 1968), pp. 51 ff. References to this edition are cited in the text.
20.   John Butler Yeats, *Essays Irish and American* (New York: Books for Libraries Press, 1969. First published, 1919), p. 58. Of the supposed murder, Yeats claims 'No one really believes it', and Christy's 'talk about the murder is a sudden freak of self-advertisement', part of the trials of 'a young poet in the supreme difficulty of getting born'.
21.   C. C. Innes, 'Naked Truth, Fine Clothes and Fine Phrases in Synge's *Playboy of the Western World*', ed. Joseph Ronsley, *Myth and Reality in Irish Literature* (Waterloo, Ontario: Wilfrid Laurier Press, 1977), pp. 67 ff., stresses the 'anti-poetic' character of Old Mahon.
22.   See for instance 'Possible Remedies', ed. Alan Price, *J. M. Synge: Collected Works*, Vol. II, Prose (London: Oxford University Press, 1966), pp. 339–43.
23.   The contrast between fantasy and realism is dealt with frequently, but see especially Edward Hirsch, 'The Gallous Story and the Dirty Deed: the Two Playboys', *Modern Drama* 26, no. 1 (1983), 85–102.
24.   See James Kilroy, *The 'Playboy' Riots* (Dublin: Dolmen Press, 1971).
25.   The Irish Times, Thursday, 31 January, 1907, p. 5, claims that *The Playboy* 'is not a play with "a purpose" in the modern sense of the word, but although parts of it are, or are meant to be, an extravagant comedy, still a great deal that is in it, and a great deal more that is behind it, is perfectly serious, when looked at in a certain light.' Cited in Kilroy, *The 'Playboy' Riots*, p. 41.
26.   Hugh Kenner, *A Colder Eye: The Modern Irish Writers* (New York:

Alfred A. Knopf, 1983), p. 130.
27. Ferdinand de Saussure, *Course in General Linguistics*, ed. Charles Bally and Albert Sechehaye, in collaboration with Albert Reidlinger, trans. Wade Baskin (London: Peter Owen, 1960).
28. Claude Lévi-Strauss, *Structural Anthropology*, trans. Claire Jacobson and Brooke Grundfest Schoepf (New York: Basic Books, 1963), and especially the famous Chapter XI, 'The Structural Study of Myth', pp. 206–31.
29. Robert Young, ed., *Untying the Text. A Post-Structuralist Reader* (London: Routledge & Kegan Paul, 1981), 'Post-Structuralism: An Introduction', p. 8.
30. As Paul Ricœur points out. See for instance 'Metaphor and the Central Problem of Hermeneutics', in *Paul Ricœur. Hermeneutics and the Human Sciences*, ed. and trans. John B. Thompson (Cambridge: Cambridge University Press, 1981), pp. 165 ff.

CHAPTER 2:   FUNDAMENTALS

1. It is worth noting that 'hermeneia' (and the verb form 'hermeneuo') are used in the New Testament. See for instance 1 Cor.2:10; 14:26, John 1:42, Hebrews 7:2.
2. *Friedrich Schleiermacher, Hermeneutics: The Handwritten Manuscripts*, ed. Heinz Kimmerle, trans. James Duke and Jack Forstman (Missoula, Montana: Scholars Press, 1977), p. 95: 'At present there is no general hermeneutics as the art of understanding but only a variety of specialised hermeneutics.' Further page numbers to this edition are cited in the text.
3. See *W. Dilthey: Selected Writings*, ed. and trans. H. P. Rickman (Cambridge: Cambridge University Press, 1976), especially 'The Construction of the Historical World in the Human Studies', pp. 170–245.
4. See Jacques Maritain, *The Degrees of Knowledge*, trans. from the 2nd rev. and augmented edition by Bernard Wall and Margot M. Adamson (London: Geoffrey Bles, 1937), pp. 51 ff.
5. See *Ideas: General Introduction to Pure Phenomenology*, trans. W. R. Boyce Gibson (London: George Allen & Unwin, 1931); *Cartesian Meditations. An Introduction to Phenomenology*, trans. Dorian Cairns (The Hague: Martinus Nijhoff, 1960); *Husserl: Shorter Works*, ed. Peter McCormick and Frederick A. Elliston (Sussex: Harvester Press, 1989).
6. Martin Heidegger, *Being and Time*, trans. John Macquarrie and Edward Robinson (New York: Harper & Row, 1962, first published, 1927), p. 62. Further page numbers are cited in the text.
7. See *Personal Knowledge. Towards a Post-Critical Philosophy* (New York: Harper, 1964; first published, 1958); *The Tacit Dimension* (New York: Anchor, 1966).
8. 'On Body and Mind', *The New Scholasticism* 4 (1969), 199. See also *The Tacit Dimension*, p. 4.

9. *Personal Knowledge*, p. 4.
10. For Polanyi on art, see especially Michael Polanyi and Harry Prosch, *Meaning* (Chicago: University of Chicago Press, 1975).
11. *Poetry, Language, Thought*, trans. Albert Hofstadter (New York: Harper & Row, 1975), 'The Origin of the Work of Art', pp. 74 and 23.
12. Edited by A. C. Cawley, *The Wakefield Pageants in the Towneley Cycle* (Manchester: Manchester University Press, 1958).
13. On coming awake and sleeping, and on the incarnation as a perpetual present, see Lawrence T. Ross, 'Symbol and Structure in the *Secunda Pastorum*', ed. Jerome Taylor and Alan H. Nelson, *Mediaeval English Drama. Essays Critical and Contextual* (Chicago: University of Chicago Press, 1972), pp. 207, 209. For a commentary on mythical, historical and present time, and the importance of charity, see Edgar Schell, 'Seeing Through a Glass Darkly. The Action Imitated by the *Secunda Pastorum*', *Modern Language Quarterly* 37 (1976), 3–4.
14. See Michael F. Vaughan, 'The Three Advents in the *Secunda Pastorum*', *Speculum* 55, 3 (1980), 484–505, for an account of this combination of eschatology with Biblical past and English present.
15. Josie B. Campbell, 'Farce as Function in the Wakefield Shepherds' Plays', *Chaucer Review* 14 (1980), 336–43. Yet Campbell also claims that the farce is itself displaced and accommodated to 'a better order' (338).
16. See Lois Roney, 'Wakefield First and Second Shepherds' Plays as Complements in Psychology and Parody', *Speculum* 58 (1983), 696–723. Roney argues against the generally received idea that the second play is a revision and replacement of the first, weaker one. Rather, both plays are about the damage done to human nature by the Fall. The first play offers an intellectualist solution, and the second a voluntarist one. According to this interpretation, the doctrines of the Fall and Original Sin are basic to both plays.
17. As Campbell points out, 'Farce as Function', 337.
18. Beckett was awarded the Nobel Prize for literature in 1969.
19. *Fin de partie* was completed in 1956. It was first performed in French in 1957, and in English in 1958. All references cited in the text are to *Endgame* (New York: Grove Press, 1958).
20. Hugh Kenner, *Samuel Beckett. A Critical Study* (Berkeley: University of California Press, 1968), pp. 155 ff.
21. Kenner, *Samuel Beckett*, p. 163.
22. See Lance St. John Butler, *Samuel Beckett and the Meaning of Being. A Study in Ontological Parable* (London: Macmillan, 1984), especially 'Heidegger's *Being and Time* and Beckett', pp. 7 ff., on which I draw in the following account. See also Sylvie Debevec Henning, *Beckett's Critical Complicity. Carnival, Contestation and Tradition* (Lexington: University of Kentucky Press, 1988), p. 96 ff.
23. Various critics have probed the puns suggested by these characters' names. The general point is widely accepted, though not precisely defined.
24. Theodor W. Adorno, 'Trying to Understand *Endgame*', trans. Michael

T. Jones, *New German Critique* 26 (1982), 119–150 (first published, 1961). The essay is edited by Harold Bloom, *Samuel Beckett's 'Endgame'* (New York: Chelsea House Publications, 1988), 9–40. Page numbers cited in the text are to this edition.

25. Harold Bloom, *Samuel Beckett's 'Endgame'*, p. 6.
26. Henning, *Beckett's Critical Complicity*, p. 88.
27. Quotations are taken from *The 'Confessions' of St. Augustine*, trans. E. B. Pusey (London: Dent, 1907), and further references to this edition are cited in the text.
28. See John J. O'Meara, *The Young Augustine. The Growth of St. Augustine's Mind up to his Conversion* (London: Longmans, Green, 1954), pp. 10 ff.; Gerald Bonner, *St. Augustine of Hippo. Life and Controversies* (London: SCM, 1963), pp. 51 ff.
29. For instance, Robert J.O'Connell suggests that pilgrimage is the key motif. See *St. Augstine's 'Confessions.' The Odyssey of Soul* (Cambridge, Mass.: Harvard University Press, 1969), pp. 11–12; John J. O'Meara, *The Young Augustine*, pp. 2–3, suggests that the verb 'confiteri' provides the structural clue. Henry Chadwick, *Augustine* (Oxford: Oxford University Press, 1986), p. 66, sees the book as 'a prose-poem in thirteen books'.
30. On Psalm 8, verse 8, in *Expositions on the Book of Psalms*, 6 vols, vol. 1, *A Library of the Fathers* (Oxford: John Henry Parker), vol. 24, p. 70.
31. *St. Augustine's 'Confessions'*, pp. 46 ff., *et passim*. I draw especially on O'Connell in this paragraph.
32. This is set out especially in *On the Trinity*, Book XII.
33. John J. O'Meara, *The Young Augustine*, pp. 2 ff.; Gerald Bonner, *St. Augustine of Hippo*, pp. 48 ff.
34. See O'Connell, *St. Augustine's 'Confessions'*, pp. 112 ff.; *Art and the Christian Intelligence in St. Augustine* (Cambridge, Mass.: Harvard University Press, 1978), p. 13; Chadwick, *Augustine*, p. 69.
35. For a summary of the Pelagian controversy, see Bonner, *St. Augustine of Hippo*, pp. 312 ff.
36. This is frequently noticed. See Jaroslav Pelikan, *The Mystery of Continuity. Time and History, Memory and Eternity in the Thought of Saint Augustine* (Charlottesville: University of Virginia Press, 1986), p. 141; Charles Taylor, *Sources of the Self*, pp. 127 ff.
37. For the clearest statement of Augustine's teaching on signs, see *On Christian Doctrine*.
38. Etienne Gilson, *The Christian Philosophy of St. Thomas Aquinas*, trans. L. K. Shook (New York: Random House, 1956), p. 184.
39. Christopher Marlowe, *Doctor Faustus*, ed. Sylvan Barnet (New York: Signet, 1969).
40. See Ernst F. Winter, ed. and trans., *Erasmus-Luther: Discourse on Free Will* (New York: Frederic Ungar, 1966), pp. 122, 132, 133.
41. *The Individual and the Cosmos in Renaissance Philosophy*, trans. Mario Domandi (New York: Harper, 1963), p. 43.
42. René Descartes, *Meditations*, trans. Arthur Wollaston (Harmondsworth: Penguin, 1960), pp. 136–7.
43. See Francis Bacon, *Advancement of Learning*, 1 ('To the King'), in

The Works of Francis Bacon, 14 vols, ed. James Spedding, Robert Leslie Ellis, and Douglas Denton Heath (London: Longman, 1858), III, 267.

44. See Thomas Traherne, *Centuries of Meditation*, III, 3, ed. H. M. Margoliouth, *Thomas Traherne. Centuries, Poems and Thanksgivings*, 3 vols (Oxford: Clarendon Press, 1958), vol. I, *Introduction and Centuries*, p. 111; Henry Vaughan, especially 'Childe-hood' and 'The Retreate'; John Earle, *Microcosmographie*.

45. 'Original Sin', in *A Philosophical Dictionary, Works*, 22 vols, trans. William F. Fleming (New York: St. Hubert Guild, 1901–3), VI, 118.

46. *Age of Reason. Being an Investigation of True and Fabulous Theology*, ed. Daniel Edwin Wheeler, *Life and Writings of Thomas Paine*, 10 vols (New York: Vincent Parke, 1908), VI, 2.

47. John Toland, *Christianity not Mysterious: or, a Treatise Shewing that there is Nothing in the Gospel Contrary to Reason, Nor Above It: And that no Christian Doctrine can be Properly Call'd a Mystery* (1696), Sect. II, ch. IV (New York: Garland, 1978), p. 59.

48. Peter Gay, *The Enlightenment: An Interpretation. The Science of Freedom* (New York: Norton, 1977), pp. 172 and 171.

49. 'The Origin of the Work of Art', ed. Hofstadter, p. 74.

50. It is worth noting that Heidegger wrote a thesis on Duns Scotus (1915), and a lecture course on 'Saint Augustine and Neoplatonism' (1921). Affinities with Augustine are noticed at several points by George Steiner, *Heidegger* (Glasgow: Collins, 1978).

51. 'Technicity' is William J. Richardson's translation. See 'Heidegger's Way Through Phenomenology to the Thinking of Being', ed. Thomas Sheehan, *Heidegger. The Man and the Thinker* (Chicago: Precedent Publishing, 1981), p. 81: 'This is the meaning of technicity (*Technik*), which crystallises for contemporary society the forgetfulness of the Being-dimension in beings.' Richardson also translates the *Spiegel* interview, '"Only a God can Save Us": The *Spiegel* Interview (1966)', ed. Sheehan, *Heidegger. The Man and the Thinker*, where Heidegger makes clear that 'technicity' is not confined to the manipulation of nature by tools: 'Technicity in its essence is something that man does not master by his own power . . . . But above all, modern technicity is no 'tool' and has nothing at all to do with tools . . . . technicity increasingly dislodges man and uproots him from the earth.' (56)

52. Victor Farías, *Heidegger and Nazism*, ed. Joseph Margolis and Tom Rockmore, trans. Paul Burrell, Dominic di Bernardi and Gabriel R. Ricci (Philadelphia: Temple University Press, 1989), documents the closeness of the links throughout Heidegger's career. Although this book is controversial, the main case it makes for Heidegger's philosophical version of Nazism is convincing.

53. Ed. Sheehan, *Heidegger. The Man and the Thinker*, p. 48. Page numbers are cited in the text.

54. Farías' book, *Heidegger and Nazism*, amasses the documentation, and gave rise to a storm of controversy. A careful statement of the controversy is offered by Luc Ferry and Alain Renaut, *Heidegger and Modernity*, trans. Franklin Philip (Chicago: University

of Chicago Press, 1990). Two further thoughtful summaries are: Tzvetan Todorov, 'Two Current Debates . . . ', *TLS* (June 17–23), 676 ff.; Thomas Sheehan, 'Heidegger and the Nazis', *The New York Review of Books* (June 16, 1988), 38 ff. I draw on these sources in the above paragraph.

55. Hannah Arendt, 'Martin Heidegger at Eighty', ed. Michael Murray, *Heidegger and Modern Philosophy* (New Haven: Yale University Press, 1978), p. 302, especially note 3 (reprinted from *The New York Review of Books*, Oct. 1971, trans. by Albert Hofstadter); George Steiner, *Heidegger*, 116.

56. Farías, *Heidegger and Nazism*, p. 60.

57. Herbert Marcuse, 'Heidegger's Politics: An Interview with Herbert Marcuse by Frederick Olafson', *Graduate Faculty Philosophy Journal* (Winter, 1977), p. 33, cited by David Schweickhart, 'Heidegger and Marx: A Framework for Dialogue', ed. Sheehan, *Heidegger. The Man and the Thinker*, p. 229.

58. *La Métaphore Vive* (Paris: Seuil, 1975), p. 395.

59. This interpretation is evident in the Rector's address (1933), and, in a variety of ways, in the works that follow. It is documented by Farías, *Heidegger and Nazism*, pp. 93, 98, 133, 140 ff., 210, 272, and elsewhere. An analysis of Heidegger's 'spiritual' interpretation is provided by Jacques Derrida, *Of Spirit: Heidegger and the Question*, trans. Geoffrey Bennington and Rachel Bowlby (Chicago: University of Chicago Press, 1989).

60. 'Why Do I Stay in the Provinces? (1934)', ed. and trans. Thomas Sheehan, *Heidegger. The Man and the Thinker*, p. 28.

61. Martin Heidegger, 'The Self Assertion of the German University', trans. Karsten Harries, *Review of Metaphysics* 38 (1985), 480. (This is the Rector's address of 1933). See Karsten Harries, 'Heidegger as a Political Thinker', ed. Michael Murray, *Heidegger and Modern Philosophy*, pp. 304–28, for further reflections on the links between *Being and Time* and Heidegger's politics. See also, Graeme Nicholson, 'The Politics of Heidegger's Rectoral Address', *Man and World* 20 (1987), 171–87.

62. Cited by Farías, *Heidegger and Nazism*, p. 282, from A. Fischer-Barnicol 'Spiegelungen-Vermittlungen', in Günther Neske, ed., *Erinnerung an Martin Heidegger* (Pfullingen, 1977), 95–96.

63. In Beckett, that is, total responsibility disintegrates the idea of the person as a traditional locus of responsibility, because the subject itself appears as wholly arbitrary and therefore meaningless. For further reflections on Beckett and personality, see Northrop Frye, 'The Nightmare Life in Death', *The Hudson Review* 3 (1960), 442–49.

CHAPTER 3: VALIDATION

1. See for instance Leszek Kolakowski, *Positivist Philosophy from Hume to the Vienna Circle*, trans. Norbert Guterman (Harmondsworth: Penguin Books, 1972); Richard W. Miller, *Fact and Method. Explanation,*

Confirmation and Reality in the Natural and Social Sciences (Princeton: Princeton University Press, 1987), especially pp. 3 ff.

2. Carl G. Hempel, *Aspects of Scientific Explanation and Other Essays in the Philosophy of Science* (London: Collier-Macmillan, 1965). Page numbers are cited in the text.

3. See Carl G. Hempel, 'Science and Human Values', ed. R. E. Spiller, *Social Control in a Free Society* (Philadelphia: University of Pennsylvania Press, 1960), pp. 39–64.

4. Jürgen Habermas, *Knowledge and Human Interests*, trans. Jeremy J. Shapiro (Boston: Beacon Press, 1971).

5. Cited without reference in Bryan Magee, *Popper* (Glasgow: Collins, 1973), p. 11.

6. Popper's opinions are developed especially in *Conjectures and Refutations: the Growth of Scientific Knowledge* (London: Routledge & Kegan Paul, 1963), and *Objective Knowledge: an Evolutionary Approach* (Oxford: Clarendon Press, 1972), aspects of which I redact here.

7. Thomas S. Kuhn, *The Structure of Scientific Revolutions* (Chicago: University of Chicago Press, 2nd edition, 1970).

8. Thomas S. Kuhn, 'Reflections on My Critics', ed. Imre Lakatos and Alan Musgrave, *Criticism and the Growth of Knowledge*, Proceedings of the International Colloquium on the Philosophy of Science, London, 1965, volume 4 (Cambridge: Cambridge University Press, 1970), p. 260. See also 'Logic of Discovery or Psychology of Research?' in Lakatos and Musgrave, *Criticism and the Growth of Knowledge*, pp. 1–23; 'Second Thoughts on Paradigms', ed. Frederick Suppe *The Structure of Scientific Theories* (Urbana: University of Illinois Press, 2nd edn, 1977), pp. 459–82.

9. Paul Feyerabend, *Against Method* (Minneapolis: University of Minnesota Press, 1970). Page numbers are cited in the text.

10. See 'How to Defend Society against Science', *Radical Philosophy* 11 (1975), 3–8.

11. See Richard Rorty, *Philosophy and the Mirror of Nature* (New Jersey: Princeton University Press, 1979); Bas C. van Fraassen, *The Scientific Image* (Oxford: Clarendon Press, 1980).

12. Richard W. Miller, *Fact and Method*. Page numbers are cited in the text.

13. See *Personal Knowledge*, pp. 352 ff.

14. The main early books by which Derrida established himself as an important figure for literary theorists were published in 1967 and subsequently translated into English: '*Speech and Phenomena and Other Essays on Husserl's Theory of Signs*, trans. David B Allison (Evanston, Illinois: Northwestern University Press, 1973); *Of Grammatology*, trans. Gayatri Chakravorty Spivak (Baltimore: John's Hopkins University Press, 1976); *Writing and Difference*, trans. Alan Bass (London: Routledge & Kegan Paul, 1978). I summarise some of the main positions here.

15. Frederick Crews, *Skeptical Engagements* (Oxford: Oxford Univerist Press, 1986). Page numbers are cited in the text.

16. Christopher Norris, *Derrida* (London: Fontana, 1987). Page numbers are cited in the text.
17. 'Structure, Sign and Play in the Discourse of the Human Sciences' was first presented as a lecture at Johns Hopkins University in 1966, and published in *Writing and Difference*, trans. Alan Bass (Chicago: University of Chicago Press, 1978). The quotations are on p. 292.
18. See, for instance, Roland Barthes, *The Pleasure of the Text*, trans. Richard Miller (London: Cape, 1976); Jacques Lacan, *Écrits: a Selection*, trans. Alan Sheridan (London: Tavistock, 1977); Geoffrey Hartman, *Criticism in the Wilderness* (New Haven: Yale University Press, 1980).
19. A. D. Nuttall, *A New Mimesis. Shakespeare and the Representation of Reality* (London: Methuen, 1983), p. 29.
20. Richard Rorty, *Contingency, Irony and Solidarity* (Cambridge: Cambridge University Press, 1989). Page numbers are cited in the text.
21. See for instance, Hans-Georg Gadamer, *The Relevance of the Beautiful and Other Essays*, trans. Nicholas Walker (Cambridge: Cambridge University Press, 1986), p. 98: 'Recognition confirms and bears witness to the fact that mimetic behaviour makes something present. However, this does not imply that when we recognise what is represented, we should try to determine the degree of similarity between the original and its mimetic representation.'
22. See, for instance, *A New Mimesis*, p. 63: 'But an episode will not be believable if it does not reproduce features which are seen to operate powerfully in the real world.'
23. Thomas S. Kuhn, 'Theory Choice', ed. Lakatos and Musgrave, *Criticism and the Growth of Knowledge*, pp. 260–62.
24. Frederick Crews, *Skeptical Engagements*, p. 174.
25. For an overview of this debate, see Evelyn Cobley, 'Sameness and Difference in Literary Repetition', *Recherches Semiotiques/Semiotic Enquiry* 3 (1983), 248–60.
26. J. Hillis Miller, *Fiction and Repetition: Seven English Novels* (Cambridge, Mass.: Harvard University Press, 1982).
27. *Grundrisse: Foundations of the Critique of Political Economy*, trans. Martin Nicolaus (Harmondsworth: Penguin, 1973), p. 111.
28. For example, see *Christ. The Experience of Jesus as Lord*, trans. John Bowden (New York: Crossroad, 1983), p. 36, *et passim*. I combine this idea with Ernst Bloch's general theory of the utopian. See *The Principle of Hope*, trans. Neville Plaice, Stephen Plaice, and Paul Knight (Oxford: Basil Blackwell, 1986).
29. References are to *The Works of Geoffrey Chaucer*, ed. F. W. Robinson (Cambridge, Mass.: Houghton, 2nd edn, 1957). Line numbers are cited in the text.
30. See especially Jill Mann, *Chaucer and the Medieval Estates Satire. The Literature of Social Classes and the 'General Prologue' to the 'Canterbury Tales'* (Cambridge: Cambridge University Press, 1973), p. 147: 'The Summoner, in other words, should be arresting the Pardoner, not riding as his "compeer."' See also, pp. 146–8.
31. These iconographical elements are noticed by a variety of critics. See

for instance W. C. Curry, *Chaucer and the Medieval Sciences* (New York: Barnes & Noble, 2nd edn, 1960); E. C. Schweitzer Jr., 'Chaucer's Pardoner and the Hare', *English Language Notes* 4 (1967), 247–50; Jill Mann, *Chaucer and the Medieval Estates Satire*, p. 146; Monica E. McAlpine, 'The Pardoner's Homosexuality and How it Matters', *Publications of the Modern Language Association* 95 (1980), 8–22.

32. For more on this pun, see D. Biggins, 'Chaucer's General Prologue, A 163', *Notes and Queries* N.S. 6 (1959), 435–6; B. D. H. Miller, 'Chaucer's General Prologue, A 673; Further Evidence', *Notes and Queries* N.S. 7 (1960), 404–6.

33. Robert P. Miller, 'Chaucer's Pardoner, the Scriptural Eunuch, and the Pardoner's Tale', *Speculum* 30 (1955), 180–99.

34. As McAlpine points out, 'The Pardoner's Homosexuality and How it Matters', 8–22.

35. H. Marshall Leicester Jr., '"Synne Horrible": The Pardoner's Exegesis of His Tale, and Chaucer's', ed. Mary J. Carruthers and Elizabeth D. Kirk, *Acts of Interpretation: The Text in its Contexts, 700–1600: Essays in Medieval and Renaissance Literature in Honour of E. Talbot Donaldson* (Norman, Oklahoma: Pilgrim Books, 1982), pp. 25–50. Leicester points out how the Pardoner sees himself as an example, and is aware of the deficiencies of moralising. Chaucer in turn uses the tale as a critique of typological ways of thinking, exemplified by the sermon. I draw broadly on Leicester in the following remarks.

36. The old man has been interpreted variously. W. J. B. Owen, 'The Old Man in the Pardoner's Tale', *Review of English Studies*, N.S. 2 (1951), 49–55; John M. Steadman, 'Old Age and *Contemptus Mundi* in the Pardoner's Tale', *Medium Aevum* 33 (1964), 121–30; Ian Bishop, *The Narrative Art of the Canterbury Tales* (London: Dent, 1987), pp. 91 ff.

37. Michel Foucault, 'What is an Author?' trans. Josué V. Harari, ed. Paul Rabinow, *The Foucault Reader* (New York: Pantheon, 1964) pp. 101–20. Page numbers are cited in the text.

38. E. H. Gombrich, *Art and Illusion. A Study in the Psychology of Pictorial Representation* (New Jersey: Princeton University Press, 2nd rev. edn, 1961).

39. References are to *The Life of Henry the Fifth*, ed. John Russell Brown, *The Complete Signet Classic Shakespeare*, ed. Sylvan Barnet (New York: Harcourt Brace Jovanovich, 1972).

40. Owen Tudor married Catherine of France, widow of Henry V. Through the marriage of their son Edmund Earl of Richmond to Lady Margaret Beaufort, the Tudors derived their claim to the throne.

41. See Harold C. Goddard, *The Meaning of Shakespeare* (Chicago: University of Chicago Press, 1951), pp. 215 ff., and especially p. 267.

42. On the conventions behind Henry's incognito visit, see Anne Barton, 'The King Disguised: Shakespeare's Henry V and the Comical History', ed. Joseph G. Price, *The Triple Bond: Plays, Mainly Shakespearean, in Performance* (University Park, Pennsylvania: Pennsylvania State University Press, 1975) pp. 92–117. Barton argues that the king's disguise is part of a motif romanticising the kingship,

but that Shakespeare's use of the motif shows the romanticism to be false.

43. For an interesting treatment of this conflict along Marxist lines, see Jonathan Dollimore and Alan Sinfield, 'History and Ideology: The Instance of *Henry V*', ed. John Drakakis, *Alternative Shakespeares* (London: Methuen, 1985), p. 206 ff.
44. See Norman Rabkin, *Shakespeare and the Problem of Meaning* (Chicago: University of Chicago Press, 1981), 'Either/Or: Responding to *Henry V*', pp. 33–62.
45. See Claude Lévi-Strauss, *Tristes Tropiques*, trans. John and Doreen Weightman (London: Cape), p. 197.
46. *Structural Anthropology*, trans. Claire Jacobson and Brooke Grundfest Schoepf (New York: Basic Books, 1963), pp. 206–31.
47. Edmund Leach, 'Fishing for Men on the Edge of the Wilderness', ed. Robert Alter and Frank Kermode, *The Literary Guide to the Bible* (Cambridge, Mass.: Harvard University Press, 1987), pp. 579–99. Page numbers are cited in the text.
48. Cedric Watts, 'King Oedipus and the Toy-vendor', ed. Laurence Lerner, *Reconstructing Literature* (Oxford: Basil Blackwell, 1983), p. 112.
49. Jürgen Habermas, *Knowledge and Human Interests*, pp. 246 ff.
50. Adolf Grunbaum, *The Foundations of Psychoanalysis. A Philosophical Critique* (Berkeley: University of California Press, 1984), pp. 3 ff. Grunbaum argues that Freud gave up the idea of 'forseeably *reducing* the clinical theory *globally* to neurobiology' (3), but continued to think in terms of neurobiological models.
51. Frederick Crews, *Skeptical Engagements*, p. 6.
52. Seymour Fisher and Roger P. Greenberg, *The Scientific Credibility of Freud's Theories and Therapy* (New York: Basic Books, 1977), pp. 341–42; Jacques Lacan, *Écrits. A Selection*, p. 72.
53. Grunbaum, *Foundations*, p. 278.
54. Crews, *Skeptical Engagements*, p. 20.
55. Besides Grunbaum, *Foundations* and Crews, *Skeptical Engagements*, see Hans J. Eysenck and Glenn D. Wilson, *The Experimental Study of Freudian Theories* (London: Methuen, 1973); Frank Cioffi, 'Psychoanalysis, Pseudo-Science and Testability', in *Popper and the Human Sciences*, ed. G. Currie and A. Musgrave (Dordrecht: Nijhoff, 1985), pp. 13–211. Studies more sympathetic to Freud but nonetheless aware of the difficulties of experimentally proving the claims of psychoanalysis are Seymour Fisher and Roger P. Greenberg, *The Scientific Credibility of Freud's Theories and Therapy*, Frank J. Sulloway, *Freud, Biologist of the Mind: Beyond the Psychoanalytic Legend* (New York: Basic Books, 1979). The following points are drawn broadly from these sources, and are commonly repeated.
56. George Steiner, *Real Presences. Is There Anything In What We Say?* (London: Faber, 1989), p. 109.
57. *The Standard Edition of the Complete Psychological Works of Sigmund Freud*, trans. James Strachey, in collaboration with Anna Freud, assisted by Alix Strachey and Alan Tyson, Vol. XIV (London:

Hogarth Press, 1957), p. 16: 'The theory of repression is the corner-stone on which the whole structure of psycho-analysis rests. It is the most essential part of it.'

58. Fisher and Greenberg, *The Scientific Crediblity of Freud's Theories and Therapy*, p. 414.
59. Richard Miller, *Fact and Method*, pp. 503 and 148.
60. Richard Miller, 'A Clinical Science', *Canadian Journal of Philosophy* 18 (1988), 659.
61. Anthony Storr, *Freud* (Oxford: Oxford University Press, 1989), p. 9. Page numbers are cited in the text.
62. 'The Question of Proof in Freud's Psychoanalytic Writings', ed. and trans. John B. Thompson, *Hermeneutics and the Human Sciences* (Cambridge: Cambridge University Press, 1981), p. 248. Page numbers are cited in the text.
63. John B. Thompson points out that Ricœur's position has modified since *Freud and Philosophy* (New Haven: Yale University Press, 1970), away from 'an emphasis on the structure of psychoanalytic theory' and towards 'the analytic situation.' But early and late, Ricœur stresses the role of language. See *Hermeneutics and The Human Sciences*, 'Editor's Introduction', p. 24.
64. References are to *The Foundations of Psychoanalysis*, and are cited in the text.
65. Anthony Storr, *Freud*, pp. 17–18.
66. Frederick Crews, *Skeptical Engagements*, p. 77.
67. These four headings are set out in Richard Miller, 'A Clinical Science', pp. 662 ff., and are closely redacted here.
68. Anthony Storr sets out similar criteria in Freud, pp. 115–16.
69. John B. Thompson, ed. *Hermeneutics and The Human Sciences*, 'Editor's Introduction', p. 7, notes that 'the recognition of the irreducible role of language and meaning in psychoanalysis brings Ricœur close to the position of Jacques Lacan and his followers.' Thompson also notes, however, that Ricœur is critical of Lacan's attempt to read 'condensation as metaphor and displacement as metonymy', on the grounds that Lacan here underplays the effect repression has of separating ordinary language from the 'quasi-language of the unconscious.'
70. The following account of the broad outline of Lacan's thinking derives in general from *Écrits. A Selection*, as well as *The Seminar of Jacques Lacan*, ed. Jacques Alain Miller, Books I and II, trans. John Forrester and Sylvana Tomaselli (New York: Norton, 1988), *The Four Fundamental Concepts of Psycho-Analysis*, ed. Jacques-Alain Miller, trans. Alan Sheridan (New York: Norton, 1978), and *The Language of the Self. The Function of Language in Psychoanalysis*, trans. Anthony Wilden (Baltimore: Johns Hopkins University Press, 1968).
71. *Écrits. A Selection*, p. 90.
72. *Seminar* I, 73.
73. *Écrits. A Selection*, pp. 76 and 83.
74. *Seminar* I, 79; 275.
75. *Écrits. A Selection*, p. 52.

76. *The Language of the Self,* p. 179.
77. Ibid., p. 180.
78. *The Four Fundamental Concepts of Psychoanalysis,* p. 239.
79. See, for instance, *Écrits. A Selection,* pp. 47, 103, 175; *Seminar* I, 287.
80. *Seminar* I, 277.
81. *Seminar* I, 274.
82. *Écrits. A Selection,* p. 105.
83. *Écrits. A Selection,* p. 1.
84. *Seminar* I, 277.
85. *Écits. A Selection,* p. 69.
86. *Seminar* I, 85; 66.
87. *Seminar* I, 249 ff.
88. T. S. Eliot, 'Ben Jonson', in *The Sacred Wood. Essays on Poetry and Criticism* (London: Methuen, 1957; first published, 1920), p. 115.
89. F. H. Bradley, *Appearance and Reality. A Metaphysical Essay* (Oxford: Clarendon Press, 1930). Page numbers are cited in the text.
90. Quotations are from *T. S. Eliot. Collected Poems 1909–62* (London; Faber, 1963).
91. See Helen Gardner, *The Art of T. S. Eliot* (London: Cresset Press, 1949), pp. 44–45.
92. Nancy K. Gish, *Time in the Poetry of T. S. Eliot. A Study in Structure and Theme* (New Jersey: Barnes and Noble, 1981), pp. 91 ff.
93. Hugh Kenner, 'Eliot's Moral Dialectic', *Hudson Review* 2 (1949), pp. 421–48.
94. Donald Davie, 'T. S. Eliot: The End of an Era' (1956), ed. Bernard Bergonzi, *T. S. Eliot. Four Quartets* (London: Macmillan, 1969), pp. 153–67.
95. Denis Donoghue, 'T. S. Eliot's *Quartets*: A New Reading' (1968), ed. Bernard Bergonzi, *T. S. Eliot. Four Quartets,* p. 213.

CHAPTER 4: IMAGINATION

1. Richard Rorty, *Contingency, Irony, and Solidarity* (Cambridge: Cambridge University Press, 1989), pp. 16 ff.; Owen Barfield, *Poetic Diction. A Study in Meaning* (London: Faber, 1928), pp. 60 ff.
2. Jacques Lacan, *The Four Fundamental Concepts of Psycho-Analysis,* ed. Jacques-Alain Miller, trans. Alan Sheridan (New York: Norton, 1978), p. 26.
3. J. Hillis Miller, interview with Imre Salusinsky, in *Criticism and Society,* ed. Imre Salusinsky (London: Methuen, 1987), p. 216.
4. The classic formulation is in Karl Marx, *A Contribution to the Critique of Political Economy,* ed. Maurice Dobb, trans. S. W. Ryazanskaya (New York: International Publications, 1971), p. 21: 'It is not the consciousness of men that determines their existence, but their social existence that determines their consciousness.'
5. See Chapter 6 for a further discussion of Althusser.
6. See *The Seminar of Jacques Lacan,* ed. Jacques-Alain Miller, trans. John Forrester (New York: Norton, 1988), Book I, pp. 247 ff.

7. *Confessions*, trans. E. B. Pusey (London: Dent, 1907), pp. 1 and 285.
8. See Gerard Watson, 'Imagination and Religion in Classical Thought', ed. James P. Mackey, *Religious Imagination* (Edinburgh: Edinburgh University Press, 1986), pp. 46 ff.; and also pp. 31 ff.; Patrick Grant, *Images and Ideas in Literature of the English Renaissance* (London: Macmillan, 1979), p. 8.
9. Patrick Grant, *Images and Ideas*, pp. 175 ff.
10. This is the general line of Hume's argument. In Book I of *A Treatise of Human Nature*, ed. L. A. Selby-Bigge (Oxford: Clarendon Press, 1888), Hume describes the differences between impressions and ideas. His thinking becomes more complex when he notices the difference between sensations of reflexion and primary sense impressions, and again when he examines how imagination can actively turn an idea back towards an impression by recovering something of the original felt impact. But basically, and despite the further and considerable difficulties with such problems as memory, space, time, and direct and indirect passions, Hume's criterion is the 'degree of force and vivacity' (2).
11. Kant's main word for 'imagination' is 'Einbildungskraft', which is fundamental to perception and to the production of fictional images and the like. Its origins remain a mystery. See *Immanuel Kant's Critique of Pure Reason*, trans. Norman Kemp Smith (New York: St Martin's Press, 1965), p. 183: 'This schematism of our understanding, in its application to appearances and their mere form, is an art concealed in the depths of the human soul, whose real modes of activity nature is hardly likely ever to allow us to discover, and to have open to our gaze.'
12. See Thomas McFarland, *Originality and Imagination* (Baltimore: Johns Hopkins University Press, 1985), pp. 90–119.
13. *Aids to Reflection*, ed. Professor Shedd, *The Complete Works of Samuel Taylor Coleridge*, 7 vols (New York: Harper, 1868), I, 119.
14. *Biographia Litteraria*, ed. Shedd, III, 345.
15. *Biographia Litteraria*, ed. Shedd, III, 363.
16. Coleridge's distinction between Reason and Understanding is discussed in many places. See, for instance, *Aids to Reflection*, ed. Shedd, I, 367.
17. See *The Phenomenology of Perception*, trans. Colin Smith (London: Routledge & Kegan Paul, 1962), p. 319.
18. See, for instance, *Aids to Reflection*, ed. Shedd, I, 129: 'It is a dull and obtuse mind, that must divide in order to distinguish; but it is a still worse, that distinguishes in order to divide.'
19. *The Phenomenology of Perception*, p. xvi. Further references are cited in the text.
20. *The Primacy of Perception and Other Essays on Phenomenological Psychology, the Philosophy of Art, History and Politics*, trans. James M. Edie (Evanston: Northwestern University Press, 1964), p. 60.
21. Jean-Paul Sartre, *The Psychology of Imagination* (London: Rider, 1950), pp. 13–4, 209 ff. Sartre's emphasis on imagination as negation draws on Hegel, whose vision of the universal reconciliation of all things in

the Absolute is described as a dialectic of affirmation, negation, and negation of the negation.

22. K. M. Wheeler, *The Creative Mind in Coleridge's Poetry* (London: Heinemann, 1981), p. 102, points this out: 'The shapes and sounds of nature are then lifted to a higher plane of metaphor, as things "intelligible", indeed as language.'

23. Thus Arden Reed, *Romantic Weather. The Climates of Coleridge and Baudelaire* (Hanover and London: Brown University Press, 1983), p. 143, concludes that 'the poem approximates a Saussurean circulation of difference.'

24. Yeats' theories are set out in *A Vision* (New York: Macmillan, 1956). This book was first published in 1925, and revised in 1937.

25. Cited by Jon Stallworthy, *Between the Lines. Yeats' Poetry in the Making* (Oxford: Clarendon Press, 1963), p. 96. As is often pointed out, Yeats admired the Byzantium of the time just before Justinian 'opened St. Sophia and closed the Academy of Plato', and in which art achieved a unity of 'religious, aesthetic, and practical life', and also a high degree of impersonality. See *A Vision*, p. 279.

26. All quotations are from *Felix Holt, the Radical*, ed. Peter Coveney (Harmondsworth: Penguin, 1987). Page numbers are cited in the text.

27. See Lenore Wisney Horowitz, 'George Eliot's Vision of Society in *Felix Holt, the Radical*', *Texas Studies in Literature and Language* 17 (1975), 175.

28. See K. M. Newton, *George Eliot: Romantic Humanist* (London: Macmillan, 1981), pp. 1 ff.; Thomas Pinney, 'The Authority of the Past in George Eliot's Novels', *Nineteenth Century Fiction* 21 (1966), 131–47.

29. See Peter Coveney, ed. *Felix Holt, The Radical*, Introduction, p. 26.

30. Barbara Hardy, *Particularities. Readings in George Eliot* (London: Peter Owen, 1982), pp. 187 ff.

31. This point is argued by Terry Eagleton, *Criticism and Ideology. A Study in Marxist Literary Theory* (London: Verso, 1976), pp. 116 ff.

32. Elizabeth Deeds Ermath, *George Eliot* (Boston: Twayne, 1985), p. 103.

33. See Fred C. Thomson, 'Felix Holt as Classic Tragedy', *Nineteenth-Century Fiction* 16 (1961), 47–58.

34. J. W. Cross, ed., *George Eliot's Life, as Related in her Letters and Journals*, 3 vols (London: Blackwood, 1885), I, 8–9.

35. *Introduction to Poetics*, trans. Richard Howard (Minneapolis: University of Minnesota Press, 1981), p. xxvi. Page numbers are cited in the text.

36. *The Fantastic. A Structural Approach to a Literary Genre*, trans. Richard Howard (Cleveland: Case Western Reserve University Press, 1973). The French title is *Introduction à la littérature fantastique*, which does not mention structure or genre. Page numbers are cited in the text.

37. See Freud, 'The Uncanny', *Standard Edition*, XVII, 219 ff.

38. *Being and Time*, pp. 321, 322.

39. Rosemary Jackson, *Fantasy: The Literature of Subversion* (London: Methuen, 1981), pp. 69, 82.

40. Jackson, *Fantasy*, p. 84.
41. C. S. Lewis here anticipates Todorov: see 'On Stories', ed. C. S. Lewis, *Essays Presented to Charles Williams* (Grand Rapids, Michigan: Eerdmans, 1966. First published, 1947), p. 103: 'To be stories at all they must be series of events: but it must be understood that this series – the *plot*, as we call it – is only really a net whereby to catch something else.'
42. See Todorov, *The Fantastic*, p. 168, on fantasy as the 'bad conscience of this positivist era.' See Jean-Paul Sartre, '"Aminadab" or the fantastic considered as a language', *Situations* 1 (1947), 56–72. Sartre claims that fantasy discovers its own realm with the emergence of modern capitalism and materialism. Because supernatural explanations of strange events are no longer acceptable in a secular society, experiences of uncanny strangeness must be interpreted as an unexplainable if unsettling dimension of the natural.
43. See George MacDonald, 'The Imagination: Its Functions and its Culture', *A Dish of Orts. Chiefly Papers on the Imagination and on Shakespeare* (London: Edwin Dalton, 1908). Page numbers are cited in the text.
44. See 'On Fairy Stories', *The Tolkien Reader* (New York: Ballantine Books, 1966), p. 55.
45. Lynette Hunter, *Modern Allegory and Fantasy. Rhetorical Stances in Contemporary Writing* (London: Macmillan, 1989), especially pp. 39 ff. The following paragraph redacts Hunter's argument.
46. G. K. Chesterton, *Orthodoxy* (New York: Image Books, 1959), p. 52. Page numbers are cited in the text.
47. *At the Back of the North Wind* ran for a year from November 1868 in *Good Words for the Young*, and was published in 1871. Subsequent references are to George MacDonald, *At the Back of the North Wind* (New York: Airmont, 1966). Page numbers are cited in the text.
48. Critics usually discuss the boundaries between worlds in this novel. See Richard H. Reis, *George MacDonald* (New York: Twayne, 1972), p. 82. Kathy Triggs, *The Stars and the Stillness. A Portrait of George MacDonald* (Cambridge: Lutterworth, 1986), p. 104, notices the same point, but uses the word 'fantasy' in a different sense from mine when she claims that *At the Back of the North Wind* is 'not a pure fantasy' because Diamond is 'a real child set in the real world of nineteenth-century London'. In my sense of the word, this point confirms the book as a fantasy. See also Michael R. Phillips, *George MacDonald. Scotland's Beloved Storyteller* (Minneapolis: Bethany House Publishers, 1987), p. 308; Rolland Hein, *The Harmony Within. The Spiritual Vision of George MacDonald* (Michigan: Christian University Press, 1982), p. 50, on the book's subject being the equivocal nature of adversity.
49. Rosemary Jackson, *Fantasy*, p. 150, notices that 'MacDonald's fantasies betray dissatisfaction with the real and seek something other. They fill emptiness with a magical, divine plenitude. Yet a strange melancholy remains, as his hollow characters arrive at their ideal visions.'

50. Aristotle, *Poetics*, trans. Gerald F. Else (Michigan: University of Michigan Press, 1970), p. 57.
51. Paul Ricœur, *Paul Ricœur. Hermeneutics and the Human Sciences*, ed. and trans. John B. Thompson (Cambridge: Cambridge University Press, 1981), pp. 165–81.
52. Christopher Norris, *Derrida* (London: Fontana, 1987), p. 24.
53. *Of Grammatology*, trans. Gayatri Chakravorti Spivak (Baltimore: Johns Hopkins University Press, 1976), pp. 141 ff. Page numbers are cited in the text.
54. *Dissemination*, trans. Barbara Johnson (Chicago: University of Chicago Press, 1981), p. 149.
55. Terry Eagleton, *Against the Grain. Essays 1975–1985* (London: Verso, 1986), p. 111.
56. Richard Rorty, *Congingency, Irony, and Solidarity*, p. 125.
57. Drawing on Paul Oskar Kristeller, I take Humanism to be a broad cultural movement beginning in Italy in the fourteenth century, and linked to a revival of interest in a set of subjects associated with the term *studia humanitatis*. Humanism emphasised the study of Greek and Latin, proclaiming how knowledge of these languages and their ancient literatures affected morality, and stressing the uniqueness of the individual. For Kristeller's influential interpretation, see *Renaissance Thought, The Classic, Scholastic, and Humanist Strains* (New York: Harper & Row, 1961), pp. 3 ff. See also Paul Oskar Kristeller and John Herman Randall, Jr., 'General Introduction', in *The Renaissance Philosophy of Man*, ed. Ernst Cassirer *et al.* (Chicago: University of Chicago Press, 1948), pp. 1–20. For a direct application of his views to England see Kristeller, 'Thomas More as a Renaissance Humanist', *Moreana*, vol. xvii, no. 65–6 (1980), pp. 5–22. By *studia humanitatis* Kristeller means a broad cycle of disciplines – grammar, rhetoric, history, poetry, and moral philosophy – which replaced a typical medieval emphasis on logic, natural philosophy, metaphysics, theology and law.
58. Giovanni Pico Della Mirandola, *Oration on the Dignity of Man*, trans. Elizabeth Livermore Forbes, ed. Cassirer *et al.*, *The Renaissance Philosophy of Man*, p. 242. All quotations are from this translation, and page numbers are cited in the text.
59. Vives never visited Italy, and seems to have held a slighly disparaging view of Italian Humanism, preferring what he found in France and the Lowlands. He might have been stimulated to imitate the *Oration* because of the good opinion Pico had established in Paris, which he visited in 1485–6, and where Vives emigrated in 1509. See Carlos Norena, *Juan Luis Vives* (The Hague: Martinus Nijhoff, 1970), pp. 25 ff.
60. Juan Luis Vives, *A Fable About Man*, trans. Nancy Lenkeith, ed. Cassirer *et al.*, *The Renaissance Philosophy of Man*, p. 392.
61. See Lenkeith, *Introduction*, p. 385.
62. Juan Luis Vives, *Against the Pseudodialecticians. A Humanist Attack on Medieval Logic*, trans. Rita Guerlac (London: D. Riedel, 1978). Page numbers are cited in the text.

63. *Erasmus. Praise of Folly, and Letter to Martin Dorp, 1515,* trans. Betty
     Radice (Harmondsworth: Penguin Books, 1971). Page numbers are
     cited in the text. To some readers, the order of this discussion might
     seem back to front, for Erasmus was twenty-six years older than
     Vives, and the *Fable* was written after Vives had met Erasmus in 1516,
     and in imitation of the older man. Yet, in another sense, back to front
     is the right way round: Vives comes from the south, imitating Pico's
     Oration in the *Fable,* into which he introduces Erasmus' characteristic
     irony and fun, and in the *Praise of Folly* we can detect all the
     major Humanist tendencies. In these various intertextual bindings
     we grasp something of Humanism's development northward.
64. See Robert P. Adams, *The Better Part of Valor. More, Erasmus,
     Colet, and Vives on Humanism, War, and Peace* (Seattle: University
     of Washington Press, 1962), pp. 166 ff, *et passim,* for an account of
     Erasmus' concern for a united Christendom. Also, R. J. Schoeck,
     'The Place of Erasmus Today', ed. Richard L. de Molen, *Erasmus of
     Rotterdam. A Quincentennial Symposium* (New York: Twayne, 1971)
     pp. 83 ff, for Erasmus' flexible use of tradition.
65. Erasmus' thoughts on the 'philosophia Christi' are conveniently
     plain in the *Paraclesis,* trans. John C. Olin, *Desiderius Erasmus.
     Christian Humanism and the Reformation* (Gloucester, Mass.: Peter
     Smith, 1973), pp. 92 ff.
66. Such arguments run through Erasmus' writings, and are present for
     instance in the *Praise of Folly,* 151, 153, 158, 172.
67. See *Praise of Folly,* 97, 98, 161, 193.
68. See *Praise of Folly,* 94, 96, 97, 161; Letter to Dorp, 68–9, 80–2. The con-
     nections between Humanist education and peace are fundamental
     to Erasmus' thinking: see Adams, *The Better Part of Valor,* passim.
69. Erasmus attributes the charge to Franciscans, in a letter dated
     December 1524, ed. P. S. Allen, H. M. Allen, H. W. Garrod, *Opus
     epistolarum Des. Erasmi Roterodami,* 12 vols (Oxford: Clarendon Press,
     1906–58), vol. v, p. 609.
70. Translated by Ernst F. Winter, *Erasmus-Luther. Discourse on Free Will*
     (New York: Frederick Ungar, 1961).
71. For details, see Vives' *Introduction to Wisdom. A Renaissance Textbook,*
     ed. Marian Leona Tobriner (New York: Teachers College Press, 1968),
     pp. 38–9.
72. Letter of More to Erasmus, 26 May 1520, ed. Allen, *Opus
     epistolarum,* vol. IV, pp. 266–9, trans. Rita Guerlac, *Vives Against
     the Pseudodialecticians,* pp. 163 ff.
73. *Hamlet,* ed. Edward Hubler, *The Complete Signet Classic Shakespeare,*
     ed. Sylvan Barnet (New York: Harcourt, Brace, Jovanovich, 1972).
     All quotations are from this edition, and are indicated in the text.
74. Maynard Mack, 'The World of Hamlet', *The Yale Review,* XLI
     (1952), pp. 502–23, points to Hamlet's 'encroaching on the role
     of providence' and assuming responsibility for the evil he sees
     everywhere. I summarise Mack's argument here.
75. This is a main argument in A. D. Nuttall, *A New Mimesis. Shakespeare
     and the Representation of Reality* (London: Methuen, 1983).

CHAPTER 5: RELIGIOUS PROMISES

1. I acknowledge the cogency of the argument maintaining that the Enlightenment won certain freedoms from religion, and despite religion. But I want also to suggest that the acculturising effects of Christianity during a millennium and a half often remain as a latent energy, informing aesthetic and moral aspirations of a post-Enlightenment culture.

2. Jürgen Moltmann, *Theology of Hope. On the Ground and Implications of a Christian Eschatology*, trans. James W. Leitch (London: SCM, 1967). The following pragraphs draw on Moltmann, especially pp. 95 ff. The idea that apocalypses forge a new view of history is a familiar one. See for instance Bernard McGinn, 'Revelation', ed. Robert Alter and Frank Kermode, *The Literary Guide to the Bible* (Cambridge, Mass.: Harvard University Press, 1987), p. 526: 'It is also becoming evident, as more work is done on early apocalypses and their later influence, that this genre not only introduced a new conception of history into Western religions but also was central in the development of the visionary tradition in Western literature and mysticism.'

3. For the rise of prophecy as a response to political threat, and the consequent opening of Israel's message to the nations, see Moltmann, *Theology of Hope*, pp. 127–9. It is interesting to consider the universalising of the exodus theme in this context. See J. Casey, 'The Exodus theme in the Book of Revelation Against the Background of the New Testament', *Concilium*, 189 (1987), 34–43.

4. Adela Yarbro Collins, *The Combat Myth in the Book of Revelation* (Missoula, Montana: Scholars Press, 1976); 'The Political Perspective of the Revelation to John', *Journal of Biblical Literature* 96 (1977), 241–56.

5. Bernard McGinn, 'Revelation', ed. C. A. Patrides and Joseph Wittreich, *The Apocalypse in English Renaissance Thought and Literature* (Manchester: Manchester University Press, 1984), pp. 2–39; Christopher Rowland, *The Open Heaven. A Study of Apocalyptic in Judaism and Early Christianity* (London: SPCK, 1982), esp. pp. 7 ff.; J. Christiaan Beker, *Paul the Apostle: the Triumph of God in Life and Thought* (Philadelphia: Fortress Press, 1980), pp. 135–7; J. J. Collins, ed., *Apocalypse: the Morphology of a Genre, Semeia* 14 (1979); Klaus Koch, *The Rediscovery of Apocalyptic: a Polemical Work on a Neglected Area of Biblical Studies and its Damaging Effects on Theology and Philosophy*, trans. Margaret Kohl (London: SCM, 1972).

6. Norman Perrin and Dennis C. Duling, *The New Testament: an Introduction* (New York: Harcourt, Brace, Jovanovich, 2nd edn, 1982), p. 73: 'The Christian Church began as an apocalyptic sectarian movement within ancient Judaism.' See also pp. 81, 89; W. A. Beardslee, 'New Testament Apocalyptic in Recent Interpretation', *Interpretation* 25 (1971), 419 ff.; Karl Barth, *The Epistle to the Romans*, trans. Edwyn C. Hoskyns (London: Oxford University Press, 1933), p. 314: 'If Christianity is not altogether and unreservedly eschatology, there remains in it no relationship whatever to Christ.'

7. Albert Schweitzer, *The Quest of the Historical Jesus: A Critical Study of its Progress from Reimarus to Wrede*, trans. W. Montgomery (London: Adam and Charles Black, 1910).

8. Moltmann's general argument informs the last paragraph: it is taken up and developed with renewed vigour by Edward Schillebeeckx, *Jesus. An Experiment in Christology*, trans. Hubert Hoskins (Collins: Fount, 1979), and *Christ. The Experience of Jesus as Lord*, trans. John Bowden (New York: Crossroad, 1983). Schillebeeckx draws on the idea of 'negative contrast' throughout.

9. See Rowan Williams, *Resurrection. Interpreting the Easter Gospel* (London: Darton, Longman and Todd, 1982), pp. 100 ff.; James P. Mackey, *Jesus, the Man and the Myth. A Contemporary Christology* (New York: Paulist Press, 1979), pp. 92 ff.

10. Especially I Thess. 4:16–17, and also I Cor. 15:20–28, and 2 Thess. 2:1–12.

11. All this is familiar enough. C. G. Jung, *Answer to Job*, trans. R. F. C. Hull (New York: Meridian, 1960), pp. 142–3, draws the contrast to the gospels, as does D. H. Lawrence, *Apocalypse: and the Writings on Revelation*, ed. Mara Kalnis (Cambridge: Cambridge University Press, 1980), p. 67. Jung also notices the images of rigidity and hardness (145), as does Amos Wilder, 'The Rhetoric of Ancient and Modern Apocalyptic', *Interpretation* 25 (1971), 441 ff. Dale C. Allison Jr., '4Q 403 Fragm. 1, Col. 1, 38–46 and the Revelation of John', points to a tradition wherein inanimate objects are presented as living beings able to praise God. But the disturbing effect of such a bizarre spectacle depends precisely on our recognising first the impenetrability and hardness of walls, pillars and so forth. The non-humanness of the effect is confirmed rather than lessened by the metamorphosis.

12. Jürgen Moltmann, *Theology of Hope*, p. 16.

13. Edward Schillebeeckx, *Christ*, p. 439.

14. See Adela Yarbro Collins, 'The Revelation of John: An Apocalyptic Response to a Social Crisis', *Currents in Theology and Mission* 8 (1981), 4–12, arguing that the author of Revelation was likely a charismatic, eschatological prophet who wanted his community to focus its life on the liturgy in the face of resentments about differences in wealth and prestige in Asia Minor, and in the context of threatened persecution by Rome. Collins also argues that Revelation was written in reaction to sporadic repression and not to the Diocletian persecution, which is unsubstantiated. See *Crisis and Catharsis. The Power of the Apocalypse* (Philadelphia: Westminster Press, 1984), pp. 104 ff. See also Stephen R. Travis, 'The Value of Apocalyptic', *Tyndale Bulletin* 30 (1979), 53–76, arguing that transcendent eschatology of an apocalyptic kind encourages responsibility towards the world.

15. Austin Farrer, *A Rebirth of Images: the Making of St. John's Apocalypse* (Gloucester, Mass.: Peter Smith, 1970), p. 36.

16. This is not to discourage those who seek a plan: indeed, we are constantly provoked to do so. Various suggestions have been offered. John Wick Bowman, 'The Revelation of John: Its Dramatic Structure

and Message', *Interpretation*, 9 (1955), 440 ff., argues for a drama in seven acts, each with seven divisions. C. E. Douglas, *The Mystery of the Kingdom: an Attempt to Interpret the Revelation of S. John the Divine by the Method of Literary Criticism* (London: Faith Press, 1915), pp. 7 ff., suggests that a four-times repeated 'in the Spirit' marks the principal divisions, and points to a main contrast between settings on heaven and earth. John Sweet, *Revelation* (London: SCM, 1979), pp. 52–4, suggests a plan of four divisions of seven elements, with an introduction and a conclusion. J. Massyngberde Ford, *Revelation. Introduction, Translation and Commentary*, The Anchor Bible, vol. 38 (New York: Doubleday, 1975), sets out a series of seven sevens (46–48), but prefers an alternative plan of six sixes, 'a symbol of incompleteness congruous with the 666, the number of the beast, expressing a lack of fulfillment felt by the Baptist and his followers before the coming of Christ (13:18)' (48).

17. See for instance William A. Beardslee, *Literary Criticism of the New Testament* (Philadelphia: Fortress Press, 1970), pp. 59 ff.; Ibon T. Beckwith, *The Apocalypse of John* (Michigan: Baker Book House, 1979), pp. 216 ff. This point about disruption from within is a main strand in my treatment of Revelation in *Reading the New Testament* (London: Macmillan, 1989), pp. 114 ff., which I redact briefly in the following paragraphs.

18. The number 666 is sometimes taken to indicate Nero's name, by gematria (ascribing numbers to letters of the alphabet). But 666 might also indicate imperfection intensified.

19. There is debate about whether the Suffering Servant of Isaiah 53 can be identified with the suffering Jesus in Mark, mainly because Isaiah 53 is not alluded to in Mark's passion sayings. D. Lorenzen, 'Jesu lidelsesudsagen i Markusevangeliet' (Jesus' Passion Sayings in the Gospel of Mark), *Dansk Teologisk Tidskrift* 42 (1979), 217–54, surveys the debate and concludes that Mk. 9:12; 10:45; 14:21–25, especially give evidence that Jesus did assume the role of the Suffering Servant of Isaiah 53. Edward Schillebeeckx, *Jesus*, pp. 284 ff., argues that a broad 'Old Testament and intertestamentary tradition of the suffering righteous one' (285) is important here, and points especially to this tradition in the Psalms; the motif is applied 'in a special way' in Isaiah 53 to the suffering prophet (285). He concludes that 'the complete motif "suffering much" and "being glorified", became general only during the first quarter of the first century before Christ' (286).

20. See Charles H. Talbert, *What is a Gospel? The Genre of the Canonical Gospels* (Philadelphia: Fortress Press, 1977); Ralph P. Martin, *Mark, Evangelist and Theologian* (Exeter: Paternoster Press, 1972), pp. 17 ff.

21. B. A. Stevens, 'Why "must" the Son of Man Suffer?' The Divine Warrior in the Gospel of Mark', *Biblische Zeitschrift* 31 (1987), 101–110, argues that the Divine Warrior mythology contributed to the emerging concept of the apocalyptic Son of Man, thus forging a link between Mark 13 and the apocalyptic genre. P. Patten, 'The Form and Function of Parables in Select Apocalyptic Literature and

244 *Notes to pp. 154–159*

their significance for Parables in the Gospel of Mark', *New Testament Studies* 29 (1983), 246–58, argues that parables in 4 Ezra, I Enoch, and 2 Baruch are enigmatic and require special interpretation to be understood by a select group, and that Mark's problems derive from this apocalyptic example. And see also G. R. Beasley-Murray, 'Eschatology in the Gospel of Mark', *Southwestern Journal of Theology* 21 (1978), 37–53.

22. William Wrede, *The Messianic Secret*, trans. J. C. G. Grieg (London: James Clarke, 1971. First edition, 1901).

23. See James L. Blevins, *The Messianic Secret in Markan Research*, 1901–76 (Washington: University Press of America, 1981).

24. See T. J. Weeden, 'The Heresy that Necessitated Mark's Gospel', *Zeitschrift für die neutestamentliche Wissenschaft* 59 (1968), 145–58, and Mark: *Traditions in Conflict* (Philadelphia: Fortress Press, 1971) argues that Mark wrote his gospel to criticise false prophets in the community, who presented Christ as a Hellenistic wonder-worker. Weeden is followed notably by Norman Perrin, *A Modern Pilgrimage in New Testament Christology* (Philadelphia: Fortress Press, 1974), pp. 92 ff., 112 ff. But reactions to this interpretation have been presented, for instance by D. L. Tiede, *The Charismatic Figure as Wonder Worker* (Missoula, Montana: Society of Biblical Literature, 1972). See also J. D. Kingsbury, 'The "Divine Man" as the Key to Mark's Christology – The End of an Era?' *Interpretation* 35 (1981), 243–57. Still, it does seem clear that Mark is concerned with how easily misunderstood are the 'signs', including Jesus' miracle working, and that he does warn us against seeing Jesus just as a powerful wonder-worker.

25. I allude to the distinction drawn by Ulrich Luz, 'The Secrecy Motif and the Marcan Christology', trans. R. Morgan, ed. Christopher Tuckett, *The Messianic Secret* (London: SPCK, 1983), pp. 75–96.

26. Qumran fragments suggest that 'Son of God' was a messianic title. See J. M. Allegro, 'Fragments of a Qumran scroll of Eschatological Midrasim', *Journal of Biblical Literature* 77 (1958), 350–54. J. D. Kingsbury, 'The "Divine Man" as the Key to Mark's Christology', p. 253, points to Psalm 2, where the king is named God's anointed, and God's son. So, Jesus 'is the Davidic Messiah, the royal Son of God, exactly as Mark also states in the superscription to his Gospel: "The beginning of the gospel of Jesus Messiah, the Son of God" (1:1).'

27. See James P. Mackey, *Modern Theology. A Sense of Direction* (Oxford: Oxford University Press, 1987), p. 3.

28. Frank Kermode, *The Genesis of Secrecy* (Cambridge, Mass.: Harvard University Press, 1979), deals with interpretive strategies in Mark.

29. There is a great deal of commentary on the disciples in Mark. For opinions that touch on the concerns of the present chapter, see S. Freyne, 'The Disciples in Mark and the *maskilim* in Daniel. A Comparison', *Journal for the Study of the New Testament* 16 (1982), 7–23. Freyne places the disciples in an apocalyptic context in which the elect play a special role because of their insight into the divine

plan, in the midst of the end-time struggle and its confusions. C. Burdon, '"Such a Fast God" – True and False Disciples in Mark's Gospel', *Theology* 90 (1987), 89–97, repeats the general point that the disciples frequently are not presented as positive models for the reader, and stresses the fleetingness of Jesus' revelatory encounters as the essential point about Christian discipleship: people can touch Jesus, but not hold on to him.

30. This is the main subject of my chapter on Mark in *Reading the New Testament* (London: Macmillan, 1989), pp. 10 ff.

31. David Daube, 'The Anointing at Bethany and Jesus' Burial', *Anglican Theological Review* 22 (1950), 186–99, suggests that Mark was concerned to show that the proper rites had been performed.

32. See D. E. Nineham, *The Gospel of St. Mark* (London: Adam and Charles Black, 1963, revised, 1968), p. 374.

33. Norman Perrin and Dennis C. Duling, *The New Testament. An Introduction*, p. 323.

34. *Jesus*, p. 652.

35. See Heribert Fischer, 'Mysticism', ed. Karl Rahner, *Sacramentum Mundi* (New York: Herder, 1968–70), p. 138: 'The Church is never without the mystic element. It has never made any universal and binding declarations on the exact nature of the mystical experience.'

36. See Jacques Maritain, *The Degrees of Knowledge*, trans. Bernard Wall and Margot R. Adamson (London: Geoffrey Bles, 1937), pp. 327, 354 ff.; R. C. Zaehner, *Mysticism Sacred and Profane. An Inquiry into Some Varieties of Praeternatural Experience* (London: Oxford University Press, 1961), passim.

37. Evelyn Underhill, *Mysticism. A Study in the Nature and Development of Man's Spiritual Consciousness* (New York: E. P. Dutton, 1961. First published, 1911), p. 72.

38. Fischer, 'Mysticism', p. 137.

39. See James P. Mackey, *The Christian Experience of God as Trinity* (London: SCM, 1983), pp. 2 ff., *et passim*; Leonardo Boff, *Trinity and Society*, trans. Paul Burns (New York: Orbis Books, 1988).

40. See Patrick Grant, *A Dazzling Darkness* (Collins: Fount, 1985), especially Chapter VI, 'Personal Progress', pp. 252 ff.

41. Cuthbert Butler, *Western Mysticism. With Afterthoughts* (London: Grey Arrow, 1960. First published, 1922), pp. 50 ff.

42. See for instance *The Interior Castle*, trans. E. Allison Peers (New York: Image Books, 1961), p. 206.

43. Jacques Maritain, *The Degrees of Knowledge*, p. 305; Cuthbert Butler, *Western Mysticism*, p. 43.

44. David Knowles, *The English Mystical Tradition* (London: Burns and Oates, 1961), p. 10.

45. See Jacques Guillet, Gustave Bardy, Francois Vandenbroucke, Joseph Regan, Henri Martin, *Discernment of Spirits*, trans. Sister Innocentia Richards (Collegeville, Minnesota: Liturgical Press, 1957); Martin Kelsey, *Discernment: A Study in Ecstasy and Evil* (New York: Paulist Press, 1978).

46. Erich Neumann, 'Mystical Man', *The Mystic Vision. Papers from the Eranos Yearbooks*, Bollingen Series XXX, 6 (New Jersey: Princeton University Press, 1968), pp. 401 ff.
47. Cited without reference in James R. Horne, *Beyond Mysticism* (Toronto: Canadian Corporation for Studies in Religion, 1978), p. 78.
48. See for instance Elaine Pagels, *The Gnostic Gospels* (New York: Vintage Books, 1981).
49. See, for instance, 1 Cor. 6:13; I Thess. 5:23; Eph. 3:16.
50. Origen, *The Song of Songs: Commentary and Homilies*, trans. R. P. Lawson (Westminster, Maryland: Newman Press, 1957).
51. For a representative selection of Gregory of Nyssa's works, see *From Glory to Glory*, ed. H. Musurillo (London: John Murray, 1962).
52. Cuthbert Butler, *Western Mysticism*, p. 188.
53. Ernesto Buonaiuti, 'Symbols and Rites in the Religious Life of Certain Monastic Orders', *The Mystic Vision*, p. 186.
54. Bonaventure, *The Mind's Road to God*, trans. George Boas (New York: Bobbs-Merrill, 1953). References are cited in the text.
55. *The Cloud of Unknowing and Other Works*, trans. Clifton Wolters (Harmondsworth: Penguin Books, 1978). References are cited in the text.
56. Jean-Pierre de Caussade, *Abandonment to Divine Providence*, trans. John Beevers (New York: Image Books, 1975). References are cited in the text.
57. Caussade refers to the transfiguration on Mount Tabor. See pp. 39, 65.
58. Edward Schillebeeckx, *Jesus in Our Western Culture. Mysticism, Ethics and Politics*, trans. John Bowden (London: SCM, 1987), p. 71.

CHAPTER 6:   SOCIAL COMMUNITIES

1. The following paragraph summarises the argument of *The German Ideology*, Part I. Quotations are cited in the text, from *The German Ideology. Parts I and III*, ed. R. Pascal (New York: International Publishers, 1947).
2. See *The German Ideology*, pp. 34 ff.
3. *Economic and Philosophical Manuscripts*, trans. Rodney Livingstone and George Benton, *Karl Marx. Early Writings* (New York: Vintage Books, 1975), p. 347.
4. *Early Writings*, pp. 421 ff. Further references are cited in the text.
5. The following quotations are from *A Contribution to the Critique of Hegel's 'Philosophy of Right'*, trans. Anette Jolin and Joseph O'Malley, *Critique of Hegel's 'Philosohy of Right'* (Cambridge: Cambridge University Press, 1970), Introduction, p. 31.
6. *Capital. A Critique of Political Economy*, Vol. I, trans. Ben Fowkes (New York: Vintage, 1977), p. 283.
7. *The German Ideology*, p. 15.

8. *A Contribution to the Critique of Political Economy*, trans. S. W. Ryazanskaya (London: Lawrence and Wishart, 1971), p. 21.
9. 'Marxism and Humanism', in *For Marx*, trans. Ben Brewster (London: Allen Lane, The Penguin Press, 1969), p. 228.
10. See 'Ideology and Ideological State Apparatuses', in *Lenin and Philosophy and Other Essays*, trans. Ben Brewster (London: New Left Books, 1971), p. 163.
11. 'Marxism and Humanism', p. 232.
12. 'The "Piccolo Teatro": Bertolazzi and Brecht', in *For Marx*, p. 144. Further references are cited in the text.
13. 'Today', in *For Marx*, pp. 30–31.
14. *Essays in Self-Criticism*, trans. Grahaeme Loch (London: New Left Books, 1976), pp. 105–61.
15. See for instance Gregory Elliott, *Althusser: the Detour of Theory* (London: Verso, 1988).
16. See Allen Wood, *Karl Marx* (London: Routledge & Kegan Paul, 1981); David-Hillel Ruben, *Marxism and Materialism: A Study in Marxist Theory of Knowledge* (New Jersey: Humanities Press, 1979). These sources are cited by Charles W. Mills, 'Determination and Consciousness in Marx', *Canadian Journal of Philosophy* 19 (1989), 421–46.
17. 'Afterword', ed. Dollimore and Sinfield, *Political Shakespeare*, p. 239.
18. 'Bertolazzi and Brecht', p. 142.
19. *Marxism and Form: Twentieth-Century Dialectical Theories of Literature* (New Jersey: Princeton University Press, 1971), p. 306.
20. See *The Modern Prince and Other Writings*, trans. Louis Marks (New York: International Publishers, 1968), pp. 59, 78.
21. *The Principle of Hope*, trans. Neville Plaice, Stephen Plaice, Paul Knight (Oxford: Basil Blackwell, 1986). The terms 'novum', 'eschaton', 'totum', 'ultimum', 'the All', are roughly equivalent, and are repeated throughout Bloch's work to indicate the condition in which alienation is overcome.
22. Cited without reference in A. Pozzolini, *Antonio Gramsci: An Introduction to His Thought*, trans. Anne F. Showstack (London: Pluto Press, 1970), p. 110.
23. Georg Lukács, *History and Class Consciousness. Studies in Marxist Dialectics*, trans. Rodney Livingstone (London: Merlin Press, 1971), p. 1.
24. Fredric Jameson, *Marxism and Form*, p. 362.
25. Ernst Bloch, *The Principle of Hope*, III, 1375.
26. David Conway, *A Farewell to Marx. An Outline and Appraisal of His Theories* (Harmondsworth: Penguin, 1987). Page numbers are cited in the text.
27. Michael Polanyi, *Personal Knowledge. Towards a Post-Critical Philosophy* (New York: Harper & Row, 1964), pp. 227 ff.
28. Louis Montrose, 'Renaissance Literary Studies and the Subject of History', *English Literary Renaissance* 16 (1986), 8.
29. *A Journal of English Literary History* 49 (1982), 765–89. Page numbers are cited in the text. All references are to *The Merchant of Venice*, ed.

Kenneth Myrick, *The Complete Signet Classic Shakespeare*, ed. Sylvan Barnet (New York: Harcourt Brace Jovanovich, 1972), and are cited in the text.

30. Barbara K. Lewalski, 'Biblical Allusion and Allegory in *The Merchant of Venice', Shakespeare Quarterly* 13 (1962), 327–43. Page numbers are cited in the text.

31. See Günther Bornkamm, 'End Expectation and Church in Matthew', in Günther Bornkamm, Gerhard Barth, Heinz Joachim Held, *Tradition and Interpretation in Matthew*, trans. Percy Scott (London: SCM, 1971), p. 38: 'No other Gospel is so shaped by the thought of the Church as Matthew's, so constructed for use by the church: for this reason it has exercised, as no other, a normative influence in the later Church.'

32. *Reading the New Testament* (London: Macmillan, 1989), pp. 30 ff.

33. See Naseeb Shaheen, *Biblical References in Shakespeare's Tragedies* (Newark: University of Delaware Press, 1987), pp. 15 ff., for an account of the bible and other associated texts that Shakespeare knew.

34. John Calvin, *Commentary on a Harmony of the Evangelists, Matthew, Mark and Luke*, trans. William Pringle (Michigan: Eerdmans, 1949), II, 408 ff. Page numbers are cited in the text.

35. Calvin's clearest statement occurs in a letter on the subject, written in 1545. See *Ioannis Calvini Opera quae supersunt omnia (Corpus Reformatorum)*, ed. G. Baum, E. Cunitz, E. Reuss (Brunswick: 1875), X, i, 245–8. For an account placing Calvin's position in context of the Elizabethan Statute of 1571, see Norman Jones, *God and the Moneylenders. Usury and the Law in Early Modern England* (Oxford: Basil Blackwell, 1989), pp. 15 ff.

36. *The New Testament of Jesus Christ* (Reims: 1582).

37. Cornelius à Lapide, *The Great Commentary upon the Holy Scriptures*, trans. Thomas A. Mossman (London: John Hodges, 1877), II, 150.

38. See Norman Jones, *God and the Moneylenders*, for an account of this literature.

39. Nicolas Sanders, *A Briefe Treatise of Usurie* (Louvain: 1568) 2v – 3r. Further references are cited in the text.

40. Miles Mosse, *The Arraignment and Conviction of Usurie* (1595), Sixth Sermon, p. 140.

41. Philip Caesar, *A General Discourse Against the Damnable Sect of Usurers* (London: 1578) 7r. Further references are cited in the text.

42. Thomas Wilson, *A Discourse Upon Usury* (London: 1572), edited R. H. Tawney (London: Frank Cass, 1925), p. 177.

43. Henry Smith, *The Examination of Usury in Two Sermons* (1591), The First Sermon, p. 17.

44. This interpretation was based mainly on Deuteronomy 23:20–21, but there are many further, complicating factors. See Jones, *God and the Moneylenders*, pp. 7 ff.; Joseph Shatzmiller, *Shylock Reconsidered. Jews, Moneylending, and Medieval Society* (Berkeley: Univeristy of California Press, 1990), pp. 44 ff.

45. Thomas Lodge, 'An Alarum Against Usurers' (1584), 5r-v, reprinted

in *The Complete Works of Thomas Lodge* (New York: Russell and Russell, 1963).

46. Anonymous, *The Death of Usury, or The Disgrace of Usurers* (Cambridge: 1594), p. 95.
47. Norman Jones, *God and the Moneylenders*, pp. 14, *et passim*.
48. It is often noticed that although Antonio is the merchant, the description might easily apply to Shylock. Even Portia asks, 'Which is the merchant here? And which the Jew?' (IV,i,173). The title page of the first quarto seems also to notice the potential for confusion: 'The most excellent Historie of the Merchant of Venice, with the extreame crueltie of Shylocke the Iewe towards the sayd Merchant . . . . ' W. H. Auden, 'Brothers and Others', *The Dyer's Hand, and Other Essays* (New York: Random House 1968), pp. 218–37, writes about the uneasy complicity between Antonio and Shylock.
49. Lawrence Danson, *The Harmonies of 'The Merchant of Venice'* (New Haven: Yale University Press, 1978), passim, notices how the binary relations throughout are resolved in images of circles, representing harmony, and how the threes (p. 90), suggest a further depth of pattern. My argument stresses disruption rather than a re-enforcement of harmony.
50. Lynda E. Boose, 'The Comic Contract and Portia's Golden Ring', *Shakespeare Studies* XX (1988), 241–54.
51. René Girard, '"To Entrap the Wisest": A Reading of The Merchant of Venice', *Literature and Society: Selected Papers from the English Institute*, n.s. 3, ed. Edward Said (Baltimore: Johns Hopkins University Press, 1980), p. 100.
52. 'Brothers and Others', pp. 234–5.
53. Terry Eagleton, *William Shakespeare* (Oxford: Basil Blackwell, 1986), p. 43.
54. A. D. Moody, *Shakespeare: 'The Merchant of Venice'* (London: Edward Arnold, 1964), p. 26, draws this distinction between aliens inside and outside.
55. See Jacques Maritain, *Creative Intuition in Art and Poetry* (New Jersey: Princeton University Press, 1977), pp. 141 ff.; C.G. Jung, 'On the Psychology of the Unconscious', *Collected Works of C. G. Jung*, ed. Herbert Read, Michael Fordham, Gerhard Adler, trans. R. F. C. Hull (New Jersey: Princeton University Press, 1953), VII, 175.
56. Amelie Oksenberg Rorty, 'A Literary Postscript: Characters, Persons, Selves, Individuals', ed. Amelie Oksenberg Rorty, *The Identities of Persons* (Berkeley: University of California Press, 1976), pp. 312–13.
57. See Marcel Mauss, 'A Category of the Human Mind: the Notion of Person, the Notion of Self', in *The Category of the Person: Anthropology, Philosophy, History*, ed. Michael Carrithers, Steven Collins, Steven Lukes (Cambridge: Cambridge University Press, 1985), pp. 14 ff., setting out the legal and moral senses of *persona* described in the following paragraph.
58. Boethius, 'A Treatise Against Eutyches and Nestorius', trans. H. F. Stewart, *Boethius. The Theological Tractates* (Cambridge, Mass.: Harvard University Press, 1968), p. 85.

59. See Edward Schillebeeckx, *Jesus. An Experiment in Christology*, trans. Hubert Hoskins (London: Collins, 1983), p. 662 ff.
60. For a developed account of this, see Jonathan Glover, *I. The Philosophy and Psychology of Personal Identity* (London: Allen Lane, The Penguin Press, 1988).
61. See Jacques Maritain, *Scholasticism and Politics*, trans. edited by Mortimer T. Adler (New York: Image Books, 1960), p. 74.
62. Leszek Kolakowski, *Main Currents of Marxism. Its Origins, Growth and Dissolution*, 3 vols, trans. P. S. Falla (Oxford: Oxford University Press, 1987. First published 1978), III, 523. Page numbers are cited in the text.
63. Review of Soame Jenyns, *A Free Enquiry Into the Nature and Origin of Evil*, ed. Arthur Murphy, *The Works of Samuel Johnson*, 2 vols (London: Henry G. Bohn, 1862), II, 492.
64. *Complete Works*, II, 5.
65. Ezra Pound, *Guide to Kulchur* (New York: New Directions, 1938), p. 179.
66. Michel Foucault, *Discipline and Punish. The Birth of the Prison*, trans. Alan Sheridan (New York: Vintage, 1979), pp. 195 ff., *et passim*.
67. All references are to *Rasselas*, ed. Murphy, *Complete Works*, II, 3–44. References cited in the text indicate chapter and page numbers.
68. There is a good deal of discussion about the interplay between experience and innocence in *Rasselas*. See J. S. Cunningham, *The Vanity of Human Wishes and Rasselas* (London: Edward Arnold, 1982), pp. 38 ff.; Harold Pagliaro, 'Structural Patterns of Control in Rasselas', *English Writers of the Eighteenth Century*, ed. John Middendorf (New York: Columbia University Press, 1971), pp. 212–15; Thomas M. Curley, *Samuel Johnson and the Age of Travel* (Athens, Georgia: University of Georgia Press, 1976), p. 181.
69. There is much discussion about what is concluded, because returning to Abyssinia does not necessarily mean returning to the happy valley. As J. S. Cunningham suggests, the book's scepticism and relativism are preserved (*The Vanity of Human Wishes and Rasselas*, p. 57), and the reader hesitates (60). A. D. Nuttall, *Pope's Essay on Man* (London: George Allen & Unwin, 1984), p. 219, notes the contrast between agoraphobia at the opening, and claustrophobia at the end, which he sees duplicated in the river's swelling and ebbing.
70. Jung, *Complete Works*, XVIII, 605.

Index

Johnson, Samuel, 210ff
  Rasselas, 210ff
Jones, Norman, 200
Joyce, James, 28
Julian of Norwich, 165
Jung, C. G., 166, 177, 207

Kant, Immanuel, 5, 10, 101, 103
Keats, John, 13
Kenner, Hugh, 10, 25, 26, 91
Knowles, David, 165
Kolakowski, Leszek, 210
Kuhn, Thomas, 56, 63

Lacan, Jacques, 1, 61, 81, 86ff, 90,
  96, 99, 100, 101, 146, 183
Lapide, Cornelius à, 198
Leach, Edmund, 77, 78
Lenin, Vladimir, 182
Lessing, G., 43
Lévi-Strauss, Claude, 11, 12, 76, 77,
  78, 100
Lewalski, Barbara, 192, 193,
  205, 206
Lewis, C.S., 21
Locke, John, 1, 2, 101, 130, 207,
  209, 211
Lodge, Thomas, 200ff
Lukács, Georg, 184, 187, 220
Luther, Martin, 41, 43, 136, 140

MacDonald, George, 120, 122ff
  At the Back of the North Wind,
  122ff
Machery, Pierre, 186
Machiavelli, N., 74, 75
Mack, Maynard, 142
Mackey, J. P., 163
Malebranche, Nicolas, 101
Manichaean, 32, 35, 36
Marcuse, Herbert, 49
Maritain, Jacques, 165, 207
Marlowe, Christopher, 40, 41
Marx, Karl, 11, 57, 68, 100, 179ff,
  210, 220
Maurras, Charles, 91
Mauss, Marcel, 208
Mechthild of Magdeburg,
  165

Merleau-Ponty, Maurice, 103,
  104, 221
metaphor, 13, 19, 20, 37, 38, 44, 60,
  84, 87, 88, 99, 102, 105, 107,
  126ff, 134, 135, 136, 139, 141,
  142, 143
Methodius, 167
Miller, J. Hillis, 67, 100
Miller, Richard, 57, 58, 63, 82,
  85, 221
Mills, Charles W., 185
mimesis, 3, 13, 25, 31, 61, 66, 78, 79,
  218, 220, 221
mirror, 86, 87, 99, 100, 152
Moltmann, Jürgen, 145, 147, 160
Montaigne, Michel, 13
Montesquieu, Charles Louis de
  Secondat de, 43
Montrose, Louis, 189
More, Thomas, 136
Moses, 165
Mosse, Miles, 199ff
mysticism, 163ff
myth, 2, 3, 4, 11, 13, 38, 44, 68, 75,
  76–8, 184, 217

narrative, 2, 13, 51, 83, 219
Neumann, Erich, 166, 177
Neurath, Otto, 54, 55
Newton, Isaac, 7, 12
Nietzsche, Friedrich, 144
Norris, Christopher, 60, 61, 127
Nuttall, A. D., 61, 62

O'Connell, Robert J., 34
Origen, 167

Paine, Thomas, 43
Parfit, Derek, 1, 2, 207
participation, 22, 28, 39, 63, 107,
  117, 126, 129, 141, 214
Paul, 32, 35, 37, 38, 147, 165, 166,
  168, 177
Pelagius, 37, 39, 41, 43, 50
perennial philosophy, 162ff, 219
person, 1, 2, 3, 5, 13–14, 19, 21, 28,
  29, 36, 38, 39, 50, 51, 52, 58,
  62, 63, 66, 72, 73, 79, 85, 86, 97,
  100, 103, 104, 106, 109, 110, 117,

Voltaire, 42, 43, 49, 51, 144

Watts, Cedric, 78
Wilden, Anthony, 88
Williams, Raymond, 186
Wilson, Thomas, 199ff
Wood, Alan, 185

Wordsworth, William, 112, 113, 114
Wrede, William, 154–5

Yeats, W. B., 106, 108ff, 111
  Sailing to Byzantium, 108ff
Young, Robert, 12